RPM

Rockin' in the
Free World

RPM
Rockin' in the
Free World

by
H.S. MEANS

ATLANTA, GA

RPM—Rockin' in the Free World
Published by H.S. Means
Soft Cover ISBN 978-0-9881752-0-4
Hard Cover ISBN 978-0-9881752-1-1
Copyright © 2012 H.S. Means
Atlanta, GA

www.ryanpmeans.com

The publisher is not responsible for websites (or their content) that are not owned by the publisher.

Once in awhile, right in the middle of ordinary life,
love gives us a fairy tale.
—*Anonymous*

*For Sophie and Elizabeth, who will only know their
father through our stories. And for Ryan, we will
always keep on rockin' in the free world for you.*

Contents

Diary of Heather Means

OCTOBER 1, 2009

"'Tis better to have loved and lost than never to have loved at all."

—Alfred Lord Tennyson

To Alfred, I say: "Absolute bullshit."

They say that human walking is controlled falling. Living, for me, is controlled dying. I manage to put one foot in front of the other and walk through each day with a smile for my children. But in reality, I am free-falling into the depths of hell with a blank stare on my face. I wonder if and how I will ever get through this alive and why I even have to try, when I'm almost certain that I have nothing left to give. More important, the question of "How did I get right here in life?" begs to be answered by a higher power that seems to neither talk nor listen to my prayers. And so they cease.

I am completely consumed by the realization that I have lost something I cannot replace. My mind works overtime to understand that death is real, infinite and, contrary to previous beliefs, it is stronger than life as I knew it. Too many life lessons have been learned in such a short period of time. I have to remind myself every few minutes that I am now the sole person responsible for an 18-month-old and a newborn.

Ryan and I should be celebrating the birth of our second daughter. We eagerly anticipated the fun and work it would be to raise two girls so close in age. Ryan was ready to protect them and love them forever. We had a strong game plan for the next 20 years. But, instead, I am alone, separating the sympathy cards from the well wishes for our new baby. For a minute, I wonder if I should just put them all into her scrapbook rather than painting a false picture of the circumstances. I decide against it. Shoeboxes filled with sympathies will remain on the deepest shelves of my closet for now.

The human mind has an amazing capacity to process or choose not to process information. Months have now passed since Ryan's death. I have moved miles from home, left our house, friends, job and identity. But still, I wait for an email, a call or text, someone to tell me that it was all a mistake or maybe a cover–up. Maybe he was accepted into the CIA and chose his country over his family. He had made this choice before— anything is possible with Ryan Means. It seems my mind will just not accept his death. He has to be coming home soon. I'll just continue to put the cards in the new baby book and write some thank-you notes until he arrives. Should I sign his name? Nobody seems to have the answers that I want. I want to know how to be a widow at age 31.

Maybe I will wake up to see Ryan laying next to me with Sophie still in my belly and Elizabeth asleep in her bed. I will realize that summer in Manhattan was all just a bad dream. It never happens. Time slips through my hands and I have no concept of future or past anymore. I am forced to live in today. I'm not sure if this is someone else's life I am living or if this is really what was in my cards.

NOVEMBER 1, 2009:

During our senior year of high school, we were asked to make a paper timeline depicting what we had planned for the rest of our lives after graduation. I planned to go straight to college for four years, get married the next day and start having children. My husband and I would travel with the kids as they got older and once they were in college, we would take the time to enjoy each other and reflect on what a great job we did and simply spend the rest of life enjoying each other's company.

Many classmates had similar stories. Nobody planned to find some- one they loved, get married, and then bury their spouse as they entered their third decade of life. But as I have learned, we don't really get to make these decisions. We make choices, we imagine timelines, but ultimately some higher power decides our fate.

In reality, I spent over seven years in college, earning my physical therapy Doctorate degree and I was looking forward to getting a job rather than being a student—for the first time in my life. While I was busy studying, my future husband was living his dream in New York City. He had the Manhattan apartment, the six figure job, exciting friends, many women, an action packed nightlife, weekends in the Hamptons, and travelled as often as possible.

On Sept. 11, 2001, all of that changed. Ryan lost his lifelong friend in the World Trade Center attacks. This re-ignited a long-held desire to protect and serve. So, at age 31, Ryan enlisted in the U.S. Army with the dream of becoming a Green Beret. After boot camp, he was stationed in Fayetteville, North Carolina. Fort Bragg was only a short drive from Wrightsville Beach, where my college friend and I vacationed every summer.

In one short weekend, my imaginary time-line became skewed and fate took hold of the drawing pen.

PART I

This is
Ryan Means

Chapter 1
Some Call This Stalking

I first met Ryan Patman Means on an August summer morning. He was on leave from his Special Forces Q–Course training and I was on my annual Wrightsville Beach vacation with my friend Lisa. I had recently graduated from the University of Pittsburgh and rewarded myself by leasing my first car, a glittering pearl white Toyota Solara convertible. My trunk was packed full of sundresses, stilettos, and my arsenal of Chanel beauty supplies.

Lisa and I made the entire 10-hour, non-stop drive from Pittsburgh with the top down. If one did not travel at warp speeds and actually stopped to relieve themselves or eat, it could take well over 12 hours. But, we were young and would never risk missing an hour of sun on the beach. Now that I am older, and, I'd like to think, wiser, I have no idea how we didn't end up in jail or splattered like one of the millions of bugs that lost their lives on my windshield. But it just so happened that those hours led to the very timing of our arrival in Wrightsville that year, which would change the course of the rest of my life.

Upon our arrival we found that the only affordable beachfront vacancies were in a cinderblock dump called the Ocean View Motel. The cement blocks were painted bright blue and the tacky wall art consisted of cheap 1970s flocked velvet sunset-over-the-ocean scenes. It was the kind of place where you would not want to meet your neighboring guests. This was in fact our case.

Our neighbors were a rowdy group of G.I.'s who had found their double-bed motel room to be satisfactory quarters for a group of eight. They were hanging like wild monkeys on the second story balcony enjoying a morning beer as we pulled into the parking lot. Lisa went inside to retrieve our keys, and I believe my first thought was to put up the top of the car and lock the doors.

Before I even had the chance, one of them walked confidently up to my car carrying a Hawaiian print shirt in a dry-cleaning bag. He reached over my head, dangled the shirt directly in front of my face and said "Hey, chick, what do you think of this shirt?"

"I don't like it," I said. I was hoping that would clue him in to the fact that I wasn't interested in meeting a group of drunk young men that not only outnumbered our party of two, but who were also spending the weekend in the same disgusting motel. It seemed like a recipe for disaster, where a girl ends up missing, only to one day be found at the bottom of the ocean.

THE HAWAIIAN PRINT SHIRT

My reply didn't seem to phase him. "My mother bought it for me, and she has very expensive taste," he said. "And it's too bad you don't like it because I'm going to wear it when we go to dinner tonight." I couldn't help but crack a smile. "We will not be going anywhere tonight," I quickly replied. Ryan told me later that this was the first of many times that I rolled my eyes at him. He introduced himself as "Ryan Means" and returned to his group of friends.

As it turns out, we did go to dinner.

Wrightsville is a small beach, and Lisa and I happened to be enjoying our first glass of wine when Ryan and his younger brother, Michael, who was visiting from Atlanta, arrived at the restaurant. They invited themselves to join us and proceeded to ask for a table for six. Two of their friends soon arrived, and we all sat down to dinner.

My first impression? Ryan Means scared the hell out of me. He was obnoxious, invaded my personal space, never censored his thoughts, and seemed to enjoy being the center of attention. He thrived on getting laughs from friends and strangers alike. Sometimes, he offended people along the way, but in the end, all that mattered was that he was having a good time. We enjoyed a great dinner and learned that the group of guys we had met had just started a grueling series of tests and training called the Q Course so that they could become, as Ryan called them "barrel chested freedom fighters" a.k.a the Green Berets. I'm embarrassed to say that I had never heard of a Green Beret and I honestly wondered if they were making up the whole story. Lisa, who grew up with two brothers, assured me that it was in fact "a real thing."

Michael and I spent some time talking as Ryan made his way around the bar introducing himself to strangers as an insurance salesman. He explained that although I felt that his older brother could come off as a bit obnoxious, he had a big heart and never truly meant to hurt (or scare) anyone.

Ryan was known for his incredibly com-petitive nature and his powers of persua-sion. He usually won the prize not by being the fastest or the strongest or even the most charming, but because of his warrior spirit— the sheer fact that he would never give up,

RYAN WORKING HIS CHARM

never back down, and by all means he would get what he wanted or die trying. Ryan would later tell me, "Your rejection only makes me stronger."

By the end of the night, Ryan proved that he would relentlessly follow us around the beach until I gave him my phone number. Just when we thought we had lost him, he literally sprang out from behind a row of bushes on our walk back to the motel—behavior that later became com-monplace to me. He had been waiting for us (some call this stalking) for at least two hours. There was only one route home on the island. I finally gave up a phone number but it was Lisa's number. Ryan called at least 15 times the next day. He eventually realized that he was talking to Lisa. During our sushi dinner she handed the phone to me, and Ryan and I decided that we would all meet up again that night. We had a great time with the group, and when they left, we agreed to do it all over again the following weekend.

DINNER AT 22 NORTH, WRIGHTSVILLE BEACH, NC

Chapter 2
"Heatwave, will you marry me?"

Ryan texted and called me every day, several times a day to remind me of his return the next weekend. I wish I could say I was unconcerned with the pending reunion, but for some reason I was eagerly anticipating his return. And then, it came. He pulled up in a 1999 Toyota 4Runner with several friends. Before I knew what hit me, Ryan ran from his car to the beach, tackled me on my beach chair and knocked me to the sand. I had never been tackled before—it was quite a new experience for me. But this was the first time I understood that this was Ryan Means. He grabbed my *People* magazine and we lay on the beach reading about celebrities and sharing stories with our friends for the next few hours. He said that he and his mother would fight over the newest issue of *People* when they were together and that I somehow reminded him of her in so many ways. I had no clue how to receive this compliment at the time.

Later that afternoon, Lisa and I got into a disagreement. At some point, she dumped a cooler of ice onto me, and Ryan took advantage of the situation. He offered to "take me away from it all" and at that point I trusted him enough to go along. Our first stop was Airlie Gardens in nearby Wilmington for a beautiful walk through lush botanicals and sculptures. It seemed odd that such a masculine soldier would choose a garden for a first date. It seemed even more strange that he should have a wealth of knowledge about the species of various flowers! I would learn that his mother was a very successful wedding planner and flower designer in Atlanta. She recruited her sons to help with much of the physical work, therefore, Ryan inadvertently gained knowledge that would someday impress and, no doubt, confuse those he would date.

We approached a beautifully constructed piece titled "The Bottlehouse." It was designed from a variety of shapes, sizes, and colors of bottles turned bottom out and cemented to form a small chapel. Ryan asked me to sit down on a bench with him.

He then got down on one knee and said "Heatwave," (This was the nickname he gave me when we met. He was terrible with names and I think he did the nicknames to compensate.) "will you marry me? We can have our wedding here at the Bottle House. What do you say?" I laughed, got back up and started walking again. He pointed out that I was "doing that eye-rolling thing again" and that I had better work on correcting my rude habit. He also said, "Go ahead and laugh, but when you end up marrying me one day, I'll be the one laughing at you for falling for my cunning ways. Haaah, haaah" he said, again in a taunting voice.

I responded with something like, "Let's go eat. I'm done, you're crazy, and there aren't enough other people around."

I thought we were going for a quick dinner downtown until Ryan pulled into the Hilton Waterfront Beach Resort of Wilmington. I refused to check in with him and told him I was sitting in the car and there was no way I was staying.

He handed the valet a tip and said, "Go ahead and park it and leave my crabby wife in it until she simmers down." Then he went inside and booked a room.

I sat in the car wondering if I should feign a reconciliation with my friend in the hope that she would come and get me or just take my chances with Ryan. He said he did not drink and drive; that he would be dishonorably discharged from the Army and shame his family if he were caught and that, furthermore, this was a separate–bed suite. After realizing I had no idea where I was compared to where I needed to be, I finally got out of the car.

Chapter 3
It Was Unsettling and Comforting at the Same Time

I believe we headed out that night knowing that we were on the same page; that we had something special. We went to every little hot spot that tiny Wilmington had to offer: a wine bar, a Goth bar, live bands, dancing, and local restaurants. We both felt at ease with each other no matter where we were that night. We could step into any situation in the world and function happily together. It was like we had been friends for years. We ate dinner at a lovely restaurant called Café Phoenix. Ryan would hold my hands and look directly into my eyes from across the table when he talked to me—it was unsettling and comforting at the same time. From this day on, I always felt perfectly safe in his care—always.

Two older couples next to us said we were a "phenomenal couple," that our love "embraced their table." They invited us to sit with them for an after dinner drink. They asked how long we had been married and if we had any children. They were old friends who met for dinner once a month, but it was still our first date. Naturally, Ryan told them that we had been high school sweethearts and that we got married once we were old enough to legally exchange vows; that children were in our future; and, in fact, I might be expecting now. They were so happy for us but seemed to start monitoring my wine intake after his comments. This is where he again recounts my eye-rolling, and also when I learned that I would be dealing with many moments that would make me red in the face if I did not learn how to join in the fun.

The next morning we went to an amazing brunch at Deluxe, another fantastic waterfront cafe and talked for hours. I had never wanted to know so much about a person in my life. But I didn't have to bombard Ryan with questions. He loved the spotlight, and he had a way of telling stories that put you right there with him and whatever he was talking about.

Ryan was raised Catholic and attended Christ the King and Marist School in Atlanta, Ga. He excelled in languages and in high school began taking a special interest in foreign affairs and world cultures. He was infatuated with how people lived and why they did the things that they did as a culture or religion. He had it in his head that someday he would be serving his country, but his parents preferred him to receive his college degree first. Ryan was fluent in German and studied abroad in Germany. He also studied in Spain, where he ran with the bulls and learned to speak Spanish, even though he had never learned the language before embarking on the trip. Through the Army, he learned to speak Arabic and Farsi and became quite fluent in Russian.

Ryan told me about his close relationships with his parents and three brothers. He described his father as stern but always guiding his sons in the right direction. To Ryan, his mother was the most amazing woman that ever set foot on this Earth. He could say nothing but wonderful things about her, and it seemed to me that she was one of his best friends as well. He had two older brothers. Alfie was six years his senior and Tommy, four. Michael was six years younger, and Ryan wasn't shy about his love for all of them.

He shared stories of his youth, when he would dress in cammo on a daily basis and spend his allowance at the Army-Navy store near his home. He would ride his bike there almost every day to see what was next on his "want list" of supplies. The Means home had a closet designated to nothing but Army gear: vests, camouflage pants, green thermal underwear, boots, helmets...Ryan was constantly adding to the arsenal.

The boys grew up in a beautiful home facing the golf course of Capital City Club in Atlanta. Ryan spent a good part of his childhood on the golf course, only he never played golf. He would don his camouflage pants and head to the lake armed with a fishing pole, knife, and spear, which he used to catch frogs, fish, and turtles. The turtles were always saved, but snakes and frogs were skinned, salted, and mounted for display to evoke reaction from anyone who would take a minute to look. He liked grabbing attention, good or bad, from a very young age.

The boys were given a log cabin for Christmas one year and it soon became Ryan's "Headquarters" fort. Eventually, he added a zip slide. He would climb onto the roof, with his shiny bullet shells worn proudly across his chest yelling "Geronimo!" as he slid down to where he and Michael would build fox-holes in the thick brush of the backyard. The two younger brothers spent a lot of time outdoors as soldiers together. Most of the stories told about Tommy and Alfie, the older of the the four boys, involved using Ryan's body in some fashion that resulted in a hospital visit and permanent scarring. He had been shot at with BB guns, darts pierced into his head, and a nostril ripped off on a glass coffee table, courtesy of his older brothers. Additionally, a major scar ran from his lower lip to his chin, caused by a glass Coke bottle and his own mischief. They all fit his character. He liked his scars and their stories.

Ryan said that he always knew he belonged in the service, but it took him awhile to find out just where he belonged. His father, Al, had enlisted in the Marines and spent some time in Paris Island when he was a young man. When Ryan was about four years old, he was visiting his grandparents with the family in Hilton Head. Al decided he would take Ryan over to the Marine Base at Paris Island. "His little face just lit up," Al would say. "He was infatuated with every aspect of the lifestyle and wanted to learn everything he could about how the soldiers lived." Quite possibly, this was the beginning of his lifelong dream to serve his country. The seed was planted.

Mary Jo would take Ryan and his friends to the 57th Fighter Group restaurant near their home. He would have all of his young birthday

parties there. He loved walking through the joint saluting everyone. As a child, he always saluted his mother when he entered a room. When she didn't consider it a high priority to sew his patches onto his uniforms, he taught himself to sew. On Halloween, Ryan would recruit an entire platoon of boys, and some girls, to march through the neighborhood streets of historic Brookhaven. Mary Jo was a nurse at the time, and she would wear her white uniform and help the kids carry a stretcher as they took turns playing the "wounded soldier" covered in blood, as the leader with the tape recorder marched in front with recorded bugle music.

From ages six to 20 years, Ryan attended or worked at Athens Y Camp in Tallulah Falls, Ga. "Indian War Games" were among his favorite part of the camp. Ryan would be the standout player decked out in full camouflage, face painted and all. He was always the last man standing. He gave 150 percent to what most considered just a fun game. I began to understand that this was the approach he used to tackle any obstacle in life, and I loved it.

Ryan's never-ending quest for adventure led him to the University of Colorado, where he joined the Chi Psi fraternity and met up with an old grade-school buddy, Adam White. Boulder was a great place for the two to ski, hike, and rock climb, but it didn't allow Ryan to live up to his full academic potential.

When I asked if he had ever been arrested, Ryan said, "Ehhh, maybe," which of course was not the answer I wanted. Why would I want to fall in love with a criminal? I wondered if it was public intoxication, theft, assault...the wheels in my mind were turning. Ryan must have noticed. He replied, "Inciting a riot." "What?" I asked. He clarified, "At a football game at Boulder, I incited a riot." That certainly wasn't the answer I expected, but for some reason it relieved my mind from wondering if he was some sort of murdering thief.

With mediocre grades, Ryan was cut off financially and his parents flew to Boulder to take him back home to Atlanta. Of course, when he got home, he jumped into a car with Adam, who was on his way back out to Colorado. Ryan failed to support himself by working at the Baby Gap in Boulder. Folding tiny toddler clothes with a hangover was not the life for which he had aspired. So, he decided to accept Al's financial assistance and attend the University of Georgia. He earned the Hope Scholarship and graduated on the Dean's list.

Two great things about Ryan were his ability to laugh at himself and the fact that he had no shame. He recalled one Halloween in Athens where he rode his bike down Sanford Drive wearing nothing but a hockey mask on his face and a tube sock on his man parts. He attempted to paint the word "BOO" across his butt, however the mirror image concept discombobulated him and he instead biked through town, ass painted with the word "OOB". The desired reaction was achieved either way, and he was quite satisfied when he landed at the bottom of the hill, where he had carefully hidden a bag of clothing for himself. Despite the antics, he made the Dean's list and graduated on time with a degree in finance and the reputation of a playboy who liked to cause a stir.

After college, he went to work for BellSouth, where he was able to get a transfer to New York City, which he referred to as "the greatest place on Earth".

Ryan's face beamed like a child on Christmas morning when he spoke of NYC. It was heaven on Earth as far as he was concerned. He started working for a company that specialized in new communications through the Internet. He thought his window of opportunity to join the Army had passed.

By the end of our afternoon brunch and walk on the docks, Ryan answered a question I had been afraid to ask. He explained that the initials "ASW" tattooed over the area above his liver were for Adam Shelby White, who lost his life in the collapse of the World Trade Center, and that was the final push he needed to enlist in the Army at age 31. My heart sank, and at the same time, I felt some type of relief as I had wrongly assumed they were the initials of an ex-lover or child I had yet to learn about. I also felt sad for sweet Adam and his family.

That afternoon, as we strolled along the boardwalk of the beautiful shores of the Cape Fear River, I felt that I didn't have much exciting to tell about myself. I had spent my entire life thus far in school. I had never lived anywhere but Pittsburgh and maybe I was ready for an adventure. Maybe

Ryan would be what I needed to make my life something worth talking about.

We later returned to the beach to meet up with our friends. We exchanged email addresses and he gave me the longest, tightest bear hug and said, "We don't say 'good-bye,' we say 'I'll see you soon.'"

The entire way back to Pennsylvania he was all I could think about, and I wondered if I really would ever see him again.

PART II

Ryan's Journal
New York, NY

Ryan's Journal, New York, NY

SEPTEMBER 16, 2001

First time writing since World Trade Center attacks. Adam was on floor 105 and certainly killed. For 4-5 days I tried to maintain hope that he was alive and able to survive the horrific scene. I've now officially given up and simply ask that my best friend watch over me as he always did.

The most difficult aspect is knowing how he died. The chaos, the fire, the smoke, falling 105 floors, leaving his body never to be recovered.

The irony of writing my best friend's eulogy on his birthday...

I rode the L train to Brooklyn for the purpose of packing his things. I asked myself, " What if someone came to you and said,' Someone close to you will be gone in six months, I'm not telling who, when or in what fashion they will pass, simply that they will be gone in 6 months?'"

How would I react? And it dawned on me that this is how Adam must have woken up on a daily basis. The reason I say this is because everything he did, he always seemed to make it special. Every trip was an adventure, every meal was an occasion, and every meeting an event.

We began packing Adam's apartment. It started off with the routine of drink a beer, move a box, drink a beer, move a box, etc... Pretty soon, boxes were taking up too much time and we focused instead on the beers and stories.

It was amazing how many neighbors stopped in to say what Adam had done for them in the short time they had been in the same building. An elderly woman stopped by saying that she had just moved in and was having her floors varnished. Not even having met her once, but knowing that her apartment reeked of chemicals, Adam took her a bouquet of flowers and invited her to his place for dinner. Others stopped by recalling numerous gestures Adam had made to invite people over, offer to help and do whatever possible to create a sense of community in their remote enclave. Eventually, many other friends of Adam came by to help and soon they were telling their favorite stories and drinking his Brooklyn Pale Ales. At one point, everyone had one of Adam's hilarious loud polyester shirts on, as we blasted the Doors from his record player. The stories and fun went on late into the night. No doubt Adam was there with us laughing.

Adam was a renaissance man. He was extremely well-read and additionally had the ability to deliver the most concise, intelligent and logical ideas from anything he read about politics and the environment. He had unshakable confidence. He may have been 5'7" and 125 pounds after a huge meal, but he had the ability to walk into a room and have a similar commanding effect as Wilt Chamberlain. He had an undying sense of adventure, the most intelligent sense of humor and an undeniably infectious laugh. He was always positive.

I met Adam in first grade. We spent four glorious years together at Christ The King elementary school in Atlanta, Ga. After that, his parents were likely pleased that we lost contact... until our freshman year at the University of Colorado in the Fall of 1992. Unbeknownst to one another, we had decided

ADAM WHITE ON RYAN'S SHOULDERS

to attend the same college. During orientation, several other students from Atlanta had approached me saying that an 'Adam', claiming to be my best friend, was looking for me. I remember clearly thinking, 'the only Adam I know is Adam White and there is no way he could be going to school here'. I did not see him in person until walking up the steps of the Lodge at the second week of rush in Boulder. It only took about 30 seconds to re-establish a notorious friendship

YOUNG CHI PSI BROTHERS, RYAN AND ADAM ARE THE TWO ALREADY LOOKING OFF INTO DIFFERENT DIRECTIONS

that would forever affect my life. Over the years, Adam was my friend, roommate, fraternity brother, climbing partner, co-worker, drinking buddy and mentor.

Our freshman year of college, Adam and I began climbing with my older brother's climbing gear, which was about 12 years old. Typical climbing gear is retired at 2 years. Remembering also, that even though he loved the outdoors,

Adam never had any formal training of how to tie knots or set anchors but he convinced me that he knew exactly what he was doing. We would be ready to climb and saw others checking one another's knots and of course we did the same. Seemed like what you were supposed to do.

I would ask him "How are my knots?"

"GREAT, PERFECT, Let's GO!" he would say.

"Are you sure?" I asked.

"NO. Let's go!"

"Okay!"

RYAN, ADAM AND SCOTT ON A
TYPICAL COLORADO CLIMB

Only by having Adam on the other end of the rope, did I know that everything would be okay.

—∘∘○❋○∘∘—

On the flight back to NYC after Adam's memorial weekend, which was overall very difficult, I find myself mentally and physically exhausted. Hoping and praying that I make a legitimate effort to alter my outlook, activities, and persona for the better. Remembering always the fragility of life and that this world has tons to offer and I must do more. I must read more, visit museums often, watch less TV, study more languages. Always find the positive, make an effort to always meet someone new, laugh until I cry, without holding back. I will stand tall, have a firm handshake, speak loudly and be direct. Adam never complained and he was never afraid.

After 9/11, checking account balance remained at $1.50. I've relied on credit cards for everything and lost my job. Despite these setbacks, I'm feeling positive that things will change for the better. I have been thinking about the profound changes I've experienced in the past 6 months, losing my best friend in the biggest terrorist attack on the US ever and losing my job when already in serious debt in a city and economy that is recovering from 9/11.

I read this today and it refreshed my spirit:

> Whatever you can do or dream you can do, Begin it.
> Boldness has genius, power and magic in it.
>
> – Goethe

OCTOBER 30, 2001

Been unemployed for over a month now and $1,875, my month's rent, is due tomorrow on my 550 sq. foot studio and I'm not sure where I will get it. The economy is on the verge of a total recession and our country is at war with an unseen enemy that may potentially be all around us. Anthrax is being found at the Post Offices of NYC and D.C. and various media outlets. Times are tough for sure, but hopes are high that I'll be able to pull out of this funk soon. Very soon. My horoscope today reads:

It's starting to happen. The first signs can be seen. Maybe though, you are like a garden that has been waiting too long for rain. Your leaves have shriveled, your stems have withered, your earth has cracked and your ability to be abundant has been forgotten. You are trying to survive; to conserve what little remaining energy you have in the hope that eventually revival will come. Here it is and, at first, even tiny raindrops feel like drums, banging in your ears. But soon, a precious hope in your heart will come right back to life.

JANUARY 5, 2002

My goal for 2002 is to become debt free. I have a steady job now and since the New Year has begun, I have felt a sense of renewed vigor towards my life. I've become more spiritual and aware of my moral direction. This self-awareness must continually be present so that I may fulfill the dreams flowing through my head.

Perception is everything. As I walk down the streets and avenues of NYC, I see nothing but beauty and joyous life, sometimes so intense that my heart feels like it may explode. I'm unable to contain my goofy smile, and I struggle to contain my spontaneous laughter so as not to scare others. I love this city... this country.

Life without Adam will always be difficult but I will continue to try to be strong and live with the virtues that he possessed, knowing that he is looking down on me, as well as looking after me. I hope to never disappoint him. From our childhood days in Atlanta to our Boulder days at Colorado University to real life in NYC, our life paths have always intersected. Adam was an inspiration to live my life fully. I've decided to tattoo his initials on my right lower ribcage: ASW.

I've established goals for marathons, reading about world history, war and politics, and intense physical training has begun.

SEPTEMBER 11, 2002

RYAN HAD NO FEAR

Exactly 365 days after the attack, I sit down to reflect on what has happened since that day and how I have hope-fully made some positive changes in my life. I miss my best friend and fellow adventurer and climbing partner. He was someone to admire and imitate. How a single man could have the courage to do the things he did was unbelievable. In the days after his death, I promised myself that I would do more with myself in various respects: personal, spiritual, physical, and professional growth. I now understand that there is always room for improvement and will forever use my friend's life as a standard. I must constantly remind myself of what needs to be done. This, in my mind, is the greatest tribute: To be inspired in such a way that you alter the greatest posses-

sion a person has... a possession granted by God, created
by love, nurtured by friends and family...the possession
is life. I pray that I do not fail. But I am courageous.
Without courage all other traits are impossible to own.

What I want:
- To do something that makes a difference.
- To be happy with my life.
- To become a better person and to leave here having
  my influence affect others in a positive way.
- To remember that stressing out is counter-productive.
- Speak fluently in three languages.
- To be a personal legend.

I am reading The Alchemist; Coelho writes:

> The closer one gets to realizing his personal legend the
> more the Personal Legend becomes his true reason
> for being.

Similarities to my own life: the feeling that life has
more to offer, that I'm here to do something great and
great adventures lie ahead. I'm too smart and too industri-
ous to be mediocre.
I don't need a lot of money because I am already rich,
as I know the value of what I have and because of the
importance I place on that value, I can never be poor.
My soul is occasionally corrupted but is inherently good.
Coupled with a strong mind, nothing can stop me.

I've literally had no cash for the past three days and I find myself totally happy and in control of my life. Not sure where I find my strength or even if it can be called that, but I know that things could be ten times worse AND that they stand to get better. Everything will be OK. Things that are good: the best friends, strong family, health, beautiful weather in NYC, and TOTAL FREEDOM. For all of this I thank God.

> The only thing that makes a dream impossible is fear of failure.
>
> –Paulo Coelho, The Alchemist

JUNE 2003

The climb of Mt. Rainier for the ASW Scholarship fund was successful in 26 hours.

I'm running back to back-to-back marathons in cities all over the world. Constantly must push to be physically fit.

AT THE START OF
MT. RANIER CLIMB

CLIMBING MT. RANIER FOR THE
ASW SCHOLARSHIP FOUNDATION

I have never experienced such success in my personal or business life as with training my body and mind to run marathons. I now realize I must train for success. I am not a natural at anything as I thought I was...nothing has been given to me. Everything comes as a direct result of the work that I put into it.

MARATHON MAN

AUGUST 2003

Thoughts on the book of stories compiled about Adam from various friends and family:

Adam had a profound effect on so many people. It is impossible to not be envious of the life that he led on a constant daily basis as it seems that every person he came into contact with had an acute awareness that they had a brush with Greatness. No doubt that kid was a shooting star with unlimited potential. This is what I am striving for in my life. I will continue to embrace life with unbri-

dled enthusiasm such that it infects everyone that comes near. There is really nothing to life but love and happiness.

I have started to have dreams where I am riding a bike or climbing a mountain, and Adam is right behind me. I take solace in his protective gaze. I am wary that my expectations and standards for myself and others are higher than most can imagine. I disrespect myself and others who think that their typical accomplishments are enough. But for me, this will change. I will work tirelessly to achieve and excel and accomplish. Not just physically, but in all areas of my life. I will squeeze every ounce out of this world because my friend could not. I am good and I will do something in this world. And, I will avenge Adam's death.

—∞∘⊰⊱∘∞—

Last entry before entering the Army in 2004:

> God has prepared a path for everyone to follow. You just have to read the omens that he left for you.
> –From The Alchemist

The decision has finally been made to answer my true calling and enter the Army with the ultimate goal of becoming a Special Forces soldier.

The reasons are obvious. It is what I was born to do and what my life path has led me to. It feels good knowing that a truly ambitious and noble undertaking is about to begin. I firmly believe this is my chance to finally accomplish something worthwhile of which I can truly be proud. A true test of the courage that I know resides in my heart. From here on in I must remain focused on this and only this as I am told that few 30 year olds are able to compete with men 10 years younger, but I've got a feeling that I can not only survive, but thrive in the environment that will soon become my life. For the next three years I will become a killer, a warrior, and most importantly, a liberator.

My decision was obviously difficult for the family to understand and I'm sure there will be sleepless nights ahead. There's only so much that I can do for this. It will be extremely important for all of us to keep an upbeat and positive attitude as well as a sense of humor regardless of the misery index. I will keep a brave and stoic face at all times.

Must remember:
- The only way to fail is to quit.
- Maintain an intense focus on everything you do.
- Achieve your goals.
- Have a sense of purpose.
- Think then Act.
- Think then Act.
- Think then Act.
- Make the right decision EVERY time.
- Confidence is the direct result of accomplishment.
- The ONLY way to fail is to quit.

Email from Ryan's mentor, Major General Julian Burns, upon his decision to enlist:

FROM: Major Julian Burns
TO: Ryan Means
SUBJECT: Another Day

You set a new course for your entire family as it renews what every generation must do for itself. Not all do so in service to country or in such dramatic fashion.

For you see, that your dad has helped build the Atlanta and the Georgia we have today in business and public works. Others have served in community and parish and police and in thousands of other ways.... the common thread is service. Consider: How empty life would be to those who can not say that they served a cause larger than themselves...

...And to the contrary, how very full the lives of those who have served, no matter what the ending.....as Shakespeare had Henry the fifth say in the great play: "We few, we happy few, we band of brothers..."

Whatever spirit possessed you to do the thing you now do, it is important it be done well. And it is for sure, that there is the spirit of your father and your mother in it...some divine spark, some motivation beyond mere words, that binds you to a larger vision of the human condition, some simple desire for distinction and honor. For what ever reason, you will stand on no higher ground than you do now.

We, in the Burns family, likewise have seemingly made this military business a family affair, that goes back to every generation over the last 3 centuries.....but in every case, we are accidental soldiers. Accidental in the sense we never really intended to be warriors. It just kinda turned out that a way. You know, Americans are not by nature pugnacious and have forever had war forced upon them. When a body of people stands for integrity, and for liberty and for the dignity of the human spirit; when some outlandish tribe, or clan, or nation like our own makes such principles their watchwords, the fight comes to them. For the world is not friends to democratic ideals and works to the advantage of the dictator and the tyrant. And war comes, surely.

And rough and ready men like you stand between them and the populace. It is that knowledge that makes the American fighting man and woman a terror in the fight, and gentle to the people when not in battle, a distinguished history of discriminated violence...Abu Ghraib notwithstanding...

...You deliver yourself into the company of the most compassionate combat force that ever walked the earth.

So do well. It is going to be what you will tell your grand-children before the end of the century.

JB

PART III

I'm in the Army Now

Email Updates from Fayetteville, N.C.

DATE: May 28, 2004
SUBJECT: Onto the next adventure...

Just wanted to give everyone a quick heads up that I've decided to make a rather drastic but overdue change in my life for a number of reasons. After some thought, I realized my life in NYC was becoming stagnant and a bit boring although immensely enjoyable, but the thought of doing the corporate thing any longer was driving me insane. In addition, I've been looking for some type of new challenge that would prove to me whether or not I was as physically fit as I thought and the marathons weren't quite doing the trick.

Naturally, a large part of my decision stems from the fact that I still continually fantasize about killing those responsible for Adam's death. So, I went ahead and signed a three-year contract with the U.S. Army with the ultimate hope of going into the Special Forces. I'll be reporting for duty at Fort Benning, Ga. in late August for basic training and airborne school, then to Fort Bragg, N.C. for SF training or somewhere in Florida for Ranger school. Pretty excited about the prospect and looking forward to the mental and physical challenges that lie ahead.

An FBI agent might be contacting some of you over the next year, as secret clearance is required should I make it to the SF. Remember, I was always a model student and citizen who never did anything bad or illegal...

Will keep you posted on how much fun basic training is and my progress. —RPM

DATE: December 17, 2004
SUBJECT: Greetings from your soldier friend.

How things have changed in the past 6 months...Crazy to think that just a short time ago I was living a very, very different life on the glorious island of Manhattan; making a stab at the pseudo-intellectual, neoconservative Bohemian lifestyle in the East Village. I now find myself a thousand miles away, literally and figuratively, usually exhausted, often times cold and wet, loaded with 60 or so pounds of various types of gear and weapons, yet strangely always happy and always having a sadistic kind of fun in west Georgia while preparing for something as horrific and frightening as war (still attempting to get my head around the fact that this is where all this is headed).

Military life is odd to say the least and I'm not sure what my expectations were except that I was in for a drastic change and that much is absolutely certain. It's funny how often I find myself on the outside looking in while shaking my head and laughing wondering if joining the Army was a dream or some perverted, drunken joke. It's even funnier when a very large, very mean and very loud drill sergeant awakens me from my mental slumber by gently screaming in my ear to do five hundred push-ups.

I've spent some time trying to develop a short, simple analogy that would allow family and friends to understand what the experience is like and the best I've been able to come up with is a 70/30 mix between summer camp and prison (thankfully without the violent homosexual shenanigans); the mix is dependent on one's ability to follow instructions and overall attitude. Imagine playing a nonstop game of Simon Says with extremely intense physical consequences.

The guys in my platoon cover the entire range. Some can barely speak in full sentences but a handful, thankfully, have completed college and are extremely bright. It's difficult dealing with the extremely lazy and unmotivated individuals who constantly complain about the harsh conditions, but we have an insane amount of fun laughing at them and making fun when they start crying (literally) when things get the slightest bit tough. It's not unlike bullies in middle school which brings unpleasant memories of course, but keep in mind we are training to effectively and efficiently kill large numbers of human beings and there is simply no place for the weak and faint of heart in the infantry.

You would not believe the entertainment in watching the drill sergeants target the weak and mercilessly work them into soldiers, or at least something vaguely similar. We are now half way through the initial 14 weeks of training and have covered the most basic of military necessities (marching, looking the part and shooting various weapons systems). Let's just say the smile plastered on my face when ripping several hundred rounds off of an M-240 medium machine gun with tracer rounds was something to see. Even the toughest and most battle hardened of drill sergeants was visibly shaken by this sight. Upon return, we move on to bigger weapons and more advanced infantry tactics. Then it's off to Airborne school and then Ranger training. From what I'm told, Ranger training is no joke and will put applicants to unimaginable physical and

mental torture. I'm busting my ass trying to get ready, but I'm
not sure if fully preparing yourself is possible.

The friends I'm making will undoubtedly last a lifetime and
the experience is something that has already paid dividends a
thousand times over and will only continue to do so. We are constantly reminded that all of us will be deployed to a combat zone
in short order and the war on terror will continue throughout our
military careers. Unfortunately, human nature has also shown
that more conflicts are sure to arise that will require extreme
violence to resolve. I pray every day that I am up to the tasks I
have committed myself to and will perform appropriately when
the time comes. Until then, keep on rockin' in the free world.

—RPM

DATE: February 22, 2005
SUBJECT: Quick update

If you hadn't heard, I survived basic and moved on to
bigger and better things, namely Airborne school. From there
I go straight to Fort Bragg in N.C. for Special Forces selection (Ranger contract was dropped for this). Should I make
selection, I'll then be in an intensive 2-year training program
around the country and most likely the world. Attrition rate for
this program is extremely high so keep your fingers crossed.

Until then, keep on rockin' in the free world....

—RPM

AIRBORNE TRAINING

DATE: April 16, 2005
SUBJECT: I am alive...barely

Just wanted to send another quick update out and let people know that although extremely tired, nearly broken and very sore, I am in fact alive.

These days, I spend the majority of my time in the backwoods of North Carolina in what is called Special Forces Qualification Course 1 Alpha which is the precursor to the official Assessment and Selection course for the Green Berets. Needless to say, the process is tough with an overall attrition rate of 60-70%. (Assessment and Selection then has an attrition rate of about 50%). We spend most of our time with about 80 lbs. of gear on our back, alone, wet, cold, hungry and moving with 1-3 hours of sleep through snake infested swamps and woods. It's an experience just slightly different than my previous wanderings through the urban jungles of New York and beaches of East Hampton.

It's crazy to discover what the human body is truly capable of and the cadre here, which are best described as looking like movie stars with the physical endurance of world class triathletes and the brains of nuclear physicists, are excellent at pushing us to the limit. It's incredible to be around such a dedicated, extremely competitive group of individuals with a common goal of being the best at what they do. When I say competitive, I mean that we compete at everything...running, push-ups, sit ups, pull ups, land navigation events, eating, drinking, walking etc...and I absolutely love it.

We are confronted with the stark daily realities of what our future holds should we succeed and it certainly serves as a strong gut check as to whether or not we really want this and more importantly whether we are really cut out for it. The missions that the cadre discusses with us would absolutely blow your minds and make Ah-nold, Bruce and Sly movies look like kids' play.

I am proud to say that with 4 days left until the beginning of Selection, I stand near the top of the class and I'm feeling strong. Hopefully, I can continue to stay healthy and drive forward toward the ultimate goal of earning my Green Beret, a process that normally takes 2 years (similar to a master's degree in counter insurgency and guerrilla tactics). I'll soon be going 'dark' after next week with no access to phones, email, mail or anything else but will hopefully be in touch with good news in a month or so. Until then, keep on rockin' in the free world.

—RPM

DATE: May 22, 2005
SUBJECT: The saga continues

I am proud and very relieved to announce that after almost 9 continuous weeks of extremely difficult mental and physical testing (aka torture), I have been selected by the Army to continue on in the Special Forces training program. This does not mean I'm a Green Beret but rather that I'm officially in the pipeline, and if all goes right and I stay healthy, I should earn my tab in about 18 months' time. After this experience, I have entirely new definitions of words like "strenuous", "difficult", "heavy" and "exhausted." Without a doubt, the most challenging experience I've ever dealt with. The Army does a very good job of ensuring that candidates are fully capable of carrying out the sensitive and difficult missions entrusted to the SF teams. For instance, the first week we were subjected to a battery of written tests that included IQ, personality, general knowledge, math and reading skills, a language aptitude battery and a few others that I have no idea what they measured. After that, it was pure physical hell: timed runs of unknown distances, day and night land navigation tests and the dreaded team week. All said and done, we marched over 175 miles with weights varying from a minimum of 80 lbs. up to 200+ lbs. in about 10 days. Unfortunately, this is the proverbial tip of the iceberg and could continue forever. Although, rumor has it that the training schedule does let up after 3 years. We shall see. Out of 425 candidates only 155 were selected and this included some incredibly strong guys who were combat veterans from both Iraq and Afghanistan. I wish I could say what the grading criteria were and why some made it while others didn't but much of the process is a closely guarded secret and we were simply too tired and confused to really give it much consideration.

Moving forward, I will begin training as a combat engineer with cross training in weapons, meaning I will build things then blow them up (i.e. explosives expert) and know just about everything there is to know about every firearm, rocket launcher and grenade ever made and then some.

I'll also be studying Arabic and German with the hopes of being picked up by 10th Special Forces Group which specializes in mountain and high altitude operations. Better yet, we have some real Jason Bourne/James Bond training coming up. We will actually learn how to steal cars (early and late models, foreign and domestic), pick locks and get out of handcuffs. How sweet is that?

The road is still very long and I'm far from being done but the first and supposedly most difficult obstacle has been crossed and for this I'm extremely thankful. In fact, I don't think I've ever prayed as much in my entire life. Apparently somebody was listening, as my spine did not snap and my heart never gave out (although I did almost gouge my eye out).

It was funny as they gave us about 45 minutes to celebrate and recover before sending us right back into the fire for more training...what's the saying...no rest for the weary? Like any good soldier, I will continue to fight knowing that somewhere at the end there apparently is a light of some sort and some terrorists still at large. Until then, keep on rockin' in the free world.

—RPM

DATE: June 14, 2005
SUBJECT: Another day at the office

Just finished with a 19-day light infantry course that culminated in one of the more hellish experiences to date (I realize that phrase may seem repetitive but this stuff just isn't getting any easier). The final exam of this course is a series of continuous combat operations over a four-day period without resupply. Before starting, we were told that our 15-man squad would be carrying 100+ lb. rucksacks over many, many miles and without food or sleep for four days. I was pretty sure they were exaggerating but unfortunately they were not. Over this period, the lucky/lazy got 4-5 hours of sleep and a meal or two. The leadership fared worse off, getting maybe 1-2 hours and almost no food.

Mother Nature decided to turn the screws on us with extremely hot, sunny days with temps in the 90+ range and humidity just as high. This was the norm with the exception of a 3-hour lightning storm that pounded us relentlessly while we prayed that God would not strike us down. It was one of the more ferocious storms I've ever experienced and we were caught in the open. If the lightning popping all around wasn't bad enough, the thunder nearly made me sick. If you weren't about to boil to death, you were shivering in soaking wet clothes in the chill of the night and the early morning. It was amazing how quickly you would go from one extreme to the other.

The first day started off with a simulated artillery attack once we jumped off the trucks. Almost immediately you were totally soaked in sweat and covered in sand from running with all the weight then diving on the ground. In the first hour, I suffered a total blowout in the crotch area of my BDUs. Since I'm training to be a commando, I have to dress like a commando, i.e. no underwear. If it wasn't challenging enough trying to lead 15 guys training to be professional killers through this type of operation, try doing it wearing something resembling crotchless camouflage chaps. I might as well have been totally naked while giving briefings. At first we had a good laugh, but as we moved out I realized that it was nearly impossible to carry my M4 at the ready while fending off pricker bushes and these brutal 1/4" thick bushes that snap up like a whip when someone passes in front of you. My poor little guy was getting pummeled while we moved silently through the forest...except of course for my occasional yelps. What was even worse was when we stopped or came into enemy contact. This required me to dive on the ground, remove my ruck and low crawl into position. I swear, I dove on every patch of poison ivy and fire ant hill in the training area. Once on the ground, it was as if I instantly communicated throughout the insect world that a new luxury condo had been built. The dark area with nooks and crannies seemingly provided ideal protection from predators so everyone moved in...ants, ticks, spiders, centipedes, demonic looking black beetles...a truly diverse group took up residence between my legs.

Now, if this wasn't bad enough, the day before we left, a buddy had to be rushed to the hospital because his penis had been bitten by a brown recluse. These bites are horrific. There's no pain with the initial bite, but the poison begins to slowly eat away at your tissue. To treat such bites, the infected area usually has to be cut out with a scalpel and, even then, the wound is a big hole that heals very slowly. This is what I had to think about while laying totally motionless with God knows what crawling all over me while waiting for an ambush.

The final straw came when we crossed the swamp of death. It was about 400 meters of going through knee-deep to chest-deep thick swamp. It looked like something out of Lord of the Rings. In the first 100 meters we spotted 12 large venomous snakes (both copperheads and the highly aggressive cotton-mouth). Our sergeant, who has 10 years of Special Forces experience and multiple combat tours, said that he was extremely frightened during this and will probably not cross the same area ever again without carrying a pistol and possibly a shot-gun as well. I envisioned myself emerging with a large serpent hanging from each testicle. Luckily, this didn't happen.

Eventually, I was able to properly clothe myself and complete the missions with 44 semi-delusional, wet, cold, very exhausted soldiers. The sight of us completing the final

10-mile march was something too fearsome to behold: four days of facial hair, covered in cammo paint, sunken eyes and faces, filthy dirty clothes, soaking wet, carrying various types of weapons. It was the first time I really felt like a soldier.

Even though it was a miserable and difficult experience, we needed no reminder that our fellow soldiers were in far worse places fighting a tough enemy who uses real bullets and dying in the process. This reminder made it a relative walk in the park.

I suppose I'll be doing a lot of construction and very loud destruction over the next few weeks which should be fun. When that's over we will have some downtime and move into the more academic phase of training. Plan on spending my spare time surfing and chasing hotties in Wrightsville Beach.

Until then, keep on rockin' in the free world.

—RPM

PART IV

Life with Ryan

Chapter 1
A Short Long-Distance Relationship

When I returned home to PA after our amazing two-day marathon date, I already had an email from Ryan.

Hey, Beautiful.

It's about 10 p.m. and I'm totally exhausted. Needless to say, the weekend was phenomenal. Absolutely loved hanging out with you. I knew from the start that we had a connection and honestly hope that we stay in touch, see each other often and spend some more time together. It's not often I find girls that I can spend time with like that. You are awesome.

I hope you got home safe and are able to deal ok with work tomorrow/today. Know that you are missed very much and I'm already looking forward to our next trip together (how's about we make it just the two of us?) I'll come up with some options if you can give me some weekends. Maybe Wrightsville, maybe somewhere else.

Miss you more than you know,
Ryan

He wrote me a letter that first week as well. In 2005, it was not common to get a handwritten letter. I was indeed impressed.

Hey Sweetness,

Sitting in my little local coffee shop studying Arabic, recovering from a brutal day of fighting and of course day-

dreaming about you. Brutal to think that it could be December until we see each other again. Hopefully, the next 5 weeks will go by quickly and I'll certainly have something special to look forward to when I return. You'd be amazed how much you inspire me. It may sound silly, corny and just plain queer but the mere prospect of seeing you again gives me a focus and intensity that wasn't there before. Regardless of what happens or where this goes, I sincerely hope that we remain friends and stay in close contact. If it's not totally obvious, a girl like you doesn't come around very often. Believe me when I say I'm not very impressionable and you haven't been out of my thoughts since our meeting in the Ocean View parking lot. Ok, I feel like I'm going a bit overboard...

Tomorrow is our last day of this class and cannot end fast enough. The final event is going to be nothing short of pure physical torture. We were practicing today (class started at 4 am) and I thought guys were literally going to die. The instructor said it's not uncommon for people to pass out, collapse, get choked out, break bones, etc. during the event. Needless to say, we will be overjoyed when it ends. Fortunately, I'll be able to recover in peace in a beautiful setting...if only I had someone to help me recover...

Time to eat, sorry for the short letter but this kid is both exhausted and busy. Will think of you often this weekend. Absolutely love the fact that we are still in touch. Some people are unable to comprehend developing an actual friendship before a relationship, maybe someday they will learn what we know.

Until then sweetness,

Ryan

This was only the beginning of a series of daily emails, occasional handwritten letters, photos and phone calls that we exchanged in the coming months. We shared so many stories about our family, friends and daily life that it seemed like we had known each other for years and that there wasn't that much of a distance between us. There was so much substance to our conversations that the weeks we had known each other felt like all of the years of our lives at times.

A few weeks after our first date, I flew to Raleigh to meet Ryan. The day I bought my ticket, Ryan sent me my horoscope:

September 22, 2005

Although it may not be visible to anyone else, you have always been open to sharing your life with someone who shares your intellect and advanced vocabulary, your capacity for abstract thought and also your restless need for individuality and freedom. If only you could find such a person, you've been ready for a long time, right? Well shine your shoes! Someone of a like mind and heart has been waiting, too, and is just about to cross your path! This is one weekend you won't want to stay home alone!

We spent a night in Raleigh going to a couple of under the radar type pubs, then a neat local diner for a southern style breakfast. I tried grits and fried green tomatoes for the first time. The next morning, we drove to Wilmington for another unforgettable date. Again, after our weekend, I had a sweet email waiting upon my return home, followed by more in the series of handwritten letters that continued to capture my heart.

Hey gorgeous,

Had an amazing time with you this past weekend. Absolutely crazy about you. Another mind blowing experience. Can't wait to do it again and again and again...

See you soon, hopefully.
RPM

Dear Heather,

So happy to get your most recent letter. It's very important for us to continue to open up to one another and learn what the other is all about considering the length of time we have known each other and what's at stake. It's very nice to know that you seem to be the exact person I thought, the same type of person I have been looking for and the same type of person I can picture myself with years down the road. Of course, time will tell for sure (time together, that is). I will readily admit that when we were together in Raleigh it all felt so very real to me. Regarding the whole Army situation...Yes, sadly enough there are many who have no morals and little compunction in cheating. However there are also many happily married long-term couples who are very devoted to one another. I believe that it's all up to the individuals involved as to what kind of relationship you have. I'm not a cheater and want nothing to do with anyone that is. I've unfortunately dealt with those types in the past and hated it. Never again. Not worth the heartache on either side. I have no problem with being celibate, especially knowing someone as amazing as you is out there thinking about a possible future together. With you I feel no need to venture, not even now after knowing you such a short time. Perhaps premature to say, all things considered, but it's such a rarity for me to feel connected to someone like this, that it is just doing what comes natural. Whoa! Sometimes I catch myself swooning over you a little too much. I guess playing hard to get is no longer possible? I take great pride in my skills as a traveler, i.e. seeing things that are off the beaten path, staying away from the usual touristy crap and of course always meeting fun and interesting people. If we stick together for any extended amount of time (how's forever sound?), then you will travel the world. But until then, we must take what we can get under the circumstances, even if it is through letters and emails and brief conversations. I will never forget how happy you make me or your incredible beauty. Two more weeks is nothing. Soon we'll be together again. Until then...

All my love,
Ryan

I sent the following letter, which he had saved through the years:

Ryan,

Thank you for the greatest weekend I have ever experienced. Not to get all mushy on you, but I really don't know how I am going to sleep well without you next to me. I've never felt this way about anyone. I thought I would be in one of those very old-fashioned couples where each person sleeps in their own bed because I couldn't share a bed with anyone. Thank you for changing my mind. I love it! I was thinking of this on the plane home...This is going to sound silly (to you) but bear with me. Working in hospitals and in nursing homes, I see some very, very sick people...my patients are often men whose wives are too frail to take them home and care for them. So the wives will come in and help feed them or dress them, watch their therapy...whatever they can do...and it has always grossed me out that no matter how sick and smelly and drooling through dirty food crusted dentures their husbands were, they could still sit there and hold their hands and kiss them on the lips and lie next to them in the hospital beds. They tell them that they will love them until death do they part, in which case, I imagine they mean after death as well. In these instances sometimes, the husband does not even recognize his own wife because he is so out of it. I always thought that I could never be like that. I could care a lot about someone, but if they didn't even know I was there? Why would I put myself through that for them? And every day? WELL, I'd do that for you, all of it...You might not understand what I am talking about and I don't see you hospitalized or in a nursing home anytime soon but that really makes me realize how much I do care about you. It's not a usual scale of measuring but it's mine. Miss you more than I knew I could ever miss anyone.

Talk to you soon.
Heather

Chapter 2
From Stilettos to Hiking Boots

In the following months, it became clear that Ryan's family, his parents and three brothers, and his close friends were the center of his universe. He often referred to his mother as the "greatest woman on earth," which seemed like a lot to live up to. But he often said that I reminded him of her, so I never let it get to me. He praised his father for instilling discipline and education as well as always making sure they went on memorable family vacations. Alfie was the generous older brother, who, while having a reputation as a bit of a playboy, had a heart of gold. Tommy was the creative genius and "not like the rest of the family," Ryan would say, explaining that Tommy was a "liberal," which led to some heated discussions. But, he was a fantastic father and he and his incredible wife, Gabrey, made up an unstoppable couple that anyone could envy. Michael, who I met in Wrightsville that first weekend, was his only younger brother and one of his best friends. They never went more than a couple of days without communicating. Ryan insisted that I meet the rest of the family as soon as possible and wanted to plan a trip to stay with his family over Christmas. I was pleasantly surprised but incredibly nervous about making such a commitment, since we had known each other such a short time. He was already trying to persuade me to move to North Carolina as well. I had never lived anywhere but Pittsburgh and was not ready to consider this as an option...yet.

Ryan continued to update his friends, family and steadily growing fan club through email updates:

DATE: October 2, 2005

Sorry I've been out of touch but things have been moving along at no set pace for the past month or so and all this waiting around has made me feel soft and weak. Been doing lots of running, shooting, studying Arabic and taking a few other courses while waiting for the next official phase of the Q Course. Being out of the field for so long makes me feel very un-soldier like which is awful. I will admit, the time off has

allowed our bodies and minds to heal and actually afforded us some time to spend with family, friends and a bit of relaxing and surfing at the beach. From what I understand this is a very good thing as the next step is one of the toughest.

I have been fortunate enough to get a number

ABOARD THE PLANE, WAITING TO JUMP

of jumps in also. During the last one, I was using my Motorola V550 phone to snap shots just prior to jumping out of the plane.

On this particular jump, I was the first to go off the ramp. The drop zone came up on me a little fast and I didn't have time to button the cargo pocket containing my phone. Upon exiting the aircraft, I inverted a little bit, which is normal, and the phone dropped out of my pocket. As soon as the parachute deployed, I realized it was gone (trying to take some shots on the way down). Seeing the distance between aircraft and the ground is 1,200 ft., the drop zone a mile long and a 1/2 mile wide, I could only assume finding the pieces was a lost cause. Amazingly enough, 30 minutes later a guy walked up to the rally point holding my fully functional phone in the air without a scratch on it.

We leave for Phase II around 3:30 AM this morning. By the time you read this, chances are team 925 will be sweaty, filthy, exhausted and already covered 15 or so miles of course and loving every minute of it. We have 5 weeks of fun and folly in the woods learning the ins and outs of Special Forces small unit tactics, hand-to-hand combat and urban combat shooting skills. During this time, we operate as a 15-man team similar to how we'll work in real world mis-sions, and like the previous phases, the possibility of being 'voted off the island' by your peers and simply dropped from the course for poor performance will result in about a 30–40% attrition rate.

Fortunately, the guys on my team seem to be strong and intelligent. However, it is amazing to see how quickly people deteriorate under these types of conditions. Other friends just out of Phase II informed me that combat vets with Ranger tabs quit after 48 hours...

Wish it was going to be as much fun as it sounds but unfortunately it's lots of high stress work with little sleep and food. While we learn some excellent tactics and techniques it comes, as with everything in this process, at a steep price. Learning here is done one of two ways: repetition and blunt force trauma. Trust me when I say repetition is the much preferred but seldom used method. Apparently, this is to be a recurring theme in my budding SF military career which is obviously a good thing considering where I'll be in about 12 months. Overall, things are still great and I'm loving every minute of it.

There are no phones or computers in the woods, only Vietnam era 127 radios that weigh about 110 pounds with a range of about 30 feet assuming there aren't any bushes between them. Actually kind of funny when communicating between positions and realizing it's easier to shout (although very tactically unsound) to the other party. So, I will be totally incommunicado until early November.

Hopefully, all is well in your world and I hope to be able to catch up real-time soon. Also look forward to getting any funny stories from phase II out upon return (assuming the experience isn't permanently blocked from memory).

Until then, keep on rockin' in the free world.
RPM

DATE: November 27, 2005
SUBJECT: The Adventure Continues

Just finished 3 weeks of some really gruesome training (on top of the previous 5 weeks). Highlights included: learning to pick locks and steal cars, being attacked by sentry dogs, eating maggot infested roadkill after going a full week with no food, being held captive and beaten on a daily basis in near freezing temperatures while wearing nothing but pajama's and flip flops. Oddly, all of that doesn't come close to conveying how bad it really was, but everything else we did and had done to us, is classified (how cool is it that I can finally say that?). Anyway, it's over, thank God and I'm now recovering mentally and physically with nothing much to do except gain weight back and look forward to the coming holidays.

We start blowing things up come January and hope to take some videos as the explosions are pretty impressive.

Keep on rockin' in the free world.
RPM

Ryan came to PA and I traveled to Fayetteville a few times in the next months. By December, I decided I was ready to spend my first Christmas away from home. I had not travelled much in my life and certainly had not left the East Coast. I obsessed over the details and eventually told him that I changed my mind a few days before Christmas. I couldn't bear leaving my family as my grandmother was 92 and I didn't want to think that I may miss what could be her last Christmas. Furthermore, I had never spent a Christmas

anywhere but Pennsylvania (where we dream of white Christmases) and
Palm Desert, California, just seemed like it wouldn't feel like Christmas at all.

ENJOYING COCKTAILS AND FRIENDS

AT A FELLOW GREEN BERET'S
WEDDING RECEPTION

Fortunately, after nights of sleeplessness, I decided that I would go
to California. Unfortunately, he had already cancelled the ticket. He
immediately bought a new flight and I began packing. Prior to Ryan, I
basically wore stilettos and dresses everywhere. I bought my first fleece
jacket and hiking shoes for this trip and never looked back; another way
in which he changed my life for the better.

The immediate days before I left for Palm Desert, I was unable to reach
Ryan. His phone was off and I was at the point where I needed a little pep
talk to get on the plane. I spoke with him a couple days sooner when he put
his mother on the phone who gave me the schedule of events. I felt like I was
ready to get on the plane. Now, after not speaking for two days, I wasn't so sure.
I wondered if he had just completely changed his mind, or if he was called to
war—who could guess with Ryan Means? It wasn't like him to not call and
see if I was on my way—but I went on ahead. I prayed that he would be at the
airport when I arrived. And, he was—standing at baggage claim waiting with
flowers, as usual! As it turned out, he started climbing a mountain and decided
he wasn't going to stop until he hit the top so, 18 hours later, he returned to
his family bruised and scraped, but at least not mauled by a mountain lion
or coyote. I could not touch his legs without him yelling in pain for the next

few days. His family later explained that this was normal behavior for him and over the years I came to expect the unexpected from him as well.

First on the Palm Desert agenda was meeting Ryan's mother, who was rocking her newest grandchild to sleep when we walked into the house. Mary Jo and I were wearing the same outfit: coral polo shirts, khaki capris and ballet flats. Ryan pointed it out in his usual taunting manner. We were off to a great start and unbeknownst to me I was about to meet the entire Means family. Not just his parents, but brothers, aunts, uncles, cousins... the list goes on. A fair warning would have been nice.

We hiked for hours every single day—once we went twice in a day—and I figured out that after 27 years of protesting "outdoorsy" activity, I actually loved it. Now I wonder if maybe it was just his companionship and conversation.

THE FOUR
BROTHERS AT
JOSHUA TREE
NATIONAL
PARK: (ALFIE,
RYAN, TOMMY,
MICHAEL)

COCKTAIL PARTY AT THE MEANS
RESIDENCE IN PALM DESERT

HIKING IN PALM DESERT

—ooo⟩⊛⟨ooo—

After the California adventure, we jetted off to our first New Year's Eve in Atlanta. We toured Ryan's old stomping grounds. I saw the gorgeous home in Brookhaven where he grew up, his first apartment, his church and clubs. The holiday was supposed to be spent as a quiet night at home, but at the very last minute Ryan decided that we were crashing a black-tie party at the request of one of his life-long best friends, Josh Cobb. Josh and Ryan together reminded me of a science experiment gone wild: two incredibly volatile substances that, when mixed, created fumes and sparks and danger...and a ton of fun.

I had nothing to wear to a last minute black-tie cocktail party. I planned on hiking, casual dinners and spending time alone. He said that I needed to be better prepared during our future travels. "You should always have a plan, an alternate, and an alternate for the alternate," he would say. Easily said by the guy who would steal his older brother's tuxedo. I knew if we ever had a family, it would function like a military operation under his leadership.

Ryan dropped me off at the door of a ridiculously overcrowded mall in the heart of Atlanta and with a devious laugh, said that I had 20 minutes to find a dress, shoes and jewelry and to remember that all of his "closest friends will be meeting me for the first time and that first impressions are lasting." No pressure. This was followed by a fast "On your mark, get set, GO!" as he peeled off in his car. He wasn't kidding either. I was in tears. I had no clue where I was or what I was looking for and I wasn't used to the diverse holiday crowds in Atlanta. It was overwhelming. My average time to get myself prepped to go out went from two hours to two minutes over the next few years with Ryan's coaching.

We went to the black-tie affair and of course stood out. But, it wasn't because I didn't pull off my end of the bargain. I found the dress, the shoes and the jewelry. And after a bit of chaos, Ryan tracked me down in the

NEW YEAR'S EVE 2005

insanity that was Lenox Mall on New Year's Eve. We stood out because Ryan had purchased a tuxedo jacket with shiny magenta photos of men appliquéd over the back and chest pocket. It was nicely made, but it still seemed odd. I didn't question it myself. I had come to expect these oddities. But this was a very, very conservative crowd. A woman immediately came over to Ryan and asked, "What is that on the back of your jacket—who are those men?" To which he replied matter-of-factly, "Serial killers." She looked disgusted. He went on: "You know, Charles Manson, Ted Bundy..."..he went on laughing as she walked away. "Why the hell did you buy that?" I asked him. "For *that* reason," he replied with a laugh. "Besides, it's made really well." This made for quite the conversation for the rest of the night.

RYAN'S FAVORITE LOCAL HAUNT,
POOLHALL BAR IN BUCKHEAD

THE SERIAL KILLERS JACKET

Chapter 3
Did You Just Ask Me to Marry You in an Email?

After the holidays, it was clear what needed to happen. I was moving to North Carolina and I was never looking back. I honestly don't remember how I broke this news to my family, but I do know that they tried to talk me out of it. Ryan worked relentlessly to talk me into it, and just as I seemed to be on board with the situation, he decided to remind me of the reality of our situation:

H,

I understand you were raised in a different world and I certainly understand the importance of taking care of your grandmother, especially now since she's getting older and more dependent. I know that you don't want to break your mother's heart by leaving or hurt anyone else in your family. I would never want to break your family apart for any reason. You simply have no choice but to stay for any amount of time if you feel that is the right thing for you to do. But understand also that I want you to be happier.

You question whether or not you are 'enough' for me. This is an interesting question that I sometimes wonder but not in the way you think. I like to think that I'm a driven person who intends on accomplishing a number of things in my life-time; whether it be avenging the murder of my friend, climb-ing mountains, running marathons or traveling the world, I want do big things. It's an attitude developed at a young age and constantly reaffirmed throughout my life. It's something that's tested every day in my current job and a big part of my current happiness and overall job satisfaction. The desire to be constantly challenged is something that I love and something that I always want in a mate, but want it in the same amount and intensity that I possess which has been a problem in past relationships. I need to learn to accept that not all people, especially women, are like this to the degree that I am...thank God.

I love the idea of you moving out on your own to a new city. Seeing someone that I care so much about, become independent and take such a big risk is amazing. If it does work out, even in 5-10 years, you will have done something that 95% of this world is unable or unwilling to do because they are afraid(one of my least favorite characteristics in people...); if it doesn't work out, the experience will prove to be more valuable than all of your schooling put together.

Moving here right now may not be practical. We need to accept that and stop wasting time on ideas that simply aren't feasible. Unfortunately, this is where reality begins to set in and the rudeness of the situation becomes apparent. I am in training at least until October. After which, I may move to Kentucky but I could also end up in Germany, Fayetteville or Colorado. Then, I could move to one of these locations for anywhere from 5 days to 5 months before deploying. Deployments could be anywhere from 3-12 months. There is no way to predict any of this. So, if it's security you want, I'm the wrong guy. Just think about what I'm going to be doing over the next 5-10 years...I'm going to be fighting in a war. At anytime during a deployment, you could very well get a phone call or visit saying that I've been seriously wounded or killed.

That is something that you need to understand. It's incredibly difficult to live with that constantly hanging over your head.

So here's the bad news: Distance relationships never seem to work, especially when the two people have spent a fraction of the time together as they have apart. Special Forces marriages have a 15% chance of success. I may see you a handful of weekends over the next two years and then die overseas. Worse, I may be horribly disfigured and live. Is this the life you want?

Given, I've painted a worse case scenario but did so because you will have it far worse than I will. The emotional pain you will suffer will be far worse and last much longer than the physical pain I will experience. I've tried over and over to help you understand what my life or lifestyle is going to be like for the next several years (again worse case) so that you can make an informed decision. Yes, it's noble and honorable to try and make it work now but we need to think about whether or not it's going to be worth it (and that sounds bad) but we may see each other for literally a handful of weekends and then even then there's little guarantee that it will work out. It sucks and I hate where we are but also wonder if we have a choice in the matter i.e. even if we 'ended' it, feelings don't change overnight—not to mention you are the only girl I've been able to potentially see myself with long term.

That being said, let's look at mid-term solutions in the not so worse case scenario: I graduate and move to Kentucky in October where I'll be for 3-5 months before shipping out for a 6-month deployment. Would I have to propose (again) for you to move to KY? These are the things I think about and sometimes wonder what the chances are. I don't want to go through the pains of a long term/long distance relationship only to realize that after 2-4 weeks of being in the same town, that person is something/someone totally different than what they were for a weekend every other month.(This goes for both of us.) When do we get a trial period that lasts longer than a week in the same region? Is it possible or do we simply put faith in our vacation time together and hope for the best?

It's a dilemma any way you cut it and we need to figure something out.

Love you,
Ryan

I replied:

Ryan:

I also understand the reality that you might not be here forever. On that note, if I make a personal choice of my own free will to put my career on hold and spend my life—and as much of yours as you will give me—being with you, then so be it. That is what I want. I understand the reality of the situation even if I don't like it.

This is MY definition of marriage: When you are married, you know that no matter where someone is, what they are going through, or even if they die (I'm tearing up here because I know you could), that they had made a life changing decision to make YOU the other half of themselves. You are the most important thing in the world to that person. You don't ever really leave them no matter how far away you are from them physically and there is a much deeper connection that transcends time or place that cannot be broken. I know those words may scare you but I am being blunt because I don't think we have time to sugar coat things and get a feel for what the other person thinks.

Hypothetically, if I was to marry you—the best case scenario is to just hold off on planting myself somewhere, work anywhere close to a base helping soldiers and make sure you have an amazing wife and comfortable home to come home to when you can come home. My job affords me the opportunity to help people in a lot of places.

You don't have to marry me to keep me local to you, Ryan. You are right. We do need to spend time in the same place together first. But, I can tell you we will be great, "it" will work, you will see that I am no different than I am on our weekend adventures. I am up for anything that my body and footwear can physically handle as far as adventuring with you.

I truly understand that there is a lot of work involved in this relationship and—like you—I love a challenge. There is no question in my mind that this is what I want. And I ALWAYS get what I want when it is up to me to make it happen, but now I have to understand it is up to you too.

In conclusion: if I need to advertise any more of my selling points, let me remind you that in my job, and especially in some wicked affiliations, I have seen people without limbs, sickly disfigured, brain dead, and literally dying in my hands. I understand what can happen to you more that most people can...more than you might.

Finally, when you are happy I am happy. That's how I know this is really love. If I didn't love you, I would not support your intense desire to avenge the death of someone you love in this dangerous manner. You are putting your life at risk, when someone who loves you immensely is right here dying to be with you. Believe me, it's hard and it hurts for me to accept that I am second to Adam, who I sadly will never know but understand is your driving force. I would never ask you to give up this fight, even though it breaks my heart over and over again to know how strongly you feel about this situation.

Still loving you,
Heather

From Ryan:

Sweetheart,

I'm all in. Here's something to chew on since you are always concerned about things being 'practical' (something that I don't do so well).

Should you move down here and things move along according to plan, after a month or so, we might want to look at doing a court house/paper marriage. Practical reasons include that we would save a good chunk of money, my pay will increase when we get married, I'd be able to actually move off base and live with you. You'd be on the Army health-care/dental plan and you'd be the recipient of the life insurance policy when I deploy, etc.

Assuming we did this, I'd like to keep this relatively low key for obvious reasons but primarily so we don't upset relatives and friends, and then in a year or so do the full on ceremony thing.

Needless to say, this would be a massive, massive step but one that I am ready to take. And yes, my head is kinda spinning a little bit after my email proposal...ha! Military romance at its finest.

Keep in mind this is the second time I have asked you to marry me, Airlie was a bit more romantic. Thoughts on secret marriages?

Ryan,

I'd never marry you for financial reasons. Not to mention, I just posted my resume today to see what was out there...I may take a pay cut, but there is not a shortage of jobs for PT/OTs near Fort Bragg—not surprising. Did you really just ask me to marry you via email!?! I'm not quite sure how to respond. Have you been drinking?

Heatwave,

No drunken empty promises here. Just an aging former bachelor letting go of his party boy ways. Move here. Now.

By the end of February, we had found a place in Wrightsville. I secured a job and plans were finally set in motion. It seemed like we had been waiting for this day for years, but in reality we had known each other for seven months and the majority of correspondence was email rather than face-to-face time, as he was often incommunicado for weeks at a time due to training. As Ryan's best friend would later write regarding my move to NC, "this may be the single greatest leap of faith that anyone has ever taken."

On March 1st 2006, Ryan again sent my horoscope:

> Because Aquarius is one of the four fixed signs
> of the zodiac you prefer things to stay as they
> are, or at least not to change unless it is you who
> chooses to change them. That is, however, asking
> a bit too much. Don't fear change. Learn to adapt.

And Heatwave, you are adapting with such class and courage. I'm so proud. This is for sure the best decision you ever made for yourself.

RPM

Ryan,

Thank you for the horoscope and sweet words. It is supposed to be 76 degrees by the time we meet in Wilmington tomorrow!!! That's 30 degrees warmer than Pittsburgh! I am thrilled about moving and I can't wait to see you and for the both of us to really get to know each other. I only wish I could shake the weight of the guilt I feel seeing my mom and grandma crying tonight. It really hurts me to know I am the cause of it. I wish I could convince them that this is as good of an idea as I believe it is...Well, it is senseless to complain. No turning back. Love you and I will see you soon!

Heather

—∘∘∘⊰⊱∘∘∘—

Ryan's email updates to the fan club continued:

DATE: April 8, 2006
SUBJECT: Almost a 'National Strategic Asset'

Believe it or not, that is one of several actual military moni-
ker's given to SF guys and I thought that it was kind of cool that in
5 weeks barring injury, I'll be able to tell the ladies 'my job; What I
do is no big deal really.... I'm just a National Strategic Asset...'

We just finished 'job training' or in military terms, MOS
(military occupational specialty) training which was 13
weeks long. It culminated in a 10 day exercise that tested our
abilities and skills as Special Forces engineers. We divided up
into 12 man teams and ran continuous missions that typi-
cally started around 2 PM and ended around 8 or 9 AM. We'd
usually walk anywhere from 10-15 miles each night. I hate to
mention, there were no shower facilities available during the
10 days and will spare you descriptions of the stench of our
team when sitting in an enclosed structure and taking our
boots and gear off.

The missions ranged from the simple; blowing up a railroad bed, airfield or bridge to the somewhat complex; a raid
on a building complex using 2 or more teams. On a typical
night, we'd conduct 3-4 of these, return to a very rudimen-
tary base camp grab a few hours of sleep a quick bite to eat
and begin planning for the next night so needless to say
toward the end we were pretty beat up.

On our final night of missions, when our team was totally
exhausted, we walked through a large swath of woods that

had recently been burnt out. It was totally blackened and reeked accordingly. There was enough moonlight that you had a decent amount of vision and could see fairly well but everything had this strange black and white or shades of blue look to it.

As we continued toward our objective, we could see a massive orange light from forest fires over a small hill a few hundred meters away. This bizarre light reflected off both the trees above the fire and the smoke it generated, setting a true scene of devastation in a combat zone.

Our target was several old railroad cars being used to store arms and ammunition—mostly 25 lb anti-tank mines, a variety of mortar rounds and a handful 105mm artillery shells. The outside of the rusted metal cars had been burnt many times over adding to the authentic look and mood of the scene around us. It was a fairly standard hit where we maneuvered into position, eliminated the bad guys, occupied the objective, established security, collected the munitions, placed our charges and moved out. The whole process took exactly 5 minutes.

We moved off this particular objective around 4:30 AM and our exfiltration route took us directly into the fires. Keep in mind we're working on a few hours of sleep for the week, haven't had much food, our faces are totally covered in soot, sweat, blood, dirt, camouflage paint and about a 5 day stubble. Our eyes are blank and sunken and the only thing we can think about is completing the next mission, walking several miles on ravaged feet so we can get 3 hours of sleep and a quick bite. During these training missions you are either: cold, wet, dirty, tired and hungry OR hot, sweaty, dirty, tired and hungry. Being comfortable just isn't in the equation.

We moved out and had to cross the fire which was just a few inches wide and about a foot high but stretched out over several hundred meters. It looked like a giant orange snake moving along the ground as it flickered in the wind. As we approached it, we were surrounded by these small campfires dotting the ground as far as you could see along with these strange fires up in the air that were actually rotten trees burning in the center that had a knot in the trunk where the flame was coming out. These elevated fires would spill sparks in a continuous fashion making it look like a flaming waterfall coming out of thin air. Very trippy indeed.

As we passed through the area, we crossed a small swamp that reflected the whole nature gone insane scene around us. Imagine 12 guys covered in soot and camouflage, carrying various types of machine guns, assault packs, and harnesses full of gear, traveling silently through waist deep swamp surrounded by these bizarre floating fires and a giant fire snake. It was completed by the obligatory smoke and fog occasionally blowing through. I kid you not, the most talented special effects guys in Hollywood could not have produced a more realistic looking situation—perhaps the closest I've seen was out of Full Metal Jacket.

We moved out of the swamp, crossed the fire line, moved several hundred meters and lay into a security position in order to make contact with HQ and get the instructions for our final hit. At this point, the moon is gone and illumination is next to nothing. We've moved from the hot and sweaty to the cold and wet in a matter of seconds. As we waited, the sun began to peek through the trees ahead of us and we saw that our position sat on the edge of a giant rolling field planted with soybeans or some crop that was just coming up and very green. A road ran along the far side that had several dogwoods in full bloom and along the middle of this field are these huge oak trees that must've been planted a hundred or so years ago. As the sun rose in front of us, the morning fog began to lift and I kid you not, several deer walked out of the far edge of the field and began to feed, completing one of the most beautiful scenes I think I've ever experienced. It was almost like there was a director calling out 'Cue the deer... ok good....I need more sunlight!!! Now give me morning mist and....birds chirping...good!!!'

Perhaps it was because we just traveled through hell, but every one of us sat in silence and in total disbelief and amazement at the whole transition taking place in front of us.

We finished our final mission around 9:00am and being point man, I had the responsibility of finding our route home. Choosing between a long dry route or a short wet one, I choose the latter. The wet area was actually a large wide opening of reeds and grass where a small creek/river fed into a lake.

As the exhausted and filthy team moved through, we attempted to find a semi dry crossing but none was to be found. As this point, I decided to cross at a seemingly shallow spot to try and keep the drying process moving forward. I took one timid step into the stream and immediately sunk up to my crotch in mud. As I took a second step, the other leg sank. Attempting to move forward looked more like a limbless upper torso squirming in a puddle as the mud literally swallowed my arms and legs every time I tried to place them.

Being exhausted and now frustrated and covered in mud, all I could say was 'don't come this way' (as if it wasn't totally obvious) followed by a string of expletives much to the humor of the rest of the guys who at this point were totally incapacitated with laughter watching a so called commando wrestle himself across a shallow creek.

My misfortune elevated the spirits enough that everyone found the energy to began throwing each other into the stream which further degenerated into a full on mud fight. The combination of completing the mission, cool water, pseudo cleanliness and my commando crossing must have made us a little insane because at some point I sobered up and looked around at a bunch of shirtless buff dudes, mud wrestling and frolicking in the water and realized I'd seen it before in an Abercrombie and Fitch catalog (or maybe it was the gas fight scene from Zoolander?). I informed everyone that should we be seen, we'd certainly be kicked out of the military for violating the 'don't ask, don't tell' rule so we regained our military bearing, geared up and moved out thus completing phase III on a high note.

We depart Monday morning for our final test of the Q course; a 5-week exercise called Robin Sage. It's played out over a 50,000 square mile area and like everything we've done so far, it will have it's fair share of pain and misery, but when surrounded by the group of guys I've been working with over the past 2 years, absolutely anything is possible and we'll do it with the usual speed, violence of action and sense of humor that has carried us this far.

After Robin Sage, we'll start language school and should

graduate sometime in October of this year. During this exercise
I will not have access to email or phones but hope to send out
some stories upon completion. The last crew that went through
wore civilian clothes while carrying concealed weapons for
most of the exercise and got to recon and rob a real bank—
complete with shooting (blanks) at actual guards and police-
men responding. Who hasn't dreamt of robbing a bank with a
highly trained team of commandos armed with machine guns?

The funny part is, I'm 32-years-old and very little has
changed since I was 10. The toys may be a little heavier and
complex, but I'm still running around in the woods playing
army and getting into mud fights with my friends. It's funny
because Tommy and Alfie always said I'd grow out of this
phase in high school...guess I showed them. The fact that this
so called fun will soon end is of course not lost on me, especially as graduation and certain deployment to either Iraq
or Afghanistan or both is just around the corner. However,
you would be hard pressed to find a group of guys who love
their job more than us. Unfortunately, I don't have the skill to
craft the words and phrases necessary to accurately convey
the meaning and feeling of these experiences, but I can say
without question that of all the decisions I've made thus far in
life, joining the Army and shooting for a career in the Special
Forces has undoubtedly been the best and it just seems to
keep getting better and better.

I'm off to Wilmington for some surfing, beer drinking
and bluegrass. I'll hope to have some time off after Sage.

Until then, keep on rockin' in the free world.
RPM

Chapter 4
He loves me, He loves me not

I made the move and we struggled to make things work from the beginning. I completed the drive from Pennsylvania in 11 straight hours and my step-dad was not far behind with our U-Haul. Ryan was to meet us and help with the move. He chose instead to stay in Fayetteville for a night out with his friends and meet me the next day, hung over. Not only did it not look good to my step-dad, who may report to my family that my boyfriend is a selfish jerk, but I thought Ryan was as excited as I was to get our place established and start living the way we had planned. This absolutely terrified me.

The early March weather was as unpredictable as my beloved boyfriend, rather than the warm and sunny days I knew from my visits. I hated my new job and found that living where I once vacationed wasn't the vacation I thought it would be. It is quite hard to get dressed for work every morning when your flip flops and bikini are staring at you, begging to go to the beach. On the other hand, my sweet little dog, Jack, was terrified of every aspect of the beach. I felt I had made the wrong decision for everyone.

Ryan visited almost every weekend. We lived for these reunions. But, as I was either working or with Ryan, I had little time to make any friends. He would often travel or disappear for work and I was left at home—which I have to admit—felt much worse than when I was in PA with my family. He had been right about this. In addition to the lonely days, it seemed like Ryan was not as ready as he thought to give up the social circuit, and I felt like we were possibly on two different pages, sometimes maybe in two different books. We rarely got to go on a date without his Army friends, which I didn't mind, but Ryan was constantly flirting with women and dying to be the center of attention when we would go out on dates with a group. It became more than irritating. I just wanted to spend time with him and get to know him better.

One day, when flipping through some papers on his desk, I found some letters from a couple of girlfriends or as he would say, friends that were girls. They were dated during the time we started long distance dating and were pretty detailed. They even included photos. It wouldn't have been so upsetting to me had he been honest with me about the situation. I had informed him that I was dating someone off and on when we met, and I expected my honesty to be reciprocated. When he said he was going out of town to see a friend, I just assumed the friend was male. Lesson learned: do not assume a thing about Ryan Means.

This would be an inaccurate account if I didn't admit that we had a series of ups and downs, and eventually, I proposed that we spend some time apart. We tried and failed. Dating other people just did not work for either of us. Through our attempts to live without each other, find someone else or just be friends, we learned that we couldn't live without each other.

By August, we had a pretty good idea that upon graduating and receiving his Green Beret, Ryan would be in 5th Group Special Forces stationed in Fort Campbell, Ky., a short trip outside of Nashville. He wishfully planned for 10th Group in Colorado Springs. I had to consider moving once again, further from my family. There were so many ups and downs and near break-ups in the next months. Looking back on all of the letters and emails, I really wonder how we made it. The Army lifestyle was wearing on me and I felt like I moved for nothing as I began to see less and less of Ryan. We took turns trying to end our relationship and then talking the other person "back from the edge," as he would say.

—◦◦◦❦❖❦◦◦◦—

DATE: August 24, 2006
SUBJECT: Email from Ryan

Sweetheart,

I tell you how and what I feel all the time, however you choose for whatever reason to ignore it and continue believing what you want. I have to believe that you are done with us.

Perhaps it really is me that makes you so miserable and if that's the case, then absolutely we need to walk away, but I don't think it is. I know that no previous girlfriend was ever this miserable to be with me (without me, yes).

I think that if you walk away for good, it would be a huge mistake. First, you'd be walking away from someone tremendously dedicated to you and who loves you very, very much. Not only that, but I happen to think I've got one of the greatest families in the world, all of whom think you are the shit. Rather than being months away from being married and living with the man who loves you very much, you'd be in Wrightsville where apparently you don't seem to know very many people OR you'd move back to Pittsburgh to be with your family and you'd be that much further away from what you eventually want.

I know I'm not perfect by any stretch, but this is a temporary situation, we absolutely make a spectacular couple and I've never been this serious about anyone before.

Sweetheart, I know you're not happy right now but look how far we've come. We've been through a lot and we've done it together. I'm 3 months away from graduating and completing a major milestone in my life. I can't imagine you not being there for any part of it.

After that, I'll be able to live a semi-normal life again and it will be different. We still spend every, or at least the majority of nights together, I won't be broke all the time ,and you will certainly be able to find a job that suits you.

You are about to walk away at the worst possible moment; right before a glorious weekend together that will provide an idea of what our life can be like. I'm out, Love, and off to bed.

I've got to work on Saturday early AM but I'll have my phone with me should you want to text me how much you still love me. I miss you tons and hate that I can't see you this weekend. I pray that you choose me over not me and decide to spend a wonderful weekend with me in the mountains.

Please let me know ASAP about your decision as I can't sleep and can hardly think straight right now.

RPM

Of course, I gave in and we took the weekend vacation together. It was rough at first, but as usual, we had an amazing time, talked things out, and decided it was for the best that we keep on working towards a future together.

WEEKEND ALONE IN CASHIERS, NC, HIKING CHIMNEY TOP MOUNTAIN

In the beginning of December, Ryan received his Green Beret. His family came to Fort Bragg for the ceremony. I was there, with the intent that I would soon commit myself to being *(gulp)* an Army wife. During the service, they played the *Ballad of the Green Berets:*

> *Fighting soldiers from the sky*
> *Fearless men who jump and die*
> *Men who mean just what they say*
> *The brave men of the Green Beret*
>
> *Silver wings upon their chest*
> *These are men, America's best*
> *One hundred men we'll test today*
> *But only three win the Green Beret*
>
> *Trained to live, off nature's land*
> *Trained in combat, hand to hand*
> *Men who fight by night and day*
> *Courage deep, from the Green Beret*
>
> *Silver wings upon their chest*
> *These are men, America's best*
> *One hundred men we'll test today*
> *But only three win the Green Beret*
>
> *Back at home a young wife waits*
> *Her Green Beret has met his fate*
> *He has died for those oppressed*
> *Leaving her this last request*
>
> *Put silver wings on my son's chest*
> *Make him one of America's best*
> *He'll be a man they'll test one day*
> *Have him win the Green Beret*

(Written by Robin Moore & SSG Barry Sadler)

THE MEANS FAMILY AT RYAN'S GREEN BERET GRADUATION CEREMONY (ALFIE, AL, RYAN, MARY JO, MICHAEL AND TOMMY)

Ryan thought that it was hilarious that all of the wives, mothers, and sisters would immediately start crying out loud during this ritual. He warned me ahead of time not to be "a typical chick" and cry. He had played this song so many times for me when we went on road trips, he

had downloaded it onto my iPod. He told me I ought to get used to it because they play it at the funerals of Green Berets and it's the most heart wrenching thing you have ever seen. Even the soldiers get choked up when they play the ballad during funeral detail. He planned on dying for his country if need be, and he always did his best to prepare me for the worst possible scenario, although I just knew Ryan wasn't

GREEN BERET
GRADUATION DAY

meant to die young, so it was senseless preparation. Either way, I still could not manage to hold back the tears when they played it at his graduation. His brother, Alfie, elbowed me throughout the song and made fun of me for crying at the ceremony. This was followed by Ryan taunting me and reminding me I had better work on getting "thick skin" soon.

THE MEANS FAMILY AT RYAN'S GRADUATION PARTY
AT THE SHADY LADY, FAYETTEVILLE, NC

After the graduation and the Special Operations Command's cautionary words on the deployment that was about to take place, it seemed Ryan had a sudden change of heart and I received this email, which came as a shock and broke my heart:

Heatwave,

I had a great time this weekend and a number of times I thought and felt that we could make it work for the long run regardless of the differences we have. But, I think that I am not going to be able to give you the attention and love you need.

Already, I have become totally focused on getting to Ft. Campbell and preparing for deployment and/or whatever school they are going to throw at me. Regardless of how we feel about each other, I just don't think that I want to continue putting you through this torture and leading you on. I have really examined what the next 2–3 years are going to be like and simply cannot make the commitment you need. Assuming I get out, then I want to either become a contractor or go into other areas, which require a similar commitment.

This is an extremely difficult decision because it means that I will likely never have a wife or kids or a normal suburban lifestyle.

This leaves us with two options. The first is to simply walk away now and try and move on with our lives. The second is to keep in touch for the next 6 months to see how things progress and see if the role of a SF wife is something with which you are comfortable. It will be brutal. I hate to keep leading you on but I also hate the idea of ending something that has so much potential. Either way it's sad.

RPM

I replied:

Thank you for being honest. That information would have proven more useful months ago—like maybe when I told you that I was prepared to break up with you for good?! Nonetheless, thank you.

That said, I do think it would be a shame for someone as exceptional as you to never bring more natural born soldiers or beautiful intelligent little girls into the world, but that isn't my choice, it's yours. Good luck with whatever you choose, even though it wasn't me.

I told (wrote) you when we first met at Wrightsville that I never truly knew what it felt like to miss anyone because I was never far from anyone I cared that much about but I missed you by the ride home from the beach... I still feel that way. You are the only one.

H

Heatwave,

I hate that this feels like a final goodbye. My feelings for you haven't changed, it's just that I am going to war for the next couple of years and it's not fair to you to be secondary in this relationship. I can't keep asking you to move and wait, move and wait. I won't be seeing other people as I love you and only you. Do you want to see me this weekend?

RPM

Ryan,

YES! I absolutely want to see you this weekend! Any time that I can spend with you is precious. That said, I hope you know (despite my sarcastic remarks) I do not regret moving here—only because of the time we have spent together.

I will never say goodbye to you as I will always want you in

my life, in whatever capacity you will afford me. Even though
you are not directly asking me to—I WILL WAIT for you. We have
no idea what will happen in the future but I refuse to risk losing
you for any reason. You never really let me go when I tried to
leave you and I love and respect you for that and I will return
the favor. We may not be in the same state—or country—but we
will stay together as long as you will have me. End of story.

I hope you appreciate what we have as much as I do. Never
ever give up on me. There will be no person who ever has a
chance to step into my heart and mind where you will be each
day. I love you, Ryan, with both emotional and intellectual
reason. If you feel the same, how can we possibly go wrong?
We can be in that small number of people who make it. I refuse
to accept anything else from myself.

CAN'T WAIT TO SEE YOU!
H

What a huge relief. Can't wait to see you either. We are
going to have a great weekend!

Love you with all of my heart,
RYAN

We spent his final weekend at my place and it was amazing. He
brought his friends and we had a huge dinner party then went out on the
town in Wilmington and Wrightsville. At the conclusion of the weekend,
the tight-knit group of now Green Berets said their goodbyes and went to
separate groups in all parts of the world... most we would never see again.

Shortly after Christmas, Ryan was moved to Clarksville, Tenn., and took his place on a team in 5th Group Special Forces. After growing up in the somewhat urban mansions of historic Brookhaven in Atlanta, Ryan had a tough time adjusting to all of the farmland and very, very rural lifestyle that Clarksville offered. He was mortified the day he arrived and never really did grow to like the town too much. His first phone call to me began with, "Heather, there are cows and tractors all over the place! There's nothing here!" It sounded like he meant a tornado went through town leaving piles of cows and tractors strewn all over the land. Really, it was just a rural area that he was not accustomed to, nor was he attracted to this lifestyle. It didn't matter much considering he was rarely at home. I met him in Nashville one weekend shortly after he arrived. As usual, we checked out some great little restaurants and took in plenty of live music. We were both pleased with what Nashville had to offer. We decided we had to do it immediately—I would move to Tennessee and we would get married.

When I returned, this email awaited:

Heatwave,

I really did have a good time with you this weekend and think that we make a fantastic couple. To think that we are moving closer to being together makes me very happy and I really do think about spending the rest of my life with you (yes, moving toward the 'M' word). Hope it continues to get better when you move here as I really look forward to seeing you more. Get here now!!

Much love,
Ryan

Chapter 5
We Can Do That?! Are You Kidding?

S hortly thereafter, Ryan returned to Wilmington and moved me to Clarksville. He and a fellow Green Beret rented an apartment in an old converted school house in town. We thought I could stay there for a few months until we got a feel for how much he would be gone and possibly look for a place that we could buy. He was now on a team. He was so proud... ODA (operational detachment alpha, aka 'A-Team') 566 in Charlie Company, 2nd battalion, 5th Special Forces Group or C/2/5.

I took a job with Vanderbilt Orthopedics Institute with the intention of starting a research project with my alma mater, the University of Pittsburgh, which benefited wounded warriors. I loved my job. I admired the amazing therapists I worked with, and if it wasn't for the outrageous price of gas that year, and the nearly four hours a day I spent in traffic with morning sickness, I would have been much happier.

That's right, within two months of moving to Clarksville I became pregnant with our first child. As two intelligent adults, who understood how such things happen, we were not surprised, and on the contrary, quite happy. I cannot say the same for our families at the time. Ryan and I had talked many times in private about the option of children and decided there is no perfect time for anyone to have a child, there will always be variables and reasons to wait. Furthermore, with the Army scheduling your life, it would be even harder to plan. So, once we moved in together, we just decided to let things take their natural course. Neither of us ever imagined that they would take course so quickly! Nonetheless, Ryan always referred to it as the "best surprise ever."

By March, we were ready to do the marriage thing. We tried to fit it into his Army work schedule, during which he was gone anywhere from two days to two months at a time for the next eight months, then possibly deployed to Iraq for six months. Nothing was set in writing and even if it was, the Army had the right to change it as many times as they wished. They weren't going to let their soldier stay home on a weekend for his wedding: Army first, family second. I was working 60 hours a week myself to compound the situation. But then came baby and she gave us the last push we needed.

We met at Vanderbilt Women's Health on a cold April morning. We had no clue what to expect. Maybe a more formal urine test or blood test to confirm the pregnancy? A question/answer session? I disrobed and we sat in the exam room making jokes about instruments when in walked Angela, our nurse midwife (CNM). Ryan made a few inappropriate jokes and she handled him well. She wheeled in an ultrasound machine and began looking for signs of life in the womb. We both expected that we would see nothing at this point and were astounded when she showed us a tiny little blur flickering on the screen. She said nonchalantly, "That's the heart beating."

I'm pretty sure all of the blood rushed out of my head as I looked over at Ryan who for once, was speechless. I can still see his expression. He was in total awe. Then he asked, "Can we have a picture of that thing? No, like a few pictures...how many pictures can I get of my baby?" She printed out two pictures of the little peanut sized blur and we were on our way.

From that day on, Ryan was in total "Daddy mode," but he wasn't just planning what sports his child would play, or where he/she would go to school. In typical Ryan Means-style, he was planning and strategizing ways to make the world better and safer for his future child. The level that this man thought on was beyond me, but I was thrilled that he would be the father of my child. Who could ask for anything more?

Ryan sent out this update to his friends:

DATE: May 24, 2007
SUBJECT: Apparently hell has frozen over.

In recent years, my ability to persuade and seduce (even with the really cool job title and fancy beret) has diminished to the point that even the most foolish and drunk of women adamantly refused to succumb to my so-called "charms." Of course that's not to say that my thinning and graying hair aren't the culprit...but I like to think it's not that obvious. So I guess the cliché "all good things must come to an end" is apropos and I'm quite happy to report that I will soon be married.

I had one last trick up my sleeve and managed to convince a very beautiful and very intelligent woman to become Mrs. Means III (the first would be my mom, the second, my sister-in-law). Fortunately she's not a military town tramp who has been around the base a few times, but rather a very moral and accomplished Physical Therapist from Pittsburgh named Heather. We've for the most part been together over two years now.

It will be a small private wedding as our schedules and desires prevented anything major. Neither of us could ever imagine being the center of so much pomp and circumstance... We'll send out some photos soon. Oh, and apparently my swimmers are also Green Berets as they were able to overcome several significant obstacles and complete their mission. We will be proud parents come December. Funny thing is, I told Heather I planned on marrying her 7 days after we met.

This miracle simply moved the schedule up a bit. We are both extremely happy and very excited. It's my gut feeling that he'll be a boy and naturally we plan on naming him after this really cool guy I once knew.

Best,

Ryan and Heather

Now, it was time to put these years of marriage talk into action. If we got married in Tennessee or Georgia, my grandmothers would have trouble traveling from PA, so we looked at venues in the North. We considered Atlanta venues since Ryan's whole family was there and his mother could plan the event. After all of the back and forth, Ryan finally decided we needed to take a long weekend, go back to the beginning—Airlie Gardens in Wrightsville and take some great photos of a private ceremony and send them to our families to break the news that we were now married and having a baby! So, that was the plan. Right in the very spot he asked me to marry him on our first date, we would exchange vows, we would each bring one friend to take pictures and witness—and that was it. He bought me a lovely dress and had his casual suit planned. We were ready to roll...but what about the engagement ring?

On March 31, 2007, Ryan took me to a small house in Clarksville in a quiet, old established neighborhood called Eastern Hills. He had found a great little house that needed some love. From the outside alone, it had two things we both desired in a home: a huge backyard and an amazing porch with a swing. He brought the video camera and we walked around peeping in the windows as he narrated for our parents, so they could see the house we may someday buy. He told me to sit on the swing and hold my dog, Jack like a baby so they could get the full effect. As usual, I rolled my eyes and played along. Then he asked, "Could you see yourself living here? Raising our children here as my wife? COULD YOU?" He put down the camera and pulled out the ring, got down on one knee and asked me to marry him with tears in his eyes. It was one of my fondest Ryan memories. After my reply, he picked up the camera and said, "OK, WHAT JUST HAPPENED?" I had to narrate with the help of his prompts. I laughed at the conclusion of the video, when I remarked that it would be hilarious if someone else gets the house before us and we have to come celebrate on their porch every year. (Ironically, the house was full of asbestos and they say that isn't the best sort of home remodeling for a pregnant woman to oversee, so we bought a similar house down the street.)

Immediately after the proposal, we drove from asbestos house to the courthouse to get our marriage license since it was on the way to the restaurant where we were having dinner.

Once at the courthouse, we filled out the paper work and returned it to the woman at the desk. She asked us if we wanted to get married. Ryan and I looked at each other as if to say, "Is she serious? I mean, we just filled out all of this—why the hell would we need a license if we weren't getting married?" She noticed our confusion and clarified.

"I mean today. Are you here to get married today?" she asked.

"We can do that?! Are you kidding?" She explained that there was a priest and it was a holy ceremony, and many people chose to do it because of unplanned deployments and he happened to be there without any appointments in the next hour, which was extremely rare—someone must have gotten cold feet. So without any discussion at all, we both said, "YES! Where do we go?"

We walked into a side room set up like a chapel and there was a sweet old man named Joe Creek who gave us some words about the importance of what we were about to do, that it should not be taken lightly and that we would be forever bound until death. He then asked us to face each other and hold hands. Ryan had on a T-shirt, cargo shorts and flip-flops, and I wore black capris, a size "too big" animal print tank top his mother had bought me for maternity gear, and flip-flops, too. We could not stop giggling at our attire and the simple fact that here we finally were, and as soon as I saw the tears in his eyes, I started tearing up myself. Poor Joe didn't have a clue what we were laughing or crying about, but Ryan gave him a look of assurance and he continued on. Throughout the vows, which seemed to last an eternity, he kept squeezing my hands as hard as he could, such a Ryan thing to let you know that he loves you and he is right here in the moment.

The kiss after the vows was awkward, as we were still in shock. We returned to the car to tell our parents. It never even occurred to us to take a picture! I don't really remember what any of them said, but the happiness seemed to be hidden by a "Dear Lord, what did they just do?" type overtone. It didn't matter; we were thrilled. We grabbed a bite to eat and went back to our apartment to break the news to our roommate, who as a true Green Beret, gave us a huge hug and genuinely happy blessings. We all watched some reality TV, and that was our wedding day. I wouldn't change it for the world.

Chapter 6
Marital Bliss

Shortly thereafter, I was glad to be out of apartment living and to walk straight into my ranch home with our groceries, rather than up and down four flights of stairs. But, I won't lie and say I loved that house. It needed a lot of love (which we gave it) and a lot of money, which we didn't have to give. It was a constant project that kept me busy though deployments and kept him busy when he was home, especially outside. Ryan's mother had a green thumb and he seemed to inherit it, and I was often jealous that the plants seemed to get more attention than the wife.

Three days after we moved into our home, Ryan was sent off to Fort Lewis for over three months. I was in charge of establishing our new home, working, and growing a baby. And, I was OK with it. I was the happiest I had ever been with my life. There seemed to be so much security and promise of happiness in being married and having a home and baby together, that not much could waver my happiness. Ryan constantly praised me on the email updates of the home, sonograms and growing belly, and gave his unsolicited advice from afar. Then, he asked me to come stay in Seattle. We planned a long weekend.

Before that weekend came, I was organizing our attic and I found a box of pictures Ryan had saved from New York. This wasn't the first time I had seen them, but it was the first time I had seen them since he promised he would throw them away. He brought them into our home and hid them! The pictures were taken long before we met, but combined with the insane amount of hormones that come with pregnancy, I actually thought I might have made a mistake by marrying him, and he was not there to defend himself. I wrote him an email, as there was no way to call him (they restrict their phones in certain Special Forces assignments), and told him what I had found. He basically had no argument except that it was dumb and he was sorry and that no matter what, I promised to love him until death do us part, not until I found a stash of photos in the attic. He jokingly threatened to call Joe Creek and tell him I was about to break my marriage vows and leave him. I wasn't amused. I include this for my children, as it was my first realization that once you are married, you are obligated to work things out, some way, somehow. You don't get to change your mind and walk away when things get tough.

Ryan replied:

Despite what you currently think about my poor actions as a loving husband and soon to be father, I feel that we have a great relationship and a tremendous amount of love. I'm confident that after your visit to Seattle we'll be set right and moving in the right direction.

That being said, I'm very sorry about not destroying the photos a long time ago. I promise you that was nothing except a story to impress my brothers with my wild NYC lifestyle. I've given up just about everything that once comprised a significant portion of my life and do not regret it for a second, primarily because it has allowed me to become the person that I have always had the potential but not the will to be and that is in large part because I met you. Now, I literally couldn't ask for anything else in the world and feel that despite my occasional bad luck and stupid mistakes, my life has truly been blessed by your presence. The fact that you are going to soon have our child makes me want to truly become a better person in every sense of the word; work harder, become a true role model through my actions and words, become the best husband, friend and father and a good and moral person. I hope that you can see how far I've come (and that I still have improvements to make) since we've met.

I hate that past skeletons are resurfacing and making you question my current goals and beliefs. I truly love you with all of my heart and promise you that our life together while not always perfect or happy or without issues, will be long and fruitful. Please give me the opportunity and trust to prove this.

Your devoted and loving husband and, of course, best friend, Ryan

Shortly after this fiasco, Ryan planned out a 'baby moon' for us and I joined him in Seattle, where we took a ferry to Victoria and Vancouver. It was the honeymoon we never got, and it was fabulous.

It was also a good indication that we still had that special bond and love of travel, people, and discovery that would keep us best friends as well as spouses and co-parents. Throughout the trip, we discussed raising our future child. We had such huge aspirations for this baby. It was also the

OUR BABYMOON, SEATTLE, WA

first time he got to see me so huge and feel the baby move. His expression was priceless. It was such an amazing moment. He talked to her every night (always starting with "BABY, I am your father," in that Darth Vader tone).

He made her a playlist of classical music and bought some Bose headphones to place on my belly. He was more than ready to be a father.

We were back to good. Over the rest of the pregnancy, we bounced parenting ideas around through emails and late night phone calls in eager anticipation of our little girl.

BUCHART GARDENS, BRITISH COLUMBIA

Chapter 7
Family Life

Ryan returned in plenty of time for the birth. I was quite miserable and ready to literally explode when a doctor finally agreed to induce me. Elizabeth Stanton Means was born on December 14, 2007, in Nashville, Tenn.

Ryan was amazing throughout the birth. He was absolutely giddy. He was thrilled to meet his sweet baby girl and would follow the nurses around the room watching everything they did to her, as he held her little fingers and toes throughout the process. He savored every minute with her from that day forward, the epitome of a proud father.

ONE LAST PHOTO IN THE NURSERY BEFORE BABY ARRIVED!

I remember the drive home from Nashville to Clarksville. The first time we buckled her into her little carrier and put her in the car was in hindsight, hysterical. We were on the highway that we drove almost every day, but this time Ryan was driving white-knuckled in the right lane. People were passing us and he was getting so angry that they had no regard for this precious cargo in the back seat. I was sitting in the back with her making sure she was still breathing, comfortable, and safe. It was as if we were the only two people that had ever had this mission of transportation providers for a newborn and it was stressful—very stressful. What if we wrecked and killed her? What if she was too hot in all of her layers in the car seat? What if she left the hospital and then decided to stop breathing?!

We arrived at the house in eager anticipation of Jack's reaction. He was Ryan's faithful best friend—the Chihuahua he never wanted, but had been my baby for five years. We set the carrier on the floor next to the coffee table and let him discover her for himself. He smelled her, looked at each of us, tucked his tail between his legs, put his ears back and slid under the sofa...for hours. He seemed hurt and this was his version of pouting. In the next year, he eventually realized that it was in his best interest to love her and just stay out of her way.

I took Elizabeth out of her carrier for the first time in our own home and we sat on the sofa staring at her little body. Ryan snuggled up next to me and played with her fingers. This was the happiest moment of my life up to this point, and I suddenly started crying. Motherhood gave me the emotions to allow me to cry tears of joy—something many women innately seem to possess. Ryan asked me what was wrong and

DAY AND NIGHT, HE JUST LOVED HIS LITTLE GIRL

I replied, "Nothing, I'm just so happy." I could tell how proud he was to have such a huge part in making me happy, as he always said it was his only goal in life, next to ridding the world of terrorism (I had some stiff competition). Yes, this was one of those moments in life that takes your breath away.

ELIZABETH'S FIRST DOLL—TALKING "W"

ELIZABETH'S FIRST HIKE WITH
DADDY, JACK AND BREWSTER

RYAN IN OMAN

Ryan was sent to Oman for two months. He would send emails like this from his 5-star resort:

Sorry I've been MIA but we've been doing some incredibly cool stuff. Can't say too much but everything so far has totally exceeded expectations and we are having the time of our lives. If only the Army could use what we are doing in a recruitment ad, everyone would try and join. Real Lawrence of Arabia kinda stuff.

For me, it's a dream come true as I'm living and breathing the culture and seeing and doing things that are mind blowing. The experience so far has given me a totally unexpected perspective and it's great to know that we are making a difference in a positive way. When I get back, you'll see some photos that will make you very jealous.

So far we've shot a lot of guns, caught tons of fish in the Arabian sea, mountain biked some of the toughest and most beautiful terrain I've been on, made some great friends and have eaten like kings. This internet connection is slow and pricey so emails will be very intermittent. I would do anything for you and Elizabeth to come here.

Wuv Woo.
RPM

'DRINKING IN' OMAN

NEVER TOO OLD TO REPEL
OFF OF A CLIFF (OMAN)

MAKING TIME FOR FUN AT WORK   LAWRENCE OF ARABIA

This is the work Ryan was subjected to while I was in Tennessee with the new baby and the worst snow the state had seen in a decade. The SF lifestyle isn't all that bad at times—for the husband, that is.

Back at home, I was a new mother anxious to be a perfect parent. I was alone in a new town, with a tiny baby, now without a job, and stuck in horrible unusually snowy weather that kept us homebound, and I became depressed. After a few weeks of feeling like the world was out of reach and that I may not be fit to be in this situation, I called the local Army hospital that our insurance required me to use, told them my situation, that I felt like I wasn't sure if I wanted to live to see the next day, but I wanted the baby safe, and there was no family or friend around to call and they told me I could get an appointment in the next couple of weeks and something to the effect of getting the right "authorizations."

"I'm sorry," I said, "I need the Army's permission to go crazy? It's a little late for that." I completely lost it on the phone with her and she finally placed me on hold, and coincidentally we got disconnected.

I gave in and drove to Blanchfield Army Community Hospital emergency room. I really believed that if I did not, I may in fact take my life. I told nobody I was going— what could they do from afar? I told the healthcare provider that I felt like I wasn't myself. I had been alone with this new baby every second of the day for over a month; no family, friends or even a baby sitter that I knew and trusted within hundreds of miles. I was sleep-deprived and breast feeding religiously every two hours for the past two months, my husband was overseas, and I was alone and very afraid that I would hurt myself. But I knew it wasn't right; it wasn't me. I thought, oh my God, this is the post-partum depression I have heard of, but how can I have it if I am smart enough to recognize it? Why can't I just use "mind over matter" and turn it off? I posed this question to the psychiatric aide who proceeded to diagnose me with an anger management issue. He told me that I could sign up for free weekly classes on the Army base and that someone there could likely watch "the kid" while I attended.

Not wanting to disprove his theory, I stood up over him at his desk, told him to quit filling out his paper work and take a good look at me. "Do you see me standing here with this baby? I'm going to put her down and drag your ass out into that hall and make an example of you, demonstrating a number of reasons why Army healthcare has the reputation it does on this base, OR, you can go back out there yourself, find me an actual educated doctor and bring him back in here. I've been waiting two hours in the E.R. to speak to SOMEONE and it isn't you! You have five fucking minutes to get me a doctor, starting NOW! GO!!!"

He looked terrified and brought a doctor in within two minutes, and believe me, I was timing the event. I looked at the doctor and said, "I had a baby two months ago, my husband left the country, and I am here in Clarksville, the armpit of Tennessee, with this child who breastfeeds constantly, and I have not slept in weeks. I cannot shut off my brain, and I am about ready to kill myself, and this jackass just told me I need anger management classes to cure my illness. What do YOU think?" He looked at the aide and said, "Have you ever heard of post-partum depression? Because this is a textbook case if I have ever heard one." He replied, "Yes, sir," and wrote the prescriptions that doctor recommended. Somehow, I felt a ray of hope.

Ryan called that night and I told him what happened. I made him promise not to tell the family. I was so afraid that someone would want to take Elizabeth from me, which I guess was a symptom of the disease. Our talk got me back on track and once he was home, I decided to go back to work for a few hours per week and everything fell into place. I made some of the greatest friends I have ever had—educated therapists whose husbands were also dragging them around per the Army's command. They may have saved my life. They were in my same situation, and we helped each other daily. I eventually went off of the medication and never had those feelings again. It was the strangest thing. Post-partum depression is a very serious life-threatening matter. Another life lesson learned.

Ryan made it back in time for Easter. His sweet grandmother, Helen Means, passed away and Al planned a family trip to Hilton Head Island to bury her ashes and celebrate Easter with a large-scale family reunion. Al has a history of planning and executing the best family trips even if they are in honor of a loved one's death.

The Means family finds a way to celebrate life regularly. It was another amazing family trip, which included much bonding time for Ryan, Elizabeth and myself.

EASTER IN HILTON HEAD, SC (AL, RYAN, ELIZABETH, MYSELF AND MARY JO)

A short time after Helen died, we lost another member of the Means family—Brewster, the perfect chocolate lab. Other than the tears of happiness during our marriage and daughter's birth, I had only seen Ryan shed a tear one time. It was during a late night conversation about Adam that we had when we first dated. So, I was shocked on May 13th, when I walked in on him tearful, composing the following sweet obituary to man's best friend:

Always the perfect gentleman, known by many names: Brewster, Brown Dog, Bud, Buddy, Brew Dog, Brew Dogger, it didn't really matter. If you called him, he would come... till the end. An animal so loved, that I seriously considered giving our first born his name (albeit the middle name). Luckily we had a girl, but even then, Heather had to con-

vince me that it was a little tacky naming your daughter after your dog, even though he was quite the anomaly and I was totally cool with it.

Amazing how rare it was to get angry with this majestic animal in so many years and even when he did misbehave you simply couldn't stay mad. Brewster was just that good. He was always remembered and loved by anyone and everyone who came into contact with him which was strangely a lot of people. More popular with the ladies in Athens than I could ever dream to be. Such a great friend that you would get offended and want to fight people who use the word 'dog' in a derogatory manner. I know that when that word was used to demean someone, I'd immediately think of Brewster and imagine, "Why would anybody be offended with being compared to him?" It's no wonder that the word God and dog are so similar.

Brown Dog had the potential to do anything: drug dog, bomb sniffer, guide dog, hunting champion, stud, Vice President, but lucky for us he was something so much more. A friend and beloved member of our family.

The uncanny obedience he possessed was matched by his handsome looks, intelligence and undying devotion to his family and of course his constant pursuit of perfecting the time honored craft of retrieving. Richard Wholters (author of Game Dog, Gun Dog, Water Dog and Family Dog) wrote that good retrievers would much rather fetch than eat and Brewster without fail would prefer chasing whatever your threw to a bowl of food. Not so much in my mind because of thousands of years of impeccable breeding or his deep and profound love of fetching but rather because it was his way of interacting and pleasing you.

Has a more perfect creature ever roamed the earth? Heidi Klum comes close but doesn't quite have the intelligence. Al Einstein had the brains but not the looks. Michelangelo had the talent but lacked the consistent fetching ability. Tom Brady may be able to hang in the pocket and throw touchdowns but he's a poor scrambler and he doesn't dive to the bottom of a pool and retrieve various items on command. Enough said.

Perhaps the neutering was a necessary precaution but certainly a crime against humanity to deprive this world of his genes. Forget cloning ridiculous sheep. Billions of dollars could have been made and world peace achieved simply from having more Brewster. I'm confident that given

enough time and a proper lab, Brewster could've cured multiple diseases, even if using the old head in the lap trick. This dog had more focus in his whiskers than 95% of today's teenagers and was probably the

RYAN AND BREWSTER

world's one and only chance to cure ADD. He was a true Champion of Champions and will always be missed.

Is the adulation and pain worth it? On the surface it almost seems cynical that in the face of so many perceived crises (high gas prices, cyclones, tyranny, war, recession, etc.) to be so wrought with sadness over the passing of an animal. But as we all know, this is the precisely the reason we loved him so much. Regardless of our mood or what may have been going on in the world or how bad the experts and pundits were telling us our lives were, at the end of the day Brewster was there ready to console us, make us feel better, protect us, serve us, make us forget all the bad and remember all the good in the world. He would generally be there in any and every way he could, always. That dog could read people far better than Dr. Phil and wasn't nearly as annoying, condescending or expensive.

I am comforted by the fact that he is in a better place fetching, swimming, eating garbage, chasing (and hopefully

BREWSTER AND RYAN RELAXING IN CASHIERS, NC

finally catching) squirrels and of course taking long naps in the shade. It will undoubtedly take a long time to fill the void left by such a wonderful dog, but fortunately we have another to hopefully assuage the pain. Consider yourself lucky to have been a part of such an incredible experience, as I know that my life was forever changed by my wise and noble best friend who just happened to be of the canine species.

Long live Brown Dog,
RPM

Chapter Eight
Living Daily Routines at a Distance

The year 2008 was filled with more frequent but shorter (less than two months at a time) deployments stateside. They included specific classes on topics like driving maneuvers and what I liked to call spy games. I would find Elizabeth's toys dissected with cameras stuffed in them or just wires that I had no clue what they belonged to and was always assured it was for schools. I once took a shirt to the dry cleaner that had a button in it that had been made into a camera. The woman at the dry cleaner happily returned it and said I had better put it back where I got it before my husband realized I took it to the cleaners.

FOURTH OF JULY, LAKE BURTON 2008

FIRST FATHER'S DAY, JUNE 2008

BABY LOVES OLD GLORY.

Even though we lived together on paper, we still had to deal with the actual distance between us and communicate in writing during these trips. I felt so overwhelmed with work and caring for Elizabeth at the time. I hated getting Ryan's emails that I felt were his way of showing me that I wasn't doing enough. When I look back on them though, I realize he just wanted us all to be better.

H,

For some reason whenever I step outside of our daily routine, I begin to examine it from an entirely different perspective and this of course leads to advice on how WE can improve ourselves as individuals, a married couple and as parents. It's absolutely not meant to be mean, critical or anything else but constructive. In the long run, I think if we can follow a fraction of the suggestions likely to spring forth in the coming weeks, then I think our lives and our daughter's will be enriched.

Developing a daily schedule is going to be important in staying sane while I'm gone. You will need to do this because there will be a ton of stuff to manage and little time to do it. You need one for Elizabeth and you need one for yourself. It should include small things i.e., making the bed when you first get up. This takes three minutes and creates a more orderly living space and gives you more space to put your piles of clothes. You also need to eat breakfast every single morning. I don't care if it's a granola bar, putting something in your stomach first thing is critical. So many benefits to this.

I also think you need to find something that YOU enjoy i.e. a hobby. Maybe you pick something to learn about for 3–4 months and read and do as much as you can. Whether it be art, studying French, learning about a specific area or whatever but make it something you like. You can then parlay this into activities done with Elizabeth and me. It sounds silly but I think it would be awesome for all of us. I can do the same. Ideally, this stuff can culminate in a full-blown trip/experience. For example, we pick a country or topic: art, cooking, France, Germany, Mexico etc…and while saving up for the trip we try and learn the history, language, cuisine leading up to the trip. Maybe we just throw a theme party based on the concept. Even if we don't make the trip at least we all learned something along the way and saved some money.

This idea came out of me and E's visit to the bookstore. Spent 2+ hours there looking at books and other stuff. It totally inspired me to be a better dad and have good, important stuff I can teach my daughter. God forbid she grows up knowing nothing but Army, absences, Clarksville and our little house.

These are just two suggestions but I think if we keep at them, then some of the disadvantages we face can definitely be mitigated. Take this in, think about it and get back to me with some ideas.

I am totally convinced that once into the realm we are happily married with a great baby. Doing things alone is no longer much fun and I only want someone with me to share in the experiences. Being cooped up in a airport hotel with no car and looking at great pics of your beautiful daughter ain't exactly a blast. Can't cook, can't drink, and being stuck in a stuffy hotel room with a painfully slow internet connection is driving me insane. You have no idea how much being away from her and you sucks. Missing these critical times in her life are things I will never get back.

Love and miss you two very much. E more.
RPM

I again travelled to see my parents and Ryan's, which would afford them time to get to know Elizabeth and give me some time to myself. The grandparents and great-grandparents were happy, and I got some relief from single-parent life, which made me happy as well.

Between these trips, I continued to work and eventually found a nanny. Shanden, who I stole from the YMCA, reminded me of myself and Ryan when we were younger. She stood out as an artsy girl with piercings, jet black hair and bright blue eyes. I knew she had a unique heart with a special place for E, and I liked her. I would never have a Plain Jane boring old lady as a sitter for my child. I could tell Shanden shared a bond with Elizabeth when she watched her during my workouts at the Y. So, I asked her to come work for us. It was terribly hard for me to trust someone with my first and only child, but I knew she was the right choice. I believe nowadays she has taken off in her career as a Burlesque dancer, and I wonder if that's where Elizabeth's uninhibited love of dance originated. I have no issue with this, as the girl had common sense and unbridled creativity and that's more important to me than any degree or formal training.

At some point during this stateside deployment, Ryan and I decided that we loved the joy Elizabeth brought to us so much, that we would start trying to have another baby. Ryan returned home the weekend of Oct. 3rd, which the doctors tell us was just one week before our second daughter was conceived. We were a very efficient couple.

SAN FRANCISCO PARK WITH ELIZABETH

Over the next three months we focused on packing in as much family time as possible while he and his team packed and prepared for their six-month deployment to Iraq. We visited Alfie, Michael and Ryan's parents and friends in Atlanta. We frequented museums, gardens, art shows and ate great food throughout the Southeast. We went to San Francisco to visit Tommy and his family. I felt like life was just getting better.

While in San Fran we had the pleasure of attending the wedding of Roger and Renee. Roger was Ryan's fraternity brother at Boulder. I finally got to meet the majority of his college friends, the Chi Psi brothers, and immediately understood

SAN FRANCISCO, 2008

why they were so important to him. They were such a unique group of people, the "Boulder Crew." You could tell that no matter how much time they had spent apart, they picked up right where they left off, and even though I had just met them for the first time, it was as if we had all been friends forever. And, we would all be friends for life.

Ryan's favorite holiday was Halloween, but this year, between training and stateside deployments, he had only two days to pull together décor. I was never one for Halloween, so I left it entirely to him. He played it low key. He hung about 100 glow sticks from the various trees in our front yard. A butcher knife wielding scarecrow sat at the door with a display of dismembered and decapitated baby dolls, pigs feet, and raw meat covered in blood at his side. Blood covered baby dolls were mutilated and their hair burnt. They were hung by noose from tree branches. Loud eerie

music could be heard from blocks away as smoke filled the air around our home. Ryan would be masked, dressed in fatigues and repel from the roof or the tree in front of our entryway and land in the faces of terrified guests. He would hide in the bushes and I would deliver his dinner and refill his wine glass throughout the night. He would never come in, even to go to the bathroom as he might miss a scare.

DINNER IN THE BRUSH, SO AS NOT TO MISS A SCARE. HALLOWEEN 2008

BEST FRIENDS: RYAN AND JOSH AT CAPITAL CITY CLUB HOLIDAY PARTY, ATLANTA, GA

Chapter Nine
We Said Our "See You Soons"

In December, the final details of the deployment were coming to light. Ryan and his team would leave Clarksville "sometime in the first week of January" and, hopefully, if all went smoothly in Iraq, he would be able to fly back for the birth of Baby #2. We managed to squeeze in one final family trip before his departure: Christmas in Punta Mita, Mexico. Al rented a beach front condo and all of the brothers were able to attend.

FAMILY PORTRAIT IN MEXICO (RYAN, ELIZABETH AND MYSELF WITH BABY #2 IN UTERO)

Tommy and Gabrey were a few minutes away in a condo with her family, the Crofts. We announced our second pregnancy. Since no one in this family can keep a secret, I think it was just a formality that we announced, not a surprise.

We spent time in the ocean and in the pool together with all of the children, and I felt like I was part of one big happy, phenomenally fun family. Every night, dinner was an event. Al and the brothers caught fish and the local restaurant prepared it for us with a feast of side dishes.

As usual, Ryan, Michael, and I spent a lot of time together. We were in our rental car one afternoon, trying to parallel park and as usual, when you got the three of us together, something goes wrong. Murphy's Law was written for us. Elizabeth was on my lap in the back seat (we really were not clear if there was a carseat/seatbelt law, seeing as how there were no actual roads in most of the town). Ryan slowly and perfectly parallel parked into a cramped space, then pressed firmly on the brake to put the car in park...only he hit the gas instead of the brake! SLAM! We all froze for a minute and then in absolute unison said, "DON'T tell Al!" The look we gave each other when those words simultaneously come out should have been caught on camera. Elizabeth laughed and applauded, we laughed, got out of the car and managed to pretend like nothing happened. No one was hurt, not even the bumpers. This was the first time that I realized I had become one of the Means' children. The words escaped my mouth so easily, that I knew I was one of them.

THE MEANS-CROFT FAMILY, CHRISTMAS 2008

The Al and Mary Jo Means family is the tightest-knit family I have ever had the pleasure of knowing. Elizabeth and Baby #2 were so lucky to be born into this clan that "put the fun in dysfunctional," as Mary Jo put it. Only they were anything but dysfunctional. On the contrary, they were a well-oiled machine, prepared for anything that would come their way. A strong matriarch coupled with a strong and driven patriarch produced four successful boys who could stand up to anyone or anything the world could give to them. Each brother has a unique set of strengths but put together, whether using their powers for good or evil, they were unstoppable. What a way to grow up and be prepared for life and everything it could deal. As we frolicked in the southern Mexico sun, we certainly had no idea what would be dealt to us in the next few months.

THE BROTHERS IN MEXICO (ALFIE, RYAN, TOMMY AND MICHAEL)

On New Year's Eve, the four brothers decided that they wanted to leave the rest of the family and drive to Sayulita, a really cool little fishing/surf town that Michael, Ryan, Elizabeth and I visited earlier that day. I got the impression that Mary Jo and Gabrey were not in favor

and this was causing a little rift in the happy vacation. Ryan looked at me and said, "Well, wife? What do you think?" At the time I was three months

pregnant, Elizabeth was completely miserable with an ear infection since we arrived in the country, and I thought it seemed like a great idea to get rid of four potentially drunk-by-midnight party goers. So, as it turned out I won the "best wife of the year" award from Ryan and they all

RYAN AND ELIZABETH IN SAYULITA

went on their way. Ironically, (and sad for the boys), their cab driver had to be back to our village by midnight, so their adventure was cut short. I'm quite certain that they made the most of it and they were almost able to convince us that they chose to be back by midnight to ring in the New Year with us. We watched the fireworks over the ocean and then climbed into bed not looking forward the end of our vacation or the return to the U.S. and the pending deployment.

The night of January 7th, Ryan spent the whole night reading to Elizabeth, making home movies with her and for her so that she would be able to see him everyday that he was gone. He didn't want to let her go to bed that night as he knew it was the last time he would see her for a very long time. The next morning, he woke her and made one final movie with her. He told her what he expected of her while he was gone. He said she should obey her mother, go to church, play sports and eat healthy, among other more specific directions. It seemed so strange that he would go into so much detail for a 13-month-old. It was as if he thought that maybe something would happen and he would not come home. He was always prepared to give his life for his country and he would have been the first to throw himself in front of a bullet to save a teammate. So, I guess it was only natural that he planned for the worst. Maybe he knew better than any of us that his time here could be cut short.

We had a few days together before I took him to the Fort Campbell Army airport and walked inside with him. He gave me a hug and said his usual, "We don't say good bye" we say, "I'll see you soon," followed by "wuv woo," probably the only mushy phrase that he ever spoke to me, and certainly never in front of another person. He hugged me tightly and I left him at the airport. I hoped for a call that said, "Come back and get me, they changed the date again," but it never came. I sent him an email that night, not knowing when or if he would have access to his account anytime soon:

Ryan,

I'm sure you won't get this for awhile, but I have to tell you while I'm feeling nice...I really missed you when I got home. I missed you even more when it got late and E and I were eating alone. It isn't the same without you. You ARE the reason we are in Clarksville and I hate it without you. I'm sure you know that I love you. But you should also know, I like you.

H

I began throwing myself into work, contracting myself to four different Rehabilitation Facilities in the local area and Elizabeth started attending The Little Country School House. I realized that even though I felt bad not staying at home with her, she LOVED being around little people her own age in a structured fun environment and it made for a happy reunion when I picked her up each day.

Ryan wrote often and asked for items to help win the hearts and support of the Iraqis as well as to make the soldier's lives more comfortable. It was nice to have little missions at home to focus on and feel like I was helping out in some way.

H,

Thanks for the care package. You can't even begin to imagine how disgusting these beds are... I'm afraid to sleep in them each night and we still haven't unpacked so I've got no pillow. I ball up some clothes and put them in a shirt which is comfy for 3 seconds before it starts to feel like a rock. Tons of fun.

You'll be happy to know that the humidifier you bought is going to a very poor family whose baby has asthma and coughs all night long. It killed me to hear that so I took it upon you to get one.

Anyways, not much is going on here. Still dirty, tired and cold. I'm going to bed since I'll be up for like 25+ hours in the next day or two. The good news is that time FLIES since we're so busy. Good for me at least. Figure it will be no time before I'm home for you guys. How's the belly? Going to be NUTS having another kid!

At some point I'm going to spend some time thinking of names. Any new ones?

Keep in touch.

Love,
Your hubby.

He also continued the tradition of updating the fan club on what was going on in his Army career:

DATE: January 13, 2009
SUBJECT: Checking in.

Sorry for the delay in getting anything out but we've been busy to say the least and the technical situation has taken some time.

Trip over was long and uneventful. Got a day layover in this cool Spanish beach town which was beautiful but chilly. Was able to enjoy a few brewskis before continuing on the final leg. The airport we landed at was insane—a huge maze of concrete barriers, barbed wire and these huge new armored vehicles. You cannot possibly imagine how much stuff has either been built or brought over in the past five years. The American war effort is amazing.

The final leg involved an hour+ helicopter flight over some heavily bombed out areas therefore some skills were on display by the pilot. A female contractor was on board and scared to death, I suppose of flying—due to the eyes clenched shut and the white knuckles. While we were flying over this bombed out section, both gunners had to do a test fire of their 240's which lasted a few seconds of full auto fire. Apparently she didn't hear the pilot say 'test fire' and almost died when they opened up. I'm sure she thought we were under attack.

The area we are in looks a lot like Punta Mita, although there are some sections with huge piles of trash and raw sewage strewn throughout the streets. Wild dogs are rampant.

This whole gig is extremely odd. Everywhere I walk within our small compound, I'm always armed (not necessarily with a long gun and kit-armor, mags etc...) and everywhere you look on the compound there are various types of weapons sitting and waiting (rockets, explosives, grenades, machine guns etc.). It's a filthy place and dust covers everything. I can't say much else except that things are going well and it's expected to be active yet safe in the coming months.

We have some very high goals in our time here and I can honestly say that the effort here is the right one and doing some good against huge odds. The Iraqis we are working with are very nice and some are good at what they do. The officers, you can plainly see, are in the good fight. They've lost thousands of good men who've been murdered in the most hideous of ways by various criminal groups and only want a stable safe country. I cannot say the same for the politicians and the sheikhs. They don't give two shits about anything except their own personal power and money. The people are dirt poor (and I mean DIRT) and are doing what they can to eek out a living. The kids unfortunately have no choice but to try and survive the insanity brought about and endured by their parents. This is the hard part, especially now being a father. Seeing the kids scared to death and not knowing why we are doing what we are doing.

In any event, this is just some rambling after my first few days on the ground. To be quite honest, although we've started working already, my work has not begun. We have a long way to go and I'm sure things are somehow going to get even stranger. I'm very confident that my training, mindset and abilities will enable me to do whatever is necessary and everything will be ok. For God's sake, you should not be worrying about anything except the souls of the guys we are pursuing, but then again, if we are going after them they are pretty much the worst people on earth and deserve everything they get on this earth and beyond.

Finally, words cannot describe how much I miss E. and H. It behooves me to stay as busy as possible so I don't dwell at all on what I am missing at home. It literally makes me physically ill thinking about missing bath time, breakfast, diapers and everything else that goes along with that baby. I know you guys will take care of them while I'm gone.

Keep on rockin' in the free world.
RPM

DATE: January 21, 2009
SUBJECT: Another beautiful day in Iraq

Things are going well here. Just working to make the world
a better place, no big deal really. Kind of like a community orga-
nizer I suppose, albeit armed to the teeth with a variety of lethal
weapons and sporting a kickin' cowboy hat. The moostache is
returning and will be in full swing in another month or so.

No worries about me never wearing my body armor and gear
(mom, Al and Heather). The pics are usually taken in a really
safe place (relatively speaking, of course). Plus my kit tends to
add 60 lbs. and makes me look short, and my face look fat.

Things have been very quiet which is good and a trend
we hope to continue. As I mentioned several times, the abject
poverty of this area is truly astounding. (Forgive me if some
of this is repetitive but I'm continually struck by a number of
things). The most difficult part is seeing the kids, especially
now being a father, who live in horrific sanitary conditions
with raw sewage, billions of flies, trash and general disarray
everywhere you look—not to mention the hellish violence that
has consumed this place for the past 30 or so years. The fact
that some children make it past the first couple of months is
a miracle. I haven't checked the infant mortality rates lately
but it's got to be high. In any event, it's extremely difficult to
make any disparaging comments about the USA after spending such a short time here. It's also hard to deny the best
part for me so far is driving anywhere in our armored gun

truck which would be sure to frighten the bejeezus out of any normal person, but these damn kids come running en masse, dead sprint, out of alleys, hovels and other cracks and crevices, leaving their soccer matches and other games to give us a thumbs up, a cheer and of course yell for candy. Makes me almost feel like one of them fancy Hollywood celebrities. They seem to be some of the only ones here who really understand or who willingly show that our presence keeps things safe.

Which brings up another point. The people I've met so far do not hate the US, Americans or our former President. To the contrary, they are almost universally trying to visit or immigrate to the states. Some simply want to see and experience true freedom before they die. Some also just want to see the ocean and women in bikinis. Either way I'd gladly trade the left coast hippies for some of these people in a heartbeat.

The days vary right now and there's a ton to do but only what seems to be 5 hours in the day. In reality we're working somewhere along the lines of 16-20 hours depending on what's going on. We're still getting settled into a routine and have been meeting all the VIPs from both our side and theirs. Trying to sort out the bad guys from the good and how to catch the former while not pissing off the latter. Our work is most definitely cut out for us and we are of course very excited about getting after it and them.

At some point I'll try and take some more interesting photos. We were lucky and got a chance to visit the ruins of Babylon and got a private tour of Nebuchadnezzar's former palace, which was rebuilt in part by Nebuchadnezzar III AKA Saddam Hussein. Interestingly, Saddam built one of his mas-

sive palaces atop a hill overlooking the original, which dates
back to 600 B.C. We sat on a terrace where he would have tea
and then proceed to massacre the dirt farmers down below by
the hundreds. He's a charming fellow who is really missed here.

The other day, we did have a big feast with the command
of our counterparts. For the most part it was delicious middle
eastern fare with chicken, rice, fresh bread, salad etc... However, there were also big plates of fish from the Euphrates
which I had zero intention of consuming. The massive Iraqi
general sitting next to me however insisted. Rather than
risk a loss of rapport, I nibbled on the fish and quickly tasted
exactly what you would imagine a fish raised in a sewage
pond tastes like. Luckily I didn't experience any ill effects but
will be sure to feign an allergy next go round.

I'll try to get a shot (photo not gun) of the Iraqi electrical
utility system. It's a hoot. They take extension cords and tie
them directly into the grid themselves. You'll drive into poor
neighborhoods and see hundreds of wires, some falling into the
street, strung up and around houses, poles and laying about. I
swear I saw some regular guy in flip flops on his metal ladder,
no protective gear or tools just tying into the 50,000 volt power
system. Driving around in the turret of the gun truck trying
to duck the cords and not rip them down with the .50 cal is a
never-ending challenge, which I thoroughly relish in.

Of course people from the states send us a bunch of stuff.
Mostly junk food and candy that I don't eat but always throw
to the kids (praying they don't chase the candy into traffic),
also school supplies, soccer balls, toiletries, lip balm and other
stuff. We live in such an awesome place (the U.S.—not our

small camp). Some second grade class sent a bunch of letters this past Turkey day which are hilarious. My favorite reads something like this: 'Deer Amerikyn Solejur, Pleeze don't dye. Thanks, your friend, Daniel.' Thanks buddy, we'll do our best.

Luckily, I was too busy to see or hear too much about the inauguration but I'll be semi-magnanimous and say that I hope for the best for him (and us). Unfortunately, it appears the stock market didn't agree too much with it though. It doesn't appear the press is apt to do its job anytime soon considering the number of scandals already at his feet. Then again, we knew his company from the start and it didn't seem to bother anyone so I guess we deserve what we get. Unlike the great un-washed masses of the left, I will do my best to resist falling into the same derangement syndrome where anything and everything bad that happens is the fault of the Anointed One. Enough of that mess, I never mean to discuss politics in an update email.

If I weren't blessed with my beloved wife and child, I'd want to do this job forever but being away from them and missing so much already is hard to say the least. I hope they one day forgive me for doing what I do and I promise to come home soon and be the best father and husband possible. From what Heather tells me, things are good (aside from E Bomb acting up and catching another cold) and I trust her fully that they are so. Very much looking forward to the next one (child that is).

The next weeks are going to be important. I promise to be safe, keep my head down, my armor on (when necessary) eating right, brushing the chompers and doing all the right things...

Until then, keep on rockin' in the free world.
RPM

RUGGED IN IRAQ

A BOY AND HIS TOY

Ryan,

Hello, hope this letter finds you well rested. I'm sure it won't so maybe you will feel better knowing that every night except one since you left, E has woken up 3-6 times per night and is not happy, but nothing seems to be wrong. I change her, give her a drink etc., and she wakes again in a few hours. Last night was no different except she got up at 5 am and was just crying CONSTANTLY. It's driving me crazy! But there's no one here to help! I hope I make it. I'd die without that Little Country Schoolhouse! I was the first person waiting to get in the doors this morning. I'm taking the whole day off to try to sleep because it's starting to take a toll. I had a dream you came home and you said that from now on you would come home for weekends. Best dream I've had in a long time.

The doctors think that she may need tubes in her ears. I feel so bad that I can't keep her happy. She goes to daycare and just smiles her little face off, looking at the toys with those 'Christmas morning' eyes and goes to anyone in there with a giant smile. She hates being home with me! This is NOT fun without you here to play with her and throw her around! Please come home.

H

MAKING FRIENDS WITH THE IRAQI CHILDREN

RIDING THROUGH
THE STREETS

H,

Yuck. That sounds awful. Take a day off, take many. That dream makes me feel good. I just talked to this guy that we are replacing and he mentioned he will likely get a divorce when he gets home. It scared the piss out of me and made me want to call you ASAP and make sure you weren't leaving me anytime soon.

This is the best job in the world but stuff like being away from you and her for extended periods makes it the worst. I hate it. You are really fun to hang out with even though I bother you so much. I really do like hanging out with you. I think a new baby will be great for E. Siblings are the shiznit.

Work today was really neat. You won't believe how poor these people are! I mean they live in 'houses' that are nothing more than mud shit stacked up and it's cold. Everyone and everything is filthy. There are disgusting dogs EVERYWHERE. Dead dogs are everywhere...probably dead from disease. It's really a horrible place. Most of the people are incredibly lazy and don't give a shit about anything. And I mean ANYTHING. They look to Americans for everything and can't do anything productive without constant direct guidance. I doubt it will ever change. The kids, I will admit are very cute. We'll drive around and they'll come running out laughing and smiling like we are celebrities and giving us the thumbs up. I really don't think it would be problem grabbing one but I'm sure it's best we continue making our own.

Talk soon and for God's sake don't abuse the little girl and don't divorce the husband. I love you more than anything and really want to spend the rest of my life with you and our wonderful kid(s). Hopefully time will continue to fly and I'll be home with you guys watching yet another birth. Mind blowing that we're making another kid. Let's figure out some names already!

ARM WRESTLING

Wuv woo.

RPM

H,

I hope you aren't totally going insane. Just a few months ago, you said you were sick of me making all the decisions and dominating the house. You wanted to live separately..."just be neighbors," remember?!?!?!? HAHA. Now you see how awesome I am!!!

How is your reading coming along? I know it's a strange question, but my brain book (which I have here) suggested several books to read one of which is called *Cheating at Canasta* by an Irish writer named William Trevor. All short stories where the characters are profoundly influenced by certain events in their lives. SHOULD YOU DECIDE to pursue some interesting short reading, get it...after you finish *A Prayer for Owen Meany* and the other 27 books I've given or recommended. I'm sure that's high on your list of things to do in all the free time you have!

If I were there, I'd love to go to a Pilates class with you. Never tried that but heard it's good. Try it and write to me about it. Today, I had to sit in a 2 hr meeting where everyone was smoking in a closed room. Let me tell you how much fun THAT was, ugh.

The most recent vid you sent was awesome. Doesn't look like much has changed. Did I mention that everything is brown and gnarly, covered in a thick layer of dirt? My point isn't so much that it's dirty and brown here but when I return, I hope to arrive at a lush, beautiful garden that has been worked to perfection by my lovely 9-month pregnant wife.... HAHAHAHAHA! Yeah right. In any event, I'm looking forward to coming home already. Had a hilarious dream last night

where we met up and I didn't recognize you. I don't think it'll
be that bad.

Got to run, wuv woo.
RPM

H,

Your birthday is coming up! And, I've been thinking...
despite our numerous protestations of getting old, I think
we've got a really great thing. Wonderful kid, soon to be 2,
jobs, pretty good health, a small but nice house and most
importantly a stable normal, loving, honest and faithful relationship. You may not think so but believe me, I see and have
seen the flip side and our 'boringness' is not a bad thing at all.
I really do love you and think you are the best thing that's
ever happened to me. I can't even begin to imagine what my
life would be like without you. I'm 99% sure that our relationship was the last chance at redemption I had. Had we not
toughed it out (and will continue to do) I'd end up growing old
alone and even more bitter than I already am.

I've said it before and I continue to believe it wholeheartedly;
you have brought more to me and my family's lives than you
could possibly imagine and we, I especially, are truly blessed to
have you. Sounds sappy, I know, but it's the truth. Funny how
when you (I) try to imagine what life would be like or what I'd be
doing I simply cannot dream of life without you and E. It's like
wondering what people who are blind think of the world, having
never seen art or read a book; No concept of colors other than
trying to imagine what cool, warm and hot look like.

That's what I think my life was like before we met, and it's not just because I was usually drunk. Long story short, I really like you. WUV WOO.

Ryan bought me a web cam for my birthday and we began using the Skype program to talk to each other several times a week. He got to see Elizabeth and she loved being able to talk to daddy, show him her toys, blow him kisses...all of the things that kept him going and made the deployment more bearable. He was so happy after our first "Skype Session":

It was great seeing your face last night. Sometimes I forget, only for a moment, how beautiful you really are. I don't think you are aging one bit. To me, you only get better. Motherhood suits you very well. I hope you know that I think of myself as both blessed and lucky to have you as my wife. It's the greatest thing ever. Although it is strange seeing you and E continue to develop a relationship while mine as a husband and father seems to be frozen in time. Hopefully pushing the play button won't be too traumatic after six months on pause...for any of us. There is nothing better in the world to me right now than watching her play in 'real time' as you follow her around with the camera. Thank you.

Wuv woo.
RPM

Another update for the masses:

DATE: February 8, 2009
SUBJECT: Greetings from the Cradle of Civilization.

It's been an interesting week to say the least. Given I enjoyed the Super Bowl, but let's say that watching kick off at 3am with no beer, chips or usual festivities made it shall we say, different. The powers that be allowed 2 beers per soldier but for some odd reason our precious supply went MIA before reaching our lonely hamlet. Perhaps they figured the helicopter flight to deliver a case or two of brewskis wasn't quite worth the cost or risk. No big deal, I under-stand. What was far worse, however, was the

ON TOP OF THINGS

fact that the Armed Forces Network (AFN) does not show commercials. So instead of hilarious Monster, Pepsi and Bud Light ads, we were treated to a steady stream of extremely boring monotone officers explaining that suicide was bad and that you should never, ever, ever shake a baby. Surely important information for some, but I could have used a little comic relief after the beer fiasco. Thank God it was a good game.

More important than watching tremendously talented and overpaid athletes run into one another was the fact that the second Iraqi elections went off in our area without a single car bomb or assassination (that we know of). Perhaps the Iraqi people are finally beginning to understand that debate and the ballot box are far better ways to settle differences than the Kalashnikov and car bomb. It is truly amazing to watch a nascent democracy continue to develop out of tyranny. Amazing that already the Iraqis understand political horse-trading and are experiencing the bittersweet reality of unfilled political promises. This recent election had hundreds of candidates and parties and a massive, peaceful turnout for the most part. Say what you want about this 'endless' war but considering the painful and bloody timeline of our own history and the ongoing saga of other so-called democracies around the world, things are on track here and will likely remain so as long as there is a stabilizing force (aka US) remains here to make sure what has been started will be given the opportunity to continue. There would be no greater tragedy in this hellish tale than to waste all that's been spent and let Iraq backslide into shit.

The novelty of being able to change leadership after a short period of time must be like experiencing electricity or indoor plumbing for the first time. The ubiquitous ink stained finger tips combined with the almost disfiguring smiles were a testament to the incredible nightmare collectively experienced by so many Iraqis over the past 30 years.

Despite my short time here, I feel that this place is finally turning the corner and the dream is slowly and painfully becoming a reality. I know that many Americans have grown tired of this war. We've spent a lot of money here. Something that was mentioned far too many times during our ridiculous election cycle. Our collective mindset has been conditioned by a stream of biased, heartless and cynical b.s. by the ruthless combination of media and politicos (most of them at least); always jockeying for the much coveted sound bite that would secure the next election.

Far more important than the billions of dollars spent was the blood of both the American and Iraqi people; sacrificed for an elusive set of ideals in these parts; taken for granted in our blessed country (for all of our faults, it is without a doubt that the U.S.A. is truly blessed by the hand of God). A former belief, now turned fact that is reaffirmed on a daily basis here. Something that will forever be etched in my mind and forged in my heart as it is with most soldiers who have spent time overseas and away from family and their homes.

I've been fortunate to come into close contact with a good number of local peeps day in and day out. A lot of which are Iraqi army officers, and soldiers who've lost thirty thousand plus over the past five years in this war, not to mention the hundreds of thousands in the previous decades. You want to talk about a country tired of war? Come have some chai with the older soldiers in the Iraqi army and believe me there aren't many that have somehow survived 3 major conflicts and a continuous slaughter over the past 30 years. There are families who are still desperately searching, not so much for the living anymore, but for both closure and perhaps a reason as to why their brother, mother, and father had to experience such a heinous and horrific end.

Ok, now that THAT is off of my chest. Let's talk about some funny stuff.

This culture is kind of odd. And by odd I mean really, really strange. For instance, we were at a sensitive facility today (FYI I am not a security guard, nor was I manning a checkpoint) and a suspicious vehicle drives up. The bomb dogs sat, indicating explosives were present. An electronic device concurred and things got a little intense. The driver was pulled out and asked why his vehicle would register explosives. He explained that it was likely due to the turbo gasoline he uses. I figured we're in the middle east, and even premium is cheap enough for the crappy cars like he was driving, but even the most pure petrol shouldn't make dogs freak

out. He explained further that this was special super turbo gas. As we began to lose patience that the bomb next to us was

TAKING CARE OF BUSINESS

going to go off at any second, the guy said that the special super turbo gas was actually a mixture of regular gasoline with a little additive to make his car run better. The secret additive was C-4 plastic explosive, which is combined with regular gas and sold on the black market. It's obviously what sent Fido and Lassie into a tizzy. Maybe it would make sense to some but if you know anything about C-4, it doesn't work like that. Classic Iraq story though.

Other than that, we continue to have fun. There's no short-age of toys on our base to keep us busy and entertained; motor-cycles, off road trucks, weapons of every sort, explosives, rockets and just recently a new camp mascot; a black puppy. So we're keeping busy and doing good things.

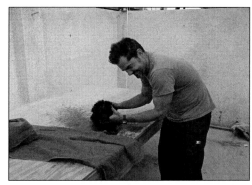

RYAN'S ADOPTED PUPPY

Hope to send a better update in a few. Time seems to fly these days.

Until then, keep on rockin' in the free world.
RPM

Back in the USA, my biggest concern was finding out the sex of our growing baby:

DATE: February 04, 2009

Ryan,

I have decided I MUST find out the sex of this baby! A
patient of mine said if you pee into a cup of Drano it will
turn a certain color if its a boy. I also hear it sizzles and the
fumes are quite bad. She's an interesting lady to say the
least. Anyhow, I understand you not wanting to know and
I can respect that but I would feel MUCH better with you
saying (in writing) that you won't be "the least bit mad or
upset with me" if I find out at this next appointment.

Thanks for your blessing in advance!

Miss you so much!
Heather

H,

If it means that much to you (It shouldn't. You're just
being weak!) then find out. BUT, the caveat is that you
cannot tell anyone including me. I'm determined to wait and
find out in the delivery room. I won't be mad or even the
least bit upset if you find out. I'm not going to deny your happiness. Have fun with trying to keep that secret! Stay sane
and give my love to the babies!

Wuv woo.
RPM

02/08/2009

I did it. I found out the sex and emailed him an ultrasound picture. I tempted him with a "bet you can't guess!" When he tried to Skype with me to figure out the answer, as usual, something broke on his computer. He could hear me but I couldn't hear him. We just had to type through it, staring at each other on the monitors while using Instant Messaging:

"You like this don't you? Every girl's dream. I can't talk but you can... enjoy it while you can." He said that he felt so unhealthy from all of the sugar and fat in the food and there were really no healthy choices to eat. He asked if the little body in the ultrasound was a boy. "Don't know," I said. He replied, "It's a girl isn't it? You wouldn't be able to wait to tell me if it was a boy. Why do you give me only girls?" He thought he should be able to get a motorcycle now that I got what I wanted...girls. And as though I would have thought any differently he typed "you know I'm totally going to love her." And I could tell even on the blurry HP monitor that he was smiling and quite proud.

Ryan said that Iraq was totally polluted and everyone seemed to chain smoke. He said that he thought Clarksville was small but now his world was limited to 10 guys holed up on a piece of land the size of a parking lot. Equipment was constantly breaking and of course the Internet connection issues were driving everyone crazy. He could not remember what wine tasted like or what women looked like. He said he could best describe the very few women he had seen there as "dressed like ultra conservative ninjas." Black robes and all but their eyes and fingertips were completely covered.

He held up his new gun and showed me how the weapon worked. He said he was working on an update for friends and family but the computer would keep shutting down, and the USB ports seemed to get messed up and malfunction from the sand that gets in everything over there. He said his face was so itchy and it was putting him in a bad mood. The call ended with me saying that he was grouchy and I was done talking to/messaging him. When I read back on that, I see the itchy skin, the feeling run down and unhealthy was just beginning. We assumed it was Iraq, why would we ever think it would be anything else?

Update to friends and family:

DATE: February 13, 2009
SUBJECT: A short hello

The weekend is upon us, which doesn't really mean much at all seeing as we are finally settling into a random routine if one could ever exist in this madhouse of a country. There's been a few groups acting up lately but not so much towards us anymore but rather targeting the thousands of unarmed religious pilgrims moving through our area; something very important to the Shia that Saddam blocked during his time so needless to say, they are walking to these parts from all over. Some have been walking for 2+ months. They don't seem to mind us at all and actually are pretty friendly. Crazy how the mass murders of 30+ people at a time is commonplace and barely registers on the news anymore. What is happening to this world?

I hate to say this, especially about the last comment, but being here is kind of like being at a summer camp for semi-grown adults. Although, a summer camp that is heavily armed with a giant wall and barbed wire around it. A camp with no pool or lake and that is surrounded by brain eating zombies that are trying to kill you day in and day out (maybe a slight exaggeration). It really does resemble the 'gasoline outpost' from Mad Max...at least it often times feels like it, but in reality, I hardly think that everyone outside of the walls, moat and wire is obsessed with destroying us. Most likely, they have no idea we exist which is ideal. I have no problem being neglected and starved for attention here.

As I've mentioned, we've got plenty to keep us busy and the current state of affairs requires us to keep a very low profile, which is fine by me. Someone from a previous rotation built a giant catapult that we've launched everything except fragmentary grenades out of, which was fun. Thinking about putting together a giant cross bow as well and maybe trying to build some giant flaming arrows. If that project gets completed without somebody getting hurt, I'll be amazed. I know I need to start taking more pictures and videos but it all seems kind of boring to me and would probably be the same for you. Next time we do something really fun like racing the trucks and motorcycles around the camp or blowing stuff up, I'll get some video. I can only imagine that considering what's going on with the economy, a little humor would be appreciated.

Luckily, through the miracle of technology, I get to see the wife pretty much on a daily basis. Not quite the same as being home but it does make the extended absence a little easier. Watching your child grow up online however is not the preferred technique and I advise against it. It's not fun for anyone involved. My girls seem to be doing well but it's obvious that kids (and parents) do a lot better when both parents are present and involved. People always mention how fast they grow up. It's a hell of a lot faster when you aren't there to see it day in and day out.

I'll likely be home before you know it, sipping on a ice cold Budweiser, watching the Dawgs blow another season, while chasing two babies around and this experience will seem more like an extended, very weird 6 month vacation to Tijuana, Mexico.

Until then, as always, keep on rocking in the semi-free, however increasingly socialist world.

RYAN WITH DISCO WHO HE
NURSED TO HEALTH

Your friend,
Ryan

P.S. We've tentatively named the dog 'Disco' but I'm not totally sold on it. I'll be sure to get a picture of the rascal assuming the wild cats don't devour him tonight.

We tried to Skype and talk through the month of March but Ryan's internet there was messed up and we couldn't connect. Elizabeth would often go to the computer and say "da-da" and then "no da–da" and shake her head when she didn't see him. We finally got the cameras coordinated to where he could see Elizabeth but she couldn't hear him, so she just stared at him and showed him some of her toys. I would follow her around the house with the laptop so he could watch her play. It NEVER got old to him. When she lost interest, we went back and forth about bills and me keeping the heat too high, trying to make it to the next pay and paying off our credit cards. In other words, the stuff every Army family deals with even when deployed. He could have spent his last three days and nights tracking the enemy, only to return to his bunker and argue with his wife about the heat setting on the thermostat and the car loan. I don't envy a soldier's life.

H,

As far as the Army deal is concerned, let's get our finances in order before we think about this seriously, but I'm ready to be permanently back at home with the three of you and Jack, I just don't want to be working as a security guard at the Clarksville Mall, so I/we have to give this some serious thought. But, it's something to think about starting now.

And, because you're the best most patient beautiful wife and mother a guy could ever ask for, I paid off our Mastercard. This money should NOT be used for diapers, cleaning supplies, tires, bills or any other items that do not directly contribute to your happiness. It SHOULD only be used for clothes, make up, gourmet food, or a good meal in the ATL. I realize this money could be spent by you in 30 seconds and doesn't really amount to much but it's more of a small token of my enormous gratitude for not killing my child during this deployment. Treat yourself from your loving and devoted husband.

Final note, if anything should happen to me, and they send

all my bags back, make sure you check the pockets of all the bags and all my pants.

Have fun on your trip to Atl. Take pics and tell everyone I said hello. Drive safe. Wuv Woo.

RPM

—∞o❀∞—

DATE: April 7, 2009
SUBJECT: Update to family and friends

All is well here. Just continuing to do God's work and hope that one day when we leave, these people will be able to handle themselves and properly govern their own country.

Things are still changing rapidly and we are trying to stay busy with a whole bunch of projects that don't involve guns or bombs, which could be interpreted as a good thing (I'll leave my interpretation out). Dealing with the bureaucratic hell on our side is probably the most frustrating thing I can imagine. We could do a helluva lot but because so many groups insist on having their say, regardless of whether or not it's apropos, things don't get done and the Iraqis get angry. Especially after so many promises are broken and more meetings are required.

Let's say that our government does not always take the most efficient route in getting things done and unfortunately it appears we'll be dealing with these issues at home on a far greater scale in the coming years.

The other sad thing is the number of great people really risking their lives to help us and for whatever reason, the powers that be (mostly in the State Dept.) are not issuing visas even though these people have repeatedly demonstrated their mettle in combat often times saving American lives.

This makes me unbelievably angry. There is absolutely no reason that they should be denied visa despite having numerous letters from generals written on their behalf. Meanwhile we open the southern borders to whomever feels the inkling to walk on over. Trying to stay apolitical here...but since the new administration, it has become considerably more difficult for Iraqis, even those with green cards to get citizenship or visas for their immediate families. If they are forced to stay, once we leave, that is the end for them.

Sorry to pontificate continuously but these are the things I'm dealing with on a daily basis and it's driving me nuts.

On an up note, our puppy, Disco has made a miraculous recovery from what we think was either Parvo or ingesting some type of poison. That tremendously raised the morale and several guys are scheming to bring him back to the states.

Days otherwise consist of training Iraqis, looking for bad guys, working out, reading and honing our skills. I hate being away from the wife and baby, but it's otherwise actually a pretty good life. On the good days, we are able to put a mass murderer or two away, or convince a kid not to take up arms thus eventually committing suicide, or directly change the perception of America through other means than the application of force (It seems like we are doing each almost on a daily basis). I really can't imagine a better job. If only I could record some of the conversations I've had and explain the type of people that I've had them with. Incredibly interest-

ing the number of hats we have to wear. Imagine sitting down
and having a civil conversation with a sworn enemy who if
the tables were reversed would have no issues in decapitat-
ing you, but during the course of talking (sometimes over 36
hours), the guy literally changes his mind and even though
he's going to jail for 30 years because you caught him, he
says that he wishes the best for you and your family, that you
have managed to smash his perception of what he thought
Americans were about and that he'll pray for your safety. It
absolutely blows your mind. Of course this doesn't mean that
I'm letting my guard down or didn't have a sidearm ready but
we've known that you have to take a different approach with
a lot of what we do since we don't have 150 Americans on our
camp, but that's exactly why we are the 'special' forces versus
regular Army.

On the bad days...well let's say that we haven't had any
real bad days yet and I pray that we don't. Like anywhere, you
will have your criminals, scumbags and folks that deserve to
die without question, but there are just as many truly good
people willing to sacrifice everything to make the country
a better place. Much of what we've discovered is that our
enemies may hate us but also do not know us (as with most
wars). We're not dealing with insurgents but in many cases
conservative, rural and overly religious patriots who are
being manipulated by the bad guys. While I'm not considering
converting to Islam or doing something outrageous like joining the peace corps or becoming a democrat, I'll say that my
experiences in the middle east haven't really opened my eyes
(since I've been studying the region since high school) but

rather reaffirmed a lot of my beliefs about people, politics and all the bad things associated with governments and war.

I still believe that what we did here was 100% right, even if it does fall apart once we leave. Anyone saying that America lost the respect of the world because of Iraq has no clue what they are talking about. A lot of these people really do like us and are extremely grateful for everything that has been done. I'd hardly call the situation we are in now a war...it's kind of like driving through the really bad parts of Detroit at night. You better have your guard up and know there are people looking to hurt you but not everyone wants to kill you. But of course that could change in short order.

One final story. We headed out on a mission not too long ago and had a dog team with us. The military working dogs are like German Shepherds but more ferocious which is pretty damn scary considering Hitler genetically created German Shepherds to be killing machines. Imagine that, coupled with a civilization that has uncanny fear or dislike of dogs, espe-cially big ones...I mean they are scared to death of them due to the fact that they just don't view dogs the same way we do. They're a filthy nuisance, not a pet right?

Disco, our 10 lb. mutt puppy harbors a similar fear and distrust of the Iraqis. Even he senses their fear...(much like I do) and barks constantly at them. So we go on this mission with this killing machine "Kim" who can also sniff out explo-sives. We roll into a place and seize a couple of houses where the suspect had been sleeping. Of course once the people (Iraqi soldiers included) see the dog, they either freeze up and start crying or just drop everything and run away. We

enter this house and the dog is acting funny so we get all our
guys in, thinking something bad is going to happen. Nothing is
found but the dog handler keeps saying something is up and
the dog is acting twitchy for some reason. (None of the Iraqis
are to be found not due to their fear of hidden bombs but rather
they didn't want to be near the dog). We break the exterior gate
down and prepare to assault the interior of the compound; fully
expecting (and sorta hoping) a big gun fight is on the verge of
breaking out. We're all amped up and as we get ready to blow
this door down, the dog stops and in the middle of the small
courtyard takes the biggest dump I've ever seen. It looked like
a Clydesdale had come straight in from the field and into this
house...Once she had finished her business she immediately
returned to normal and started sniffing around like nothing
had happened as 10 commandos were stacked on this door
prepared to do a dynamic/explosive entry. Needless to say, we
all immediately understood where the 'twitchiness' was coming
from. Unfortunately, we didn't have any doggy bags, not that
we would've used it if we did, and decided to leave it for the SOB
that we missed. As we filed out, the Iraqis went in and starting
laughing figuring that one of us had left him a message...maybe,
had I been a few years younger...

Still no name for #2 yet. I like Georgina W. Means but
Heather says 'absolutely not'. I'll keep thinking, but in the
meantime feel free to provide some input...

Until then keep on rockin' in the free world.
RPM

—∘∘∘◦)◉(◦∘∘∘—

One last update for the masses from overseas:

DATE: April 20, 2009
SUBJECT: Pirates

Brief update that can be sent over the net:

We are still working. This city on the surface is showing remarkable progress with all kinds of economic activity
and very little violence. It is still very much of a third world
country but there is a collective effort to make it better. We
continue to get out and meet people and oddly they continue
to be very positive about our presence (ranging from kids, to
mayors, to religious leaders). I always try and make it very
clear that we are doing our best to help out but they need to
know that we'll soon be leaving and that peace and stability
are most important. Sadly, the inevitability of a relapse into
something similar to a civil war is also accepted. The various sides continue to stockpile arms and prepare for what
may happen once we leave and it's very unfortunate. There
really are a lot of very good people here trying to make Iraq
a safe democracy—and make it last—but, due to the current
circumstances we are no longer able to go after the bad guys
like we once were.

Life otherwise really isn't too bad for us. I've certainly
got plenty of projects to keep me busy and except for a few
random disorganized incidents here and there, it's been relatively safe. Of course the other caveat to what I said before
was that this town is a well-known hideout for bad guys i.e.
after committing their deeds elsewhere they come lay low

here. We know where they are, what they've done and how to catch them but because of the corruption, we simply can't get them. This is what's going to bite them later but it's all in the name of keeping the peace and hoping it holds.

It unfortunately appears that the Commander in Chief is everything that we expected and knew he would be which does not bode well for the world. Being over here and doing what we do has absolutely reinforced what I knew earlier; that we are not an imperialist nation out for oil, as the liberals love to say. We are not committing atrocities on a regular basis against innocent civilians. Mistakes have happened but all in all American troops are incredibly restrained and very professional and believe me, I've seen what the 'other side' does both the good guys and the bad. Sad that there are still large segments of our society who will always view the military in a bad light. Those fools are so incredibly ignorant when they talk about Iraq or Afghanistan it's almost unbearable to listen or watch them act out. I actually began to write 'if they had any clue as to what was really going on...' and then realized that most of them probably do but prefer to slander our country and our efforts in the name of their political agenda. I better be careful what I write so I am not targeted as a radical and a threat to the government, who is susceptible to recruitment by racist organizations...

It's not an easy job nor is it always fun, but it's extremely rewarding and one that I love. In any event, this probably isn't too different than my previous updates. Know that we are doing well, we are safe and we continue to do God's work regardless of what people think. I only hope that in our short time here, we continue to make progress in the never ending fight against the evils that exists in this world and that we are able to help at least a few people in the process.

Looking forward to a safe return and the birth of #2 who will likely get at least the middle name of Reagan.

Keep on rockin' in the free world,
RPM

04/20/09

Ryan said that he had been throwing up frequently. He continued to complain about all of the filth and raw sewage. He reported that the dog they rescued was still quite healthy since their miracle work, although, he may not live too long since he decided to start chasing cars and barking at Iraqis with guns.

When he could get online, Ryan would spend his time searching Home Depot and Lowe's websites, planning his lists for when he returned home. He was excited to get back into his gardening groove.

His first day home would be spent loving me and E while we watched him do yard work and then have a healthy dinner and a glass of wine. Or, at least that was the plan. I sent him some pictures of the plants that had begun to come back from the winter. He instructed me on what perennials to buy and how to space them. He asked about every single plant he had planted the previous year. It amazed me the level of detail he knew about that garden.

Spring was on it's way and I wanted Ryan back home more than ever. The grass was finally growing in our huge yard and I didn't like yard work when I wasn't pregnant, let alone at seven months and huge. My dad and brother visited and helped me restore the garden to its beautiful state in preparation for Ryan's return. We performed above and beyond Ryan's expectations and sent before and after photos that gave him a renewed energy.

04/26/09

Ryan had fantastic news. Plans were in action for a possible new job in Alexandria, Va. He said he would never be able to tell me exactly what he would be doing, but he would be "living the dream." Polygraphs and such had to be passed, but if all was successful, we would move to a fun town, full of life and great restaurants, closer to the beach than landlocked Tennesse, with plenty of biking and hiking opportunities and culture. Not to mention, we would only be a train ride away from the greatest city on earth...New York City! Something we were both craving badly.

—ooo❧ooo—

I was instant messaging Ryan from the waiting room at the doctor's office. I had been really short on energy by late April and thought maybe I was getting signs of post-partum depression, if that was even possible when you are still pregnant. Turns out it was a glucose issue. When I told Ryan about my thoughts, he said that he was depressed shortly after 9/11 and never since...but right now, he was worried that he may be depressed since he had no energy and was not feeling like his usual high-power motivated self. He felt like things were not getting accomplished there, and he desperately felt that he needed to get home for some reason.

Over the next few weeks, it seemed like we had both reached our breaking point. We started to argue more about the finances and the fact that we only had heard that savings accounts existed, but had never actually had one. I told him that he was bossy and always gets to make the decisions. It wasn't until a year later that I realized how much I loved his bossiness, or more importantly how much I needed his bossiness. I never knew how many things he took care of without my knowledge.

By May 1st, Ryan said he thought he had a stomach ulcer. He thanked me for the Easter package I sent him but said that his stomach couldn't handle anything except maybe water. He started having very vivid nightmares. One where he was in a loft apartment, half wakes up feeling horribly hung over, and sees his mother and I standing over him and I am crying and looking at him with hate. He feels an arm try to wake him fully and turns to see a naked woman in bed with him. I run out, still pregnant and he wakes in a cold sweat feeling the horror. In another, he is driving down the road and he knows he is extremely drunk and doesn't want to be in the car but cannot stop to get out because he is on a highway and there is a roadblock in front of him. Again, he woke up in a cold sweat and said he could not sleep and thought about the dreams during the day, as they were so real and terrifying. He tried to find the positive and said "I think it's just God's way of reminding me that I have an awesome life and doing stupid shit isn't worth it." And he was still getting sicker.

I continued working on his garden requests and although I hated getting all muddy and mosquito bitten, I loved the way it made him so happy and proud of me. Aside from chatting with Elizabeth, his favorite thing to do was have me walk around the outside of the house showing him plant by plant how they were doing. Like a child with a noisy toy, he just never seemed to tire of it. And it was the only way I could appease him when he was heartbroken that E was always in bed by the time he called us. His mornings were our evenings, and since they did most of their work at night, he missed Elizabeth frequently.

—ᴏᴏᴏ⫩◈⫨ᴏᴏᴏ—

05/17/09

We were using the IM on Skype this night when Ryan said, "I've got a full body itch all over, no rash, no bumps, no bug bites. It's SO itchy and I drink fluids constantly to hydrate but my urine is always dark, very dark. Plus everything I eat, especially fatty food, makes me very gassy and just sick to where I can't sleep."

I told him I thought that maybe his kidneys and/or gallbladder/liver had an issue. Who knows with the filth over there? He said he would tell his medic.

That same night, a prisoner escaped from the Montgomery County prison near our home. He was in for a shooting death in 2007. I wished we had an alarm system, or even better, I wished Ryan was home. I never felt safe without him. Now I was worried about his safety.

05/20/09

Ryan emailed me a picture of his eyes and he said, "My eyes turned yellow, like jaundice. Medic can't seem to figure it out." I told him that it sounds like liver issues, too much bilirubin. I told him to not drink alcohol or take any medicines like Tylenol. He said his medic gave him erythromycin ointment for his eyes. I told him I thought that was for pink eye infections, and that he needs a doctor, pronto. I told him to stop messing around with those symptoms. He heard the worry in my voice and changed the subject.

He asked, "Do you think they will let me bite through the umbilical cord when you deliver at Vandy?"

"No," I said.

"That story would live on forever," he replied. "I'm gonna ask, can't hurt."

I told him that those things are pretty damn tough and I didn't think a human could bite through one. Well, that was the worst thing to say. He was determined to find out if it was possible.

"How about we just save it and make you a bracelet or something? Not quite as disgusting but still as unnecessary," I joked.

"No, it will be a beautiful act of love and commitment. I will show them how Green Berets do it!" he said.

"Al-righty then, go practice on a goat. You are gross." I said.

He was adamant. "Heather, that would make the news for sure. Green Beret returns from war zone still hungry for blood, must have hardcore PTSD. Would be a great photo too, right?"

"No, I don't think it would. Besides, the guys at Lowe's think my chances of delivering there are pretty good since I'm there more than many employees. The guy in the window department told me he was a retired paramedic, so I'm good. But thanks for the strange offer. I think you need to get home ASAP." How we always got into such strange discussions is beyond me.

Ryan said he would spend much of his day trying to imagine what the first moments with E after the six month deployment would be like. Would she remember him? Would she go to him? Would she fear him? How long would it take for it to come back to her? Will the bond be the same as before he left? And what will we do that first day? And then he would start counting the days till until he left Iraq and recount to be sure, again and again. He said being away from her was the toughest thing he had ever done. And he had done some tough stuff! It wasn't like him at all to say such a thing. I sent him more frequent pictures and video clips of Elizabeth over the next days. We talked about how we were glad that we waited until we were a little older to have kids because we truly enjoyed our time with her, we realized she would grow up fast, and we just wanted to enjoy her and get all we could with her while she was young and make sure she had a bright future.

05/23/09
Email from Ryan:

Hey,

My eyes are still yellow. I've been trying to eat more veggies but they're not really ever available so, I'm drinking more V8 and trying to get some sun every day. Bad news on the hair front; wearing a helmet all the time doesn't do it much good.

I also don't like hearing that you are having all these problems and I'm still over here. I'd do anything to be there with you guys now but our command just isn't very understanding. I swear to God I'd be suicidal if I had to spend another week over here than absolutely necessary. It would be a lot better if we were doing what we should be but we can't for all kinds of fucked up reasons so it's mind numbing.

I'm totally exhausted. This heat is unbearable and we wear full uniforms with 60 lbs. of gear and drive around in vehicles with no air conditioning that blow hot air. It's not fun and wears you out like you wouldn't believe. But, I know that another day is gone, and I'm one step closer to you and baby and that's what's pulling me through and keeping me sane. Just wish I could've seen you guys via Skype today. Shaved the mustache and got a haircut. Now people are seriously freaked out when they see me. They don't recognize me.

Wuv woo.
RPM

That email terrified me because it was certainly not in Ryan's nature to complain. I didn't know if it was just the situation in Iraq or the illness that was getting him down, but I did know that it was completely out of character.

05/26/09

H,

I didn't want to mention this, but we are down to 9 days. Now I'm just trying to play it cool and not go insane waiting. I've got to stop looking at calendars. I'm literally counting the number of days several times a day expecting it to somehow change. I packed some stuff up last night. It's like the longest Christmas Eve ever. I keep imagining what E is going to do when I first see her and of course how big you are going to look in person and whether or not I'll be able to get my arms around you. I'm thinking yes, but Skype could totally distort the actual size. I'll do my best to get them around you. I just imagine every little detail a thousand different ways and I can deal with time crawling by. Soon, I will be leaving here and coming to you.

Obviously, I'm also very excited about seeing the house. I've got zero concern that everything you've done is going to look great (translation: I'm sure you did a great job). Happy to see that you are physically done so I can resume my role as the one messing everything up with my misguided projects. Which brings up a disturbing new trend...

During a meeting we had the other day I got on a survivalist kick. Nothing serious but a couple of things happened and

as the head of the house, I want to make sure that we are prepared for just about anything. I've got most of the stuff already
but want to put together 3–4 duffle bags that would allow us
to live for at least a week in our house during any conditions if
we lost electricity or something silly like that (a Katrina like
deal or when the house lost power for 4–5 days when I was in
Oman). Like I said, it's mostly just putting camping gear we
have together in a single place. I'm not burying my guns or stor-
ing up 5 months of food or anything. Just want to make sure
that the family has what it needs. Anyway, I've made a list.

OK, I'm going to work. Hope you wake up in time to read
this novella and it puts a smile on your face.

Wuv woo.
RPM

The next day, 05/27/09
(IM) Instant Messaging session:

"Did you get to a hospital yet? It's been a week now since you showed
me the yellow eyes, you need more help than a medic can give you. Go
to a hospital, please." I begged.

"Well," he said, "they took my vitals and sent them up to command."

"You are kidding me right? Yellow eyes, itchy skin, runny poop,
fatigue, night sweats...who cares about vitals? These are textbook signs
of a liver dysfunction!" I said. "You need blood work and imaging. This
is serious! Some of those signs are red flags for cancer, Ryan! Although
I'm sure it isn't, you still need to check." I wanted to cry. My hands were
so tied. Years of medical training for nothing.

"Heather, you don't understand, we are in the middle of nowhere. I need a helicopter to get to a hospital, that's where they have to take me to get tests and blood work done. I HATE this place! I know what those signs are, too. Should I be concerned? I mean, I am trying to play it down but I got a little freaked out reading the research online last night. But hopefully, those in charge will make a decision in the next day or so. Do you think I have cancer or cirrhosis?" he asked.

"No, you are too young and healthy" I said. "I'm sure it is something to do with being in an unsanitary country and after three decades of taking care of your body it all goes to shit for six months. Maybe Hepatitis, or a virus, liver fluke, gall bladder disease? I don't know."

"Well, I am packed and ready to go as soon as they say the word. I'll hopefully hear something tonight. I need to get those tests done ASAP." He started to sound desperate. This terrified me. It was completely uncharacteristic of Ryan Means.

"Get well and un-yellowed, please. I have to go to work," I said. "Love you."

"Wuv Woo, too," he said.

05/28/09

"You there?" He typed on IM.

I heard the beep. It was 3:29 a.m.

"Yes! I couldn't sleep," I said.

"Yay. Why can't you sleep?" he asked.

"No idea" I replied. "So I did the usual. Long, hot bath and reading. Any news?"

"I guess they are sending a bird to get me today. Weird because I feel totally normal right now, which makes me nervous," he wrote.

"You are going to the hospital? And getting the tests?" I asked.

"All the tests will be done," he said. "Thinking it's Hep."

"Did you tell your mom yet?" I asked.

"Yes! I did, thank you!" he replied sarcastically.

"No, thank you," I replied. "I'm glad you did."

"I'm not. It is exactly what I told you. She calls her 78-year old retired doctor friend that isn't my doctor and never has been and gives him third hand information. Might as well use Web MD," he said.

"She is your mom and she wants to help from across the world. It means she must be concerned about the news though," I said. "Besides, you and I are going to be doing that stuff to E and Baby #2 one day. Parents are supposed to be that way; it's how they care…Where is this hospital anyhow?" I asked.

"Baghdad", he said. "I hope they say what I have is super common in this filth and they say it's no biggie. I know they see some trauma here. Probably makes Detroit's trauma centers look like daycare. I hope they give me a shot and send me home," he said.

"I don't," I replied. I'd kill myself if I was to permanently raise two kids alone. Deployments with one kid are rough but two kids, while you are on the eternal deployment? Nope, can't do it. I'm convinced single moms deserve sainthood if their kids turn out well."

"Ha," he laughed. "When they do a good job yes, they do. You should have some help this week, right? Isn't my family coming?"

"No, I told them not to worry about it. Everyone wants to come during the week when I am paying for full-time childcare already. Nobody can come on the long weekend or Memorial Day when I can use the help. Why does it always seem to work that way? People say, 'let me know if I can help' but only to do only what they want. That's not so great for the one who needs the help, is it? I'm sure they mean well…oh my God, I sound like a miserable pregnant woman," I sighed. "Anyhow, be safe and get your ass on the helicopter." Maybe you can steal someone's cell for a bit and send me a text to let me know you are OK?"

"I didn't think you cared," he smirked.

"I don't have a lot of time to express emotions right now, Ryan! It's been a hell of a month. I care!! There." I replied.

"Ha, I was joking. If anyone is emotionless, it is me. Wuv woo. Talk soon," he said. "Goodnight."

That same night, someone broke into my car and stole Elizabeth's DVD player and DVDs along with my navigation system, just when I was beginning to feel safe in our house in Clarksville. On top of Ryan's sickness, it was the straw that broke the camel's back, so to speak, and it sent me into a major meltdown. I awoke to an email from Ryan saying that he was requesting to be flown into Nashville when he returned. Thank God. I started mentally planning the homecoming party.

PART V

30 Days to Live

Chapter One
The Call

The last five months were filled with the usual ups and downs, highs and lows of a deployment. The wife gets fed up with the fact that she is left to take care of the children, the home, the finances—everything. In turn, she learns to appreciate the often unnoticed tasks that her husband took care of when he was home. Soldiers are enthusiastic to leave home and set forth on their missions in Iraq and eventually learn the most important adventure is raising their own family. They both long for the time when they will meet at the airport and all of the excitement that was there when they first met will be again. Those reunions are as happy for us as our wedding days. There is so much anticipation leading up to it, especially when kids are involved. Our reunion was side tracked. It was certainly not what we hoped for or envisioned.

It has been one long year since I received "the call." I cannot account for my exact mental whereabouts in most of the days that have passed since that night. But I remember May 29, 2009, like it was yesterday.

It was 3 a.m. I was wide awake already, thanks in part to a strange sound outside of my bedroom window. My car was broken into the night before, so I suppose I was on high alert. But this sound was definitely an animal—just not one that I had ever heard. Also, I was eight months pregnant and not getting quality sleep any night of the week. I was prowling around the open bedroom window, hoping to catch a glimpse of the moaning creature, when my phone rang. It wasn't completely out of the ordinary as Ryan had been in Iraq for five months now and sometimes forgot that we were in opposite ends of the time zone. I expected the call was regarding his transfer from the front line to a hospital in Baghdad.

For months, he complained of decreased appetite, sleeplessness, night sweats, and lack of energy or motivation. Next, yellowing of the eyes and terrible itching all over. And to my knowledge, the team medic had done nothing but monitor his vitals and give him erythromycin ointment for his eyes. I understand that eight percent of men are color blind, but find it hard to believe that they were all stationed together in a remote area of Iraq. Pink eye...yellow eyes...How these symptoms were allowed to go untreated and misdiagnosed for so long was and is beyond my comprehension. These men comprise one of our nation's most elite fighting forces; they are Green Berets. How on earth did this situation escalate to this point?

However, the important thing now, was that they got him to a hospital so that he could be treated before he would be sent home to watch the birth of our second daughter. I warned him that if it was in fact hepatitis, he may not be coming to our house when he got back to the states. I made it clear that this wasn't the best timing for him to decide to get ill. We had a 17-month-old and another soon to make her appearance and I needed a healthy partner. I somehow felt like he owed it to me as I spent the last five months of my miserable pregnancy taking care of our home and child alone. Now it was time for him to help his own family instead of the Iraqis.

The phone only rang once and I knew it was him. I don't think I gave him much of a chance to say anything. I started in telling him that his call had perfect timing. I put the phone near the window and asked him what the animal was, and he said it was probably an owl and to not worry about it. He asked if the baby was sleeping. I said yes. He asked if I was back in bed and I said, "Yes, and I wish you were too." He said that he had finally made it to Baghdad and that they did an MRI.

"Finally!!" I said relieved.

I remember hearing him inhale, there was a brief moment of silence, then with a cracked voice he said, "Heather...I have liver cancer," followed by another very deep intake of breath and a shaky exhale. He was crying. It was the first time I heard fear in his voice—ever.

I was completely unable to speak. I could not make a single sound escape from my lips. I felt all of the blood rush out of my hands and my heart fell into the pit of my stomach. I think I was nauseated as my mouth began to water, preparing me to be sick. Then it all came out. "WHAT?? Is this some kind of sick joke? What is Elizabeth going to do? My God, we're having baby! NO! NO, NO!!! Elizabeth is so in love with you...are you sure this is right?"

I started crying. It was the strangest cry—I thought I should have been crying so much harder, but somewhere in my brain I guess I thought it was a bad dream, it really wasn't true. To this day, I wish I would have said something else—something to comfort him. He was so alone there in Baghdad. But this was what came out of my mouth. Instinctively, my main concern was the child he already had and the fact that she was so madly in love with her perfect daddy; that I would have to one day explain to her that she would have been raised by the best father in the world, but this happened to him. I had to shift my thoughts back to the real main concern—Ryan.

He said, "I wish to God it was a joke, it's not." He went on to say that the doctor in Baghdad told him that the MRI showed a walnut sized tumor in the common bile duct between the gall bladder and the liver. He called it Cholangiocarcinoma. It was a word that we had never heard before but it would soon roll effortlessly off of our tongues more times than we ever cared to say it. It happened to be a very rare cancer, mostly affecting men in their 50s. Ryan was 35. He was in impeccable health when he left for Iraq in January. He had been training for months for this deployment.

He lived a healthy athletic lifestyle consisting of daily workouts, an uber–healthy diet, and of course the extreme amount of training required to be a member of the Special Forces. He passed the health physical before the deployment. In other words, he was in remarkably great physical shape. But somehow, despite the youth, diet, exercise and health monitoring, he was told he had 30 days to live—just a few days past our due date for the birth.

That moment in time was surreal. I had used that word before, but I had no idea how a true 'out of body' experience felt until that night. It was as if my mind had been elevated above my body, which was left abandoned perfectly upright in bed. I was watching this happen from outside of the actual situation. In retrospect, I truly believe that this is the human mind's way of coping with the trauma. It is a protective mechanism that I would inadvertently come to use for weeks and months. Maybe I still use it.

Imagine finding out that you have cancer. Awful. Imagine finding out that you have cancer when you are in your 30s and have a baby on the way and a child that you are madly in love with at home. Even more awful. Now, imagine that you have just been told that you have cancer, you spent the last five months of your life liberating the people of Iraq instead of spending time with your own family. And at the moment when you need your wife and child to hug you the most, you are literally half a world away from anyone you know in a foreign hospital. I can't imagine what he went through before he even dialed our phone, and I never did ask him. He would have lied and said he was fine. He never wanted me to know when he was in danger. I'm sure that calling me that night was more difficult than any of the challenges of war he had experienced.

Upon hearing me cry, Ryan stepped into his usual hero mode. He said, "Heather, stop crying and let's talk about this calmly and reason-ably." His voice was once again strong and commanding and, like always, it made me feel safe. Despite the desire I had to comfort him, he didn't want my pity or help. He just wanted me to be tough and take care of Elizabeth and baby in the womb and start researching this disease. He continued, reminding me that the socialized system of Army heath care never proved to work well for the majority of active duty recipients or their spouses, at least none that we knew. There were plenty of horror stories that spread around the bases, so maybe this was another terrible mistake in diagnosing. He said, "Let's hope he's wrong and it's just a chicken bone or something." He hadn't lost his sense of humor.

I told him that we would get him home and find the best doctor in the country even if we had to sell our house and everything in it to pay for treatment. Nothing mattered except him getting well. I began searching the Internet for information before we ended our phone call. Sadly, this led to more tears. The symptoms were a textbook match for Cholangiocarcinoma and the prognosis for this type of cancer was grim. Very, very grim. I kept this to myself as I was sure he would find the same thing once had access to the Internet.

We sat in silence. I tried to comfort him from afar. I felt so inadequate and helpless. There was nothing I could do to help him from where I sat. He assured me that the fact that I wanted to be by his side through the hell that he was about to endure was all he needed to get his positive focus. How he could think that I would ever leave him, especially at a time like this just goes to show you what a deployment will do to your head. Ryan said, "I'm going to do everything I can to make sure that you and E and Baby #2 don't get hurt." And that was all he could say.

Ryan decided that he was going to find a workstation where he could compose an email to his family explaining the events leading up to this diagnosis as well as the treatment plan itself. As if he even really knew. As a mother myself, I immediately thought of his mother. I would die to hold my child or at least hear her voice if I received this news. An email would not suffice nor would it make the news any easier to digest. I told him that I wanted him to hang up the phone and call her at once. He wanted to wait until the morning so that he wouldn't interrupt his parents' sleep. For some reason, I could not bear the thought of any mother not knowing that her child is dying. Maybe I was pregnant and hormonal; maybe it wasn't necessary. Especially since none of us would sleep for the next few months. But I thought she had to know; his father had to know. And then, the brothers. It would be a long tearful night.

The call ended with the most heartfelt "I love you" either of us ever spoke and then a dead quiet. No owl outside the window. Just me, alone in a silence that was finally interrupted by an uncontrollable cry that terrified me. I never cried so hard in my life. My body actually convulsed as this incredible cry of terror and sadness overtook it. I had no control, none at all. It was paralyzing. Never in a million years could we have seen this devastation coming our way. It turned our world upside down.

After I regained composure I wrote him an email:

Ryan,

You are likely talking to your parents by now. I cannot imagine what they are thinking. I'm so sorry you are there alone, a world away from all of the people who love you. It breaks my heart.

I just wanted to write you that no matter how long it takes and whatever happens, I am by your side 100 percent and I will never leave. I would never ever, ever in a million years have thought that I might have to spend my life and our girls' lives without you. I was looking forward to the days when the Army was done and we could finally have you all to ourselves, and now this? I'm ready to put on a strong face and get you the best help possible to keep you in our lives. This isn't supposed to happen. I just know it. I cannot wait to put my arms around you. I love you so very, very much more than I ever tell you. I really, really do.

All my love,
Heather

Now the game begins. There was no plan as to how or when he would make it back to the U.S. I assumed that he would be back in Tennessee in a couple of days, given the current situation. If a man is given 30 days to live, one would hope he is returned to his family immediately. This was not the case. Not only that, but the decision makers did not seem to agree on where he should be treated in the U.S. Luckily, I had been an Army wife long enough to know that I should not get a ticket to meet him until he is physically in the said meeting location. Until then, it is all subject to change in the blink of an eye. Just like life.

Chapter Two
Hurry up and Wait

The days following the phone call seemed to drag on for eternity. I wanted him back home more than I have ever wanted anything in my life. I couldn't possibly go to work and put my patient's lives at risk when my brain was somewhere else. So I spent the days taking care of Elizabeth, researching Cholangiocarcinoma and constantly repeating the contents of that horrible phone call to those who were concerned. He never got home to see the garage conversion to a playroom or the landscaping. I lived both of our lives while he was deployed, but through emails and webcams, it often felt like he was there and he was still part of every decision. He was so excited to finally see all of the changes in person. He loved our house and his backyard haven.

Within the next two days, Ryan was flown to Germany. He then had to wait two days to get a flight back into the U.S. It really irritated me that they could not arrange something on a commercial flight or let us arrange it. But in the Army all property is equal, and he was just another piece of Army property on deployment that needed to be returned to the U.S. to get repaired. Our hands were tied.

Medically, he heard much of the same news as in Iraq. Cancer. May have 30 days to live. Have to get to United States. We, his family and our doctor contacts had done some research and found that because of the rarity of this cancer, the best place for him would be Sloan-Kettering Memorial Hospital in NYC or MD Anderson in Houston, Texas. Sadly, the Army felt that although Walter Reed Hospital had little to no experience with Cholangiocarcinoma in young adults, they would go ahead and take on the responsibility. After all, Ryan was their property. I hate to think this had anything to do with controlling costs of paying for healthcare outside the Army healthcare system, but I am only left to speculate as to why else they would try to even touch him with that diagnosis.

He emailed me:

First, I love you very much and we are going to get through this. Walter Reed may just be a layover to get another MRI from what they tell me. Hopefully, they can confirm (again) and send me elsewhere for treatment. Let's get over the initial shock and look forward to beating this thing. I have age and health on my side.

I emailed him:

Ryan,

I can have a baby at any hospital. I want to be wherever you are. I want to see and read the results and I want copies of the records to take to outside specialists for second and third opinions. This seems like the longest day ever. I cannot sleep and I have more (nervous) energy and strength than I have had in weeks. It has been killing my back to lift Elizabeth and suddenly, I have super human strength. It is like I can handle anything—the break-in, our belongings stolen, sleeping in the house alone, pregnancy, heavy babies both in and out of my body, they all seem trivial. I just pray to God that we can live happily ever after.

I already had my 'coming to Jesus' moment this morning where I promised God that we would live a perfect life, go to church, anything if he just lets us keep you in our life. But as the words slipped through my lips, I wondered in my head, can you even bargain with a God? In any case, it was a cold hard promise and I will not break it throughout what we are about to endure. I wish I could say I didn't cry until morning, but I did, and I think I'm still crying—it's just not a cry you can hear. I'm starting to see the light and wish we had done things differently—spent more time together when you were home, less time on the computer and working. The minor arguments, the major fights were all such a waste of our short time together. We should have spent more time in each other's arms. Maybe there really is a God and he will watch over our lives closely, as I can't imagine he would not want the two of us—the four of us—to stay together. Despite my agnostic beliefs at times, I know there has to be some higher power to facilitate the medicine and the doctors on this road that lies ahead, right? We always knew that love involved work when we married and we have prevailed through the small tests these past four years. Now, it's final exam time. Seems a bit early to me...just in time for year number five...Happy Wedding Anniversary. This year I actually would like a present: you—safe at home.

Ryan Wrote:

Let's add that to the list of things that have surprised us about our relationship:
1) Meeting in the parking lot of a cheap motel
2) Initial marriage proposal 24 hours later
3) Elizabeth
4) $20 wedding
5) Anniversary #2 spent dealing with a cancer scare

At this point, nothing should really surprise us anymore. Seriously, aliens could land in our front yard and I'd be like, "Oh, the aliens are here; what's on TV?"

The only time I get sad is when I think about you and E. I can deal with anything except hurting you guys. Will do my best to make sure that doesn't happen.

The doctors seem pretty sharp and very nice, although more of trauma surgeons than oncologists. I have this horrible full body itch and am completely unable to sleep so they allowed me some Ambien. I'm amazed at the critical care transport facilities they have set up. They really do make every effort to take care of the injured in Iraq. Everywhere you look there are things sent from people in the States. That really helps.

It is also amazing to see the young guys that are banged up and yet are still incredibly patriotic and all about their buddies and the mission.

I can't wait to see you guys. Please try not to stress too much right now. I know it is hard, but we've got to remain positive (I'm already sick of hearing the phrase), but we've got no choice.

In any event, I am totally dedicated to beating this for you, E and the mysterious #2. It can and will be done. And we will go on with our lives together. I love you very, very much and I can't imagine doing this with anyone but you and certainly not alone.

I will be home soon, until then—chillax and take care of the babies. Wuv Woo.

RPM

I replied:

> I'm taking good care of E. I just can't look at her right now.
> I had to take her to daycare. All I see is you two together and
> I think about what I will have to tell her. I think about how I
> feel that if only one parent can live, I would pick you. I want
> her to be like you—JUST like you. So many reasons that I am
> with you—I have never told you—actually have to do with the
> qualities that you have that I wish I had and being with you
> has made my life the way I could not have made it myself. You
> have always been a positive influence and made me a much,
> much better person. You are my idea of the perfect father, and
> I saw that in you before you ever knew it. You have gone above
> and beyond what a father does for a child and ours isn't yet
> two years old. You try to change the world to make it better
> for our girls. You plan and live everyday for their future. I felt
> safe with you on our first date and every day since then and I
> do not want to lose that feeling! You make me feel that noth-
> ing can hurt us, we are invincible. I don't want our daughters
> to not know what that feels like!!! You have to be OK. This has
> to be a mistake, an awakening...something else.

I love you.
Heather

Mary Jo drove alone from Atlanta to Tennessee to stay with me while
we waited to hear if and when Ryan would make it to Walter Reed. It
seemed that we didn't know for sure where he would go until the plane
took off with him in it. I wrote Ryan that his mother, Elizabeth and I were

driving to Walter Reed which may take two days, as no one would let me fly with only a couple weeks left in the pregnancy and I just needed to get out of the house and start heading his way.

He wrote back that he was just told he would fly to Fort Campbell and get the MRIs at Blanchfield Hospital. So, we were to stay put. He felt he was getting excellent care as an inpatient in Landstuhl Regional Medical Center in Germany. Additionally, he felt that leaving the desert and seeing colors and breathing fresh air was definitely "recharging his batteries." He was still able to joke and make people laugh, which in his opinion couldn't be bad.

The next day, Ryan heard talks of a transfer to Fort Gordon in Georgia or even Vanderbilt where the baby would be induced. However, they ultimately decided on Walter Reed, just to get the MRI and make sure no infection had set in, and then on to another hospital for treatment/second opinion or follow-up. I think that follow-up talk was to appease us for the time being because once he got to Reed, they were not in any hurry to get him on his way. The internist in Germany said that in his 25-plus years he has never seen a tumor like this one. It was connected to the bile duct and the liver rather than the bile duct and the duodenum. He said a stent to open the blockage will NOT work. The doctor further stated that this could hopefully be a tumor excised with surgery, but he could not tell without the MRI and biopsy; he had only a CT scan to go by this far. For some reason, he had to wait to get the MRI in the States.

Mary Jo and I kept ourselves and a team of soldiers/friends busy with cleaning, preparing the house for Ryan, and redecorating a room as a surprise for his welcome home. We wanted his home to be a comfortable, maintenance free place to recover. She bought us new furniture for our empty room and got me pumped up about his return to the house. It was looking fantastic, and decorating our home was the perfect distraction. I could not wait to show it to him. I knew he would be thrilled.

My dad spent the prior week planting, gardening and getting the outside of the house up to par so that I could impress Ryan upon his homecoming. Mary Jo put on the finishing touches, so that Ryan would have nothing to do but relax. The soldiers organized the mess I had made in his dear little gardening shed. We found a turtle living in there, which was interesting since Ryan found one and set him free when we moved in—possibly he liked it in there and was waiting for his liberator to return. Everything was coming together and ready for his arrival. He was going to be amazed by this refurbished oasis that he deserved.

Mary Jo and I took Elizabeth to mass that Sunday. Across from the church, was Hooker's Funeral Home. Mary Jo insisted that I take her photo with Elizabeth in front of the sign and send it to Ryan with a caption suggesting that we were spending time attending the funerals of hookers as there wasn't much interesting to do in Clarksville. We spent the rest of our free time looking for Mary Jo's car keys, which she misplaced on her first day there. We assumed they were accidentally discarded by some well-intentioned helpers. And although we never did find them during her stay, looking for them became a constant distraction when the reality of the sit-and-wait situation set in too heavily.

Tommy sent this email from San Francisco:

Hey everyone,

I was about to get on a plane home from NYC this morning when Mom told me about Ryan. I'm emailing you from the plane now. I'm sorry that I did not get a chance to talk to Al about it.

When Mom told me the news I was stunned and really unable to process it. I think my initial reaction is that we should all remain positive, upbeat and direct our energy and thoughts to hoping and praying for the best. I remember feeling much the same emotions 25 years ago when mom got sick. We struggled through it and here we are.

It goes without saying that we need to be super strong for him and Heather when he gets back. At least until he gets a final diagnosis and all of the tests back. We obviously need to do everything we can to be strong for Heather as she goes into having their second child.

Ryan is an incredibly strong individual. Similar to Lance Armstrong, his body is in the best physical shape. And similar to Lance Armstrong, Ryan has a mental toughness that comes from a lifetime of being a fighter. Whether it was trips to the emergency room as a kid, tackling guys twice his size on the football field, climbing high altitude mountains in the dead of winter, helping the White family cope after 9/11, or surviving Special Forces training, Ryan has struggled and prevailed in every facet of his life. In short, he is a total badass and if anyone can beat this thing he can.

Our family is totally awesome and we'll get through this as a team. I love you all and look forward to sharing thoughts or feelings as we begin this process.

Love,
Tommy

Chapter Three
The Downward Spiral

On May 31st, 2009, our wedding anniversary, Ryan arrived at Walter Reed in Washington, D.C. He told me that the MRI was done, he was eating a ton and feeling way too good to be sick in any way, shape, or form! I was beyond ready to go. I wanted to be there before he arrived. But since I was due to have the baby in less than four weeks, everyone suddenly seemed to have an opinion about why I should stay put and "take care of myself and the babies."

Al, Ryan's father, and his eldest brother, Alfie, arrived at Walter Reed to greet our hero. They instructed me to stay in Clarksville with Mary Jo. I became irritated because Ryan had taught me to be an actor in the play of life, not a prop. He welcomed my insight and I wanted to be there to provide it. I was the one who planned to live with this man for the rest of my life and I felt as though I was responsible for helping ensure that he had a long life ahead of him. Alfie and I got in a heated battle of words. Suddenly, I was no longer the responsible adult that prevailed through all of the deployments. The woman who was raising a toddler, pregnant while her husband was deployed, making all financial and health decisions, taking Elizabeth for ear surgery alone, renovating a home alone, hundreds of miles from family, the strong and independent Army wife, was now to sit at home knowing that Ryan was finally back in the free world and I could not be with him? All the credit that had been given for what I had accomplished up to this point was disregarded, and I was directed around like a lost child that was unable to make a decision for herself. Control of my life was completely taken by well meaning family members and healthcare providers. I had done nothing to prove myself incompetent. I felt that everyone in the family had teamed against me by trying to protect me. My heart was breaking.

I would like to say I have no regrets in life, but I have two. First, I regret that we did not take pictures on our wedding day. Second, I regret not being there to greet my husband with babies in tow upon his most sought after return. I learned a million things about myself and life in general through this tribulation. I became stronger, converting my sense of helpless sorrow into action. I had to get on a plane. I just wondered how, without the family's support I was going to care for Elizabeth as well as be at the hospital with Ryan. Financially, I couldn't afford to do it. So at first, I stayed, defeated. The Special Forces motto is De Oppresso Liber, to Free the Oppressed. It is the creed by which Ryan lived. How is it that I was in fact oppressed by his family and our situation? The downward spiral began to accelerate. As the situation was extremely dire, emotions flared.

The day that Ryan was admitted to Walter Reed, he was able to eat and walk around freely. He walked through the doors of that hospital in one piece. His father sent pictures of him that gave me hope that things were possibly not all that bad. He was finally eating a gourmet meal. He had his favorite: salmon with rice and broccoli from a local Bistro that Al had tracked down for him.

Then, for some reason, instead of just performing an MRI and getting Ryan to a cancer hospital as planned, they decided to insert a drain into him to lower the bilirubin levels. If I was there, I know I would have fought the decision, but I would have been just another cook in the kitchen. I would not give consent to a military hospital to treat a rare cancer that even certain cancer centers send to specialists! There are ALWAYS risks in any medical procedure, and Ryan was in such a fragile and rare state with Cholangiocarcinoma that I don't see why anyone but a specialist should perform any procedures without a clear strategy. If his leg was blown off, fine, proceed. But, why not send him to one of the hospitals specializing in Cholangiocarcinoma? Were they simply following the chain of command? Why else would they take such a risk? I wondered how this could be happening to Ryan after all he had been through these last few months in Iraq.

But there I was, in Tennessee, unable to speak a word. And as it happened, something went terribly wrong and he began to bleed internally. I felt responsibility because of negligence. I should have been there. He was infused with blood and platelets but despite the transfusions, he eventually lost near his entire volume of blood. Four units turned to nine units. He became weak. And it then became clear that he was not the same Ryan that left for Iraq or even the same one who returned from Iraq. He was now released from the war overseas to the bloody war here at home—in his body. Fear tore through all of us as the unknown began to manifest signs that our indefatigable champion was suffering.

On June 2nd, Mary Jo and I were suddenly told that we were to come to Walter Reed. I knew there was something wrong. I had cried and cried over the fact that I wasn't "allowed" to go see my husband who was given 30 days to live. Now, suddenly they wanted us there immediately. I had to get there and never leave his side again. The next morning, Ryan's generous Uncle Bo arranged for a private plane to pick us up at the local airport. It was likely the only way I could make the trip so far along in my pregnancy. We packed our bags, along with 18-month-old Elizabeth for a three-day stay, to see Ryan for ourselves. That three-day stay turned into a 37-day stay, a race to NYC's best cancer hospital, and a childbirth. It goes without saying that I was under-packed and unprepared.

When we arrived at the hospital, Ryan was changed to NPO (nothing by mouth) status and began to basically starve. The procedures he had to undergo required that he not eat for 24 hours and one procedure ran into the next. Days were going by and he became thin, more yellow and was wasting away. He could not stand up to greet me when we arrived. He was too weak. He tried but he looked like a baby bird trying to stand and open its wings for the first time as he attempted to hug me, and then he slowly descended back into the bed with a thud. I sat at his bedside. Elizabeth recognized him instantly despite the five months apart but didn't understand why her fun daddy wasn't fun anymore. He tried to hug her at their reunion and it caused him a tremendous amount of pain. I could see that it was killing him. He just stared at her constantly.

I kept a smile on my face while I was in the room with him. We tried to joke about the fact that we had envisioned a number of different scenarios for our reunion...I would pick him up at the Nashville airport with Elizabeth. We would take our trip to Vanderbilt to induce the baby at the end of the month. But now we sat in a cold room at Walter Reed along with his parents, unable to hug or do anything but hold hands and have our conversations interrupted by nurses who did not knock, and who were not friendly. Perhaps they were jaded by the callous crawl of death.

Ryan would ring for a nurse and the alarm would be silenced. Or someone would walk by and say, "Please don't ring that, I have other patients to tend to, I will be around as soon as I can." I felt like that awful family member I had seen so many times coming to the desk, telling them that they simply cannot just shut off the bell. He needs them. He would never ask for anything if he didn't really need help. He was unable to move from his right side in bed. He wanted to use the urinal, which was nowhere to be found. He couldn't use the sink because there were bloody bandages that the nurse left in it, and there was no red bag I could find to dispose of them. I was chastised for helping him to the bathroom when no one else would. They actually told me I needed to focus on the fact I was having a baby and leave him to rest. He asked me not to go. He told me that he felt like something was seriously wrong now and the hope he had before was fading.

The doctors reassured him that they were doing all that they could, but the time he spent alone without contact with a nurse made him wonder if anyone would notice if he began to die. It was my first true experience with having a loved one in a hospital, and after working with critically ill patients for eight years myself, I began to wonder if they were not giving us the entire story.

Through this entire ordeal, I saw some of the best nurses and doctors, and I saw some of the worst. It made me realize that what people always told me was true: Healthcare requires a special person. Sadly though, not all people in the field are special in the right ways. It made me hurt to know that my husband was just a job to many people that summer. I pray that I never ever made any of my patients or their families feel this way. As a great friend once told me, "Nothing is more disarming than being next to a young living soul knowing that their life could possibly be saved by diligent and focused care". You cannot allow yourself to get jaded by the history of your work when you are caring for living people.

I was told that after the first drain failed, they tried a second attempt with a smaller catheter, and it seemed to be successful on one side of the liver. However, this 'working' drainage catheter moved out of its appropriate site and was not able to be corrected due to the bleed caused by the first drain, which now compressed his organs and caused a massive subcapsular hematoma. I prayed it wouldn't ruin his chances as a surgical candidate.

I would like to one day understand why Ryan was sent for the operation at Walter Reed. I don't want to believe this ultimately killed him. I couldn't live with myself for not stopping it. But I don't have the answers.

This will likely haunt me for the rest of my life. Maybe he would not have lived for more than a few months or years with this cancer—how can anyone know? Those weeks or months would have meant everything to us! But instead, these procedures he underwent not only led to massive blood loss, but caused major issues with his lungs, a huge hematoma over the cancerous organs, significant weight loss from all the back-to-back procedures being NPO…there was nothing left for the doctors to work with by the time he got to NYC! The complicated situation was now much more complicated. And to think, he was walking around laughing when he came into this facility! He had to be flown out on a gurney by helicopter. Someday, I just hope to understand why this happened.

Socialized practices of military healthcare are fine for healthy young people who need a check up or immunizations; in most cases this is sufficient. But what about when there is a life-threatening problem that needs to be diagnosed? The system doesn't work. Ryan and I joked about this when we found out that he would not be sent directly to New York. We joked that he would likely be given 30 immunizations and a bag of naproxen (or as he called it, "Ranger Candy") and sent home. We didn't joke after the emergency surgery. We just said, "Let's get out of here. ASAP."

I had spent one night in D.C. when I asked my mom to fly in and take Elizabeth. I quickly realized that there was no way I was going to be able to focus on Ryan and take care of a toddler, as she was not allowed in the hospital. But there was also not a chance I could make it through this ordeal without seeing her face at the end of each day. At that point, I had never been away from Elizabeth since the day she was born. My mom packed her bags and never hesitated to board her first flight ever. Michael, Tommy, and Josh were en route as well.

We were at our hotel the next morning when we received the urgent phone call. My heart sank as it did the night Ryan called from Iraq with the news. The surgeon said that he needed to see the family immediately. The situation suddenly became a matter of life and death. The 30 days to live were taken prematurely.

The doctors sat us down that morning and told us about a plan for emergency embolization. They said they needed my signature and that Ryan would be wheeled into surgery at that moment. I looked at the doctor and point blank asked him, "Are you asking my consent now?" Basically, as the wife, I had to say "go" or "no." Prior to my arrival it was up to Ryan and Al. Neither of which, God bless them, had been exposed to these types of medical events. If you aren't in the field, you tend to have a "the doctor is always right" attitude and will sign your life away (literally) without ever knowing what exactly your body is about to endure.

I wasn't there on those first days to say "No, don't touch him," a rerun I will have in the front of my mind every day of my life. Sometimes I find the guilt hard to live with as I wonder what could have been different. I would have gotten on my knees and begged those doctors to send him to NYC. Now, I was forced to say "go," or he would bleed to death and die before his chance in New York. He was not stable enough to fly.

Ryan departed into the surgical ward, and we headed for the cafeteria. We feasted on what little hospital food our stomachs could handle. Then the Means left to attend a mass in the hospital chapel while my mother and I entertained Elizabeth outside.

During the mass, there was a knock on the door. The doctor entered and said "I'm sorry," and before he could continue Mary Jo screamed, "Sorry about what? Oh, God, what happened?"

He continued, "I'm sorry to interrupt your mass! The surgery is done and we have embolized the bleed." We reunited, exchanged hugs and tears of joy, then rushed to visit Ryan who was still sedated. We did not know at that point if he would still be a candidate for surgery in NYC, only that there was a slightly better chance that he would live to see the end of the day.

The Means family has an amazing way of finding the positive in any situation and making every event seem like a sporting event or a cocktail party. This uplifting email was composed for friends and family:

Hello Everyone,

Thank you all for your thoughts and prayers.

On this date, 65 years ago, our troops landed on the beaches of Normandy. It's been one of the most poignant days to celebrate our troop's commitment to our country. Specifically, we have experienced up-close an incredible team of doctors and support staff at Walter Reed Army Medical Center (WRAMC) who have not only given Ryan world class medical care, but have also been amazing care advocates for our family.

We can only thank the Special Forces for creating such a strong bodied and strong willed human being. In fact, the doctors yesterday referred to him as a "genetic freak" which made us all feel very confident!

During the week, a few complications have developed during the course of his treatment to prepare him for surgery. He is now stabilized, and hopefully he will be moved out of ICU today. If he remains stable until Sunday, he will be medevac'd via the Air Force to NYC's Memorial Sloan-Kettering Cancer Center (MS-KCC).

As Ryan struggled with complications this Wednesday, Bo Means was gracious enough to fly Ryan's wife, Heather, 18-month-old daughter Elizabeth and Mary Jo on a charter to D.C. We are very grateful, as their arrival greatly lifted Ryan's morale.

Tommy arrived from San Francisco and Michael and Josh Cobb, one of Ryan's best friends, also arrived from Atlanta.

Having the family together has been key because on Friday, Ryan's condition became critical. We met with his team of liver specialists, who are in constant contact with Ryan's ultimate surgeon Dr.Fong at MS–KCC. The decision was made to send Ryan into surgery for an emergency embolization.

During this meeting with his surgeons, the family huddled around on the floor of the waiting room as if we were all on a football team. The surgeons, being the quarter backs, diagrammed the play for us sketching the procedure on graph paper. It felt as if it was fourth down, in the fourth quarter and we were going for a "Hail Mary" to win the game. Tommy gave the surgeon a high-five and told him to get his "game face" on.

Michael and Tommy then went into Ryan's room to pump him up before the procedure. They got Alfie on speaker–phone and they chanted things like, "Beat it down, Ryan!" and "Strength and Honor!" and "You're the man!"

During his procedure, the family attended a Mass held in Ryan's honor at Walter Reed's chapel. Just after we received communion, his surgeons pulled us out of the Mass to inform us that his surgery went extremely well. BOOM! Touchdown! At that moment, we were all reminded that miracles do happen!

Ryan has since stabilized although we are taking things day by day. We are hopeful that he will remain stable so that he may be transferred to MS–KCC for further treatment.

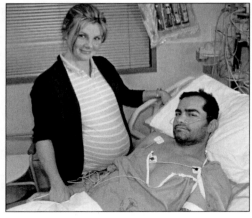

AT WALTER REED AFTER THE "HAIL MARY"

We want to thank all of you for your prayers and support for Ryan's family. Love the Means family.

Al Means

—∞o⚶oo∞—

After the procedure, Ryan stayed in the MICU (Medical Intensive Care Unit) rather than returning to a general nursing floor. The difference in care was like day and night. The nurses were specialized, knowledgeable, and compassionate. Many were contracted to the facility for a short period, then would travel to another, but the communication between shifts was flawless. We had many visitors from fellow Special Ops soldiers, Army soldiers we had never met, friends who were able to take a train into town. Ryan's friend took a flight from Florida to see him. She was the first in a rather long series of ex-girlfriends of Ryan Means that I would come to know in this journey. I told him I would wait until he was well to hear an explanation of why he never mentioned that he dated at least a dozen different women that he referred to as "good friends," little details that I'm sure he never imagined would arise, especially not in this sort of situation. Had the final outcome been different, I think we would have had to have a discussion about it and he would have been quite busy sorting out his explanations.

A colonel from the Pentagon stopped by stating he had to see this "genetic freak" that everyone had been buzzing about...the man who would not die. He reminded us that Green Berets require significantly higher doses of narcotics than normal patients, a fact each doctor along the way would find as Ryan woke up on every operating table.

I spent the next few days at Ryan's bedside. His parents, family, and Josh remained at his side as well. Each day seemed like an eternity. I would leave to let him rest and take the shuttle bus to the other side of town and meet my mom and Elizabeth in the park for a play date or for dinner. We did our best to make sure Elizabeth thought she was on a vacation and that nothing was wrong. At that age, it was easy to pull off...for her, at least; not so much for us.

Whenever I returned to my hotel or left for a meal, I was on edge. I felt like my hotel was too far from the hospital, but that is where the Army directed me to stay. Everyone at the hotel front desk knew my situation, and they had more compassion than most of the nursing staff at the hospital. They made sure that I could get a cab quickly and held the shuttle for me when I was running slow and pregnant.

In addition to feeling on edge, I started having anxiety about my phone. As strange as it sounds, I remember the ring tone on my phone that caused my skin to crawl and made me instantly nauseated and light-headed. I was terrified it would be another "come quickly" call from the hospital. It became a sort of Pavlovian response that continued to happen almost a year later. The ring tone haunted me. I couldn't bear another hospital call saying we may lose him before I made it there to say goodbye.

—∞○❂○∞—

Chapter Four
Kickin' it in NYC with Three Hotties

Ryan had come full circle, back to the city he loved, the city he left to avenge his best friend's death. I didn't know if I should take this as a sign of closure or a sign of hope, so I decided to accept it as neither for the time being.

Once we were informed that Ryan was medically stable, waiting for the helicopter that would get him to NYC became unbearable. Ryan feared something else would go wrong before he would make it there. He wanted to get the cancer out of his body. He said, "No matter what happens to me, the only thing I will ever regret is not being there for you, E and #2 and the pain that you will have to go through. I'm trying to beat this, but it seems I've some things working against me. Why didn't they take me to New York? Do you think I'm going to die?" I can remember the first time he said those words like it was yesterday.

For once, I didn't speak my mind. And in my usual calm manner that I reserved for my patients, I replied, "Do you think you are going to die?"

"No," he said.

"Good. Don't," I said with a smile. And we left it at that.

Mary Jo spoke with a nurse and asked her how she felt Ryan was progressing. She replied, "He looks tough." Mary Jo asked for clarification. "You need to get him out of here." Mary Jo relayed the message to Al. He became our hero, arranging to pay for the medevac transportation to NYC in a last-effort to hurry to transfer. Then, on June 8th, he was ready, and finally, so was the chopper.

Myself, my mother, and Mary Jo packed up Elizabeth and flew to NYC with our Special Forces liaison, Phil. Al met us there. We had made arrangements to stay at the Helmsley Medical Towers on the Upper East

Side, just a couple of blocks down from Memorial Sloan-Kettering Cancer Center and adjacent to New York Presbyterian Hospital/Weill Cornell Medical Center. We were no longer in Clarksville, Tenn., or Washington, D.C. Our new home address was 1320 York Ave, Room 914, New York, N.Y.

I was at the hospital with Mary Jo when Ryan was scheduled to be flown in. He was a few hours late as the team was not familiar with this particular medical center and proceeded to wheel him around the streets of New York on a gurney to find the correct entrance to admit him. He was incredibly irritated with this as he was in pain and every crack and crevice in Manhattan felt like a speed bump as he lay helplessly strapped to the bed on wheels. He wasn't happy when he finally arrived, but we were elated. All I could think about prior to his arrival was waiting in NYC for Ryan as he took a turn for the worse, and here we would sit as he was suffering alone. So his arrival in NYC was a very happy day, nonetheless.

They immediately went to work on him, replacing the drain that had been a huge source of discomfort. The new drain began working immediately and Ryan said he just felt "better" about the whole situation. There was a

FINALLY AT SLOAN-KETTERING, NYC

refreshed sense of confidence in his new caregivers. They did an exploratory procedure, which they said was not simple, and may not work, but they had to buy time. They wanted him much stronger for the surgery. Once again, I thought of how different things would be if he had been flown straight there, feeling that his caretakers were laser focused on his diagnosis and ready to battle cancer versus rewinding other procedures.

We met with Dr. Fong the next day. He drew out a diagram of the proposed surgical treatment. He said that the subcapsular hematoma, as well as the right hepatic arterial embolization would complicate the surgery, but he planned to proceed, as Ryan wanted to get rid of this cancer. We had no choice but to press on. Dr. Fong informed us that Ryan would need about three weeks to gain weight and strength before he could perform the operation.

Ryan needed to eat as much as possible and then eat even more. His body was in for plenty of torture, and he had lost too much weight and strength. We were going to stay in NYC for this period of time, as it seemed things could possibly go downhill at any point now. Ryan stayed in the hospital and I began the homestead process again.

During this time, my mother and Mary Jo teamed up to take care of Elizabeth. I had plenty of time to spend with Ryan in the hospital while the two grandmothers made sure that Elizabeth was experiencing a fun life as a "city kid." One day, they decided to take our Special Forces liaison, Phil, and head to the Children's Museum. To think a month ago, he was tracking terrorists, and now he was chasing a toddler and two grandmas around New York City. These are the Green Berets, the Gentlemen Defenders. Their fighting skills are matched by a compassion for life and their brotherhood.

We decided that I would have the baby at NY Presbyterian since it was next door to the Helmsley. My mother took me for a check-up so that I could meet the staff. We spent hours there, just as we did at Walter Reed, to get someone to look at me and for what? People have babies all of the time, naturally. Why all this commotion? Well, as it turned out at this particular appointment, they suspected the baby's heartbeat was irregular. That was news to me. Perhaps the stress had changed conditions in my womb. Nature would press her will, and baby #2 was knocking on the door. They put monitors on my belly. Actually, we got an intern who didn't really know how, so it ended up being a group effort between him, my mom, and myself. After a few hours, and what was probably the worst and most painful pelvic exam ever, he decided we were clear to head out and return when the baby would be delivered. I headed back to tell Ryan about my adventure. He could only laugh and say that, for once, he had some idea of what I just went through. We found ourselves in one of the most profound of human oxymorons, of life and death.

That night I decided there was no way I could function without sleep any longer. I knew the baby would be here in the next few weeks, so I decided to take an Ambien. I knocked out. In the middle of the night, I awoke my mother, telling her I thought I had to go to the bathroom, but I couldn't, and I kept getting up and down. Luckily, her pharmaceutical background and mother's intuition led her to figure I was in labor and in an Ambien induced dream. She called Phil, who was there to help us with pretty much anything we needed assistance with during our stay. He managed to pull a wheelchair out of thin air, plop me into it, and along with my mother and Elizabeth, set off racing down the streets of Manhattan at 3:30 a.m.

The great thing about New York is that it didn't seem strange to anyone. During his sprint, Phil managed to maintain composure and time my contractions. He told the admissions clerk that they were about five minutes apart. I still insisted that I was not in labor. I vaguely remember trying to explain to the nurses how we were all related, or not related, as I think she thought Phil was with me and wanted my mother to stay out in the waiting room while he went with me to have the baby. I was still quite confused, a side effect of awaking soon after taking Ambien.

Once introductions were established, in typical Means family story fashion, my anesthesiologist walks in and says, "Heather Means? Are you related to Gabrey Means?"

"If I say yes, will you give me the epidural—NOW??" I asked.

"Yes, you are Ryan's wife! I went to school with Gabrey." He went on to tell me details that I will never recall. The thing is, Gabrey lives in San Francisco. I lived in Tennessee. I was having a baby in New York. This was just too strange for a girl in labor on Ambien and on pain medication to comprehend.

As we cleared the confusion and attempted to deliver a baby, Phil frantically ran down the block to Sloan-Kettering and managed to get through their doors. Security is tight there, but he somehow got to Ryan's floor to alert him. Phil, being a medic, removed Ryan's IVs himself, found a wheelchair and rushed back to my bedside with the father-to-be. Ryan's legs were swollen to four times their normal size because of fluids administered to him and he surely wouldn't have been able to make the arduous walk. Not even 20 minutes later, around 5:30 a.m. (her daddy's usual wake-up time), we welcomed baby Means #2 at 6 lbs 14 oz. She had no name, as we were obviously focused on other things over the last few weeks. Mary Jo and Al arrived minutes later and we took some photos as if nothing in the world was wrong. Ryan was there to see his second baby girl come into the free world that he had helped to protect. He was filled with pride.

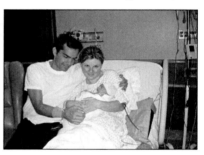

BABY GIRL MEANS #2 MADE IT TO NYC IN TIME TO MEET HER DADDY

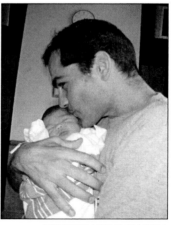

INSTANTLY IN LOVE AGAIN

I remember having this strange, what in the hell just happened feeling for the next 24 hours. I didn't get to sleep, as it was morning once the baby was there and they took me to my room. I was not ready to be a new mom again. I sat in my room, unable to cry, just shaking my head. What was I going to do with a newborn right now? Would I have to send Elizabeth to stay with someone else? How could I give Ryan the love and care I promised him and take care of a new baby? Why did she come early? She was beautiful and I loved her, but I wasn't ready for her. I felt like the worst, most ungrateful mother ever. I was too consumed with worry over Ryan's new battle.

The nurses on my floor were amazing. They did everything they could to help make our situation easier. Ryan made it over two or three times during my stay to see and hold the baby. We started a list of names on the marker board and people would give their opinions as they visited. We thought of naming her Ryan, but it seemed like that would be admitting defeat at this point. So we used it as a middle name and Ryan decided on the first name. He told the nurses and then told me, "This is Sophie Ryan Means."

"Sophie?" I asked. That wasn't even on the board! Sophie? Not even Sophia?"

"She isn't Italian or one of the Golden Girls. She's a Sophie," he said matter of factly. And so it was: Sophie Ryan Means. And she looked just like Ryan—black hair, dark brown eyes and dark skin; quite different from the blonde hair, blue-eyed baby we had been raising! She was indeed a little, baby-girl version of Ryan.

It seemed pathetic and became a bit depressing that Ryan and I were stuck in hospitals across from each other. Who would have ever thought? This wasn't one of the many ways we pictured our reunion after Iraq or the baby's birth. I went to all of the required parent classes and meetings alone in order to be discharged. I watched as the new daddies helped the new mommies, and people smiled telling their birth stories. There was no way I would share mine. I couldn't imagine changing the mood of the room like that, so I kept to myself. I was the only one there without a husband, which I thought strange these days. But at that point it wasn't the worst of my worries. I just hoped that wasn't the way the rest of my parenting years would go. What could be worse than what we are going through?

Almost on cue, a doctor entered my room and told me that Sophie had some abnormal blood work and they would have to do more tests. So we began that routine. Anything else?, I thought. Bam! Herniated disc in my neck. Somehow during labor, I managed to actually herniate a disc! As a physical therapist, I knew the signs and I hoped I was wrong. The MRI confirmed it. I couldn't move my head at all. It caused horrible pains shooting down my neck and my right arm. I had to wear a neck brace. It helped somewhat but I still couldn't lie down without wanting to scream in pain. Lisa, who is an occupational therapist, had taken Elizabeth for the day and brought me dinner. She had to help me get in and out of bed. I couldn't bear sitting up and I couldn't take lying down. It got to where no position was comfortable. I couldn't hold Sophie. I had to stack pillows up to bring her to me without lifting her to feed her. And that's when I finally lost it. What the hell kind of life is this?! Is the cancer patient husband not bad enough? The newborn with possible issues? Now a herniated disc? I cried and it hurt my neck even more. I felt like I was trapped in hell. What little faith I had was exiting my body, and I could feel it departing.

The next day, I took my Percocet and signed myself out of the hospital. I called my mother and asked her to come and help me. She never questioned my decisions, and she came immediately. I planned to get the baby the tests she needed as an outpatient in all my free time, and then get back to see Ryan. I strapped on my neck brace, put Sophie in a stroller, and slowly walked back to the hotel. I couldn't walk at a normal pace without feeling like each step was jarring my neck to where my head would roll right off into the street. It was at this point I became very pissed off. No prayers had been answered, as far as I was concerned. Where was my God? Why do horrible people get to live long happy lives without this pain my family is going through? All we had done is pray, pray, pray and love each other, and this is what we have been reduced to now? I was determined more than ever to get past all of this. I felt like someone was asking for a fight now, and my competitive nature took over. Nobody was going to knock me down again. I remember that day, on York Avenue in Manhattan, when I went from putting my faith in God to putting my faith in Ryan and myself. Ryan had taught me that together we could handle anything.

Once I settled Sophie into her new home, I did a Google search for neck pain treatment in the Manhattan area—specifically, alternative medicine. As a physical therapist, I knew how to treat a herniated disc conservatively, and I also knew how long it could take to recover. More important, I was sick of doctors and hospitals.

I came across Reiki therapy by a woman named Julie. She had a phenomenal amount of feedback from pleased clients—or at least she had a lot of friends pretending to be clients. Either way, I was willing to try. I took a cab completely to the other side of the island and arrived at a very sketchy looking building. I attempted to use the elevator, but when I stepped inside, the floor felt like it might give way and I jumped back out. I took three to four flights of stairs and arrived in a hall only lit by windows. There was a door with the correct numbers next to it, but no sign. I hesitated to open it for fear it was a "Happy Ending" style massage parlor.

After a few minutes of trying to call the number with no response, I reasoned with myself like this: "Heather, after all that you have been through, this cannot end with you getting killed in an abandoned building in New York. And you only have an hour before Sophie needs your breast back. Get your ass in there." I knocked, no answer. So I opened the door and, to my surprise, there was a tiny waiting room. Phew! I signed my name on the tablet, which made it the only name on the list, and I took a seat. I assured myself that it must be her usual day off, and she came in just for me. It smelled pretty spa-like, so I tried to relax.

Julie came out, looked at her list and said something about "Hedder," which I assumed was me, and motioned for me to follow her. We went into a small room with nothing but an ancient massage style table and a laboratory-style countertop lined with a handful of glass jars. After breaking the language barrier with some creative sign language, she seemed pretty clear on my diagnosis and left me a towel to don after removing my tank top. She returned a few minutes later and positioned me upright on a wooden chair facing the massage table.

She motioned for me to turn my head as she made a mental note of my range of motion. "Not good. This hurts?" she asked.

"YES!" I shouted. She placed my arms on my lap and positioned my forehead on the massage table. She immediately started scraping my neck with what felt like a smooth but blunt wooden spatula. She did this for about five minutes straight (it felt like 20) and requested I sit up. What in the hell? I thought. Are we done? This was $75 per 15 minutes, so we had better not be. I noticed she had set a timer for 15 minutes and I still had 10 left. Then she motioned me to turn. I was so guarded because it was horribly painful for me to turn my neck at all. In just a few days, I subconsciously began to compensate by turning my whole body.

Julie held my shoulders still. "Turn head, Hedder," she commanded. So I did. And I gained at least 15 degrees of motion on the side she had been working on. "Good?" she asked.

"Good!" I said with surprise. She shoved my head back down and continued for the next 10 minutes. It was rather painful and I felt like I may be on candid camera here. My seven years of college and doctorate in PT were no match for Voodoo Julie and her wooden spatula.

I let her beat the crap out of my neck, and every few minutes she stopped to let me turn my head and gasp in awe at the improvement. When the timer went off we did one last range of motion check. I was still guarded but amazed when I had almost my full range back. She asked if that was all I had problems with and I told her about the subsequent headaches I had been getting. She held up the timer as if to say, "$75 more, Hedder?"

And I said "Yes."

She went to work on my scalp in the same manner. Oil was everywhere in my hair and down my back. I looked like I had been through a greasy tornado by the time I left that hole of an office. But my head felt weightless and my neck had full range of motion. I was blown away. I was healed. I wanted to call of all my colleagues and tell them that we are stupid for thinking we know it all. I believe! I believe! Chinese alternative medicine in the right hands is phenomenal. She told me to bring my sick husband, as she knows how to fight off cancer as well. Had I been able to get him out of the hospital, I just might have let her try. My neck continued to improve with only a few minor setbacks, and I did not need to revisit Julie. Nor could I have afforded to, anyhow.

Now that I was mobile, I began the frantic search for a doctor who would take our active duty military insurance. Of course, she was on the other side of Manhattan. When we finally got an appointment I realized I had no clue about how to take a baby in a cab. Luckily I had a plan. During his few days out of the hospital, I dragged Ryan on an adventure to purchase a stroller I found on Craigslist. He didn't want me to go alone, but the cab ride there nearly killed him. Like most cab drivers in NYC, it was hit the gas, slam on brakes, hit the gas, slam on breaks, and Ryan's drainage tubes were really giving him pain, so the jarring motions were making him miserable.

We arrived at Wall Street, and the streets were still blocked off with security guards to where you could only walk down them, so we had a bit of walking to do after the awful ride. Ryan reminded me that just because it was a nice building didn't mean the people wouldn't want to harm us or kill us. I reminded him that he was hunched over and frail, not to mention yellow, and that alone would likely change their minds. We went upstairs to find a very lovely couple and their daughter who was napping. No murderers here. We proceeded to tell stories and make new friends. They were the type of people we would have surely asked to join us for dinner had we not been busy fighting cancer. We got the stroller and headed back for rest.

The top of the stroller was removable and served as a bassinet. Perfect. We had a bed, car seat, and stroller in one. I planned to take the bassinet in the cab and just hold it next to me. I really don't know if that was OK or not. But I do know that when my stepmom and I ventured out across Manhattan in a monsoon that day, white-knuckled holding onto the baby bassinet between us on the back seat of that careening cab, neither of us thought we should try it again.

Fortunately, Ryan had a large support group of friends still in Manhattan. They brought us everything from car seats and strollers to DVD players. His Boulder fraternity brothers and their wives made sure that we had friendship, food, shoulders to cry on, tour guides, baby gear... anything we needed. A few lived in Manhattan, others were in town for business or just flew in to see him in the hospital.

One evening, we used the lobby at Sloan-Kettering to throw an impromptu pizza party and it lifted Ryan's spirits tremendously. His only complaint was that, after they left, he had to double-up on the pain medication because his gut was literally killing him with pain from laughing so hard. With all of the gifts from our family and friends, I think we had more toys and baby clothes in NYC than we would have had at home! My friends in Clarksville dug through my 110-degree attic a number of times to find my cold weather clothes, as it was still quite chilly in the north. Besides, I had only packed for a three-day stay, and now it looked as though, with recovery, it would be at least three months.

THE ONE EXISTING PHOTO OF THE FOUR OF US TOGETHER

We were making it work. So much so, that we actually talked about one day moving back to NYC if his job permitted. I would have done it in a heartbeat. The way I felt in New York doesn't compare to anywhere else I have ever been. Despite all we went through there, I can't help but still be head-over-heels in love with that city.

DATE: June 18, 2009
SUBJECT: Update from Ryan Means

I know that bits and pieces of the drama have been put out by various people but I want to give you a full and complete (OK, it's pretty abbreviated) rundown. I'm typing on an archaic keyboard that insists on double typing every letter so this may read as if a robot high on Percocet wrote it. Due to drugs and crazy travel circumstances, some dates may not be exact.

May 28th: I was airlifted to Baghdad for some additional testing including a CT scan of my liver. This scan indicated an abnormal cell mass on my bile duct, which gave us the initial (and correct) diagnosis of Cholangiocarcinoma, a rare form of cancer that is usually fatal. The doctors told me that it was fatal and it was unknown how much time I had to live. Needless to say calling Heather that morning at 3 a.m., waking her up to say that I had liver cancer was not very much fun. The ONLY upside at this point was that the doctor was very clear in explaining that he was giving me the worst case scenario and it could change. Some upside.

For the next 2-3 days I flew from Iraq to Germany where I heard much of the same.

May 31st: I arrived at Walter Reed Medical Center. The doctors examined me and determined that a stent needed to be placed. We discovered the tumor had effectively killed the left half of my liver. There were several complications that developed from this procedure and without getting too detailed (most of which I was not privy to) things got real bad, real quick.

Shortly after, I had to go into what is being referred to as the 'Hail Mary'. Basically, the doctor said if they didn't attempt a very risky procedure to close a bleeding artery in or near my liver, I was done. My family put together an email about this since I was out of it (probably busy telling the grim reaper to fuck off and go see someone else). Doctors were obviously successful, I lived and we moved to the next step.

All of the aforementioned work was done in order to stabilize me enough so that I could travel to the Sloan-Kettering Cancer Center in NYC where the foremost expert on liver cancer and perhaps the only man in the world capable of removing this tumor, Dr. Yuman Fong aka 'The Miracle Worker' lives and works.

June 9th: I arrived in NYC and was admitted Sloan-Kettering. The current plan is for me to stay here in NYC until I am strong enough to go through the MAIN EVENT. The Main Event will involve removing a lot of things including 70–80% of my liver, gall bladder and a few other things, not to mention, rework the lower intestine a bit. Dr. Fong assures this is not an easy procedure on a good day and unfortunately I've got a few complicating factors going against me but also ton going for me (age, physical condition, beautiful wife, great kids, attitude, good looks, family, desire etc...). He's giving me a 40% chance of surviving which is a 100% better than the other prognosis I've received.

June 13th: 5:23 AM Heather had our second daughter across the street at Presbyterian Hospital. A humbling and beautiful event, which did nothing but strengthen my resolve to kick this thing. Baby and mother are both doing well.

We've got an apartment here along with tons of friends, family and support. As of now, we plan on keeping the family unit together as long as possible, which is great for all of us. This surgery is by no means a gimmee, recovery will be long and arduous, and we still have a number of hurdles but things are looking better by the day.

It's been a very long, strange trip in a very short time. I cannot stop shaking my head and laughing at the situation. That's all you can really do at this point. I love the challenges and can't wait to add cancer survivor to my list of achievements. Perhaps one of the most important things I've experienced thus far, is the importance of family and friends in this situation. The absolute low point of this ordeal came after getting the worst-case scenario in Iraq, sitting alone in a room for two days and being totally cut off from anything and everything familiar except my thoughts, which were becoming exceedingly difficult to control.

Another major source of inspiration came from the guys with me on the AIRVAC bird, who were much worse off in the short term. Of course on the surface I looked a little yellow but otherwise fine. These guys were far from it and some would likely never see family or friend again. It became almost easy at this point to deal with my situation and my overall perspective could not have been any better; so many soldiers' lives are ended in an instant while I had practically been given years extra already.

Once in Germany my luck got better and better as I teamed up with a Group guy, and started hanging out. From that point on, the number and variety of friends who have come out and supported me in so many ways has been insane. I don't see this as any sort of popularity thing or ego trip but rather a validation of the choices I've made in my life. Starting with my wife, who somehow raised a toddler while pregnant for six months alone and then dealt with this without so much as a whimper or a tear (at least that she's shown me). I've never witnessed such strength, beauty and grace. What I did to deserve her will forever be a mystery. My family has always and will continue to be my foundation and I hope to build my own with the same values and ethics. They've been incredible.

Finally, I've somehow managed to build this network of friends who are now coming out of the woodwork to provide an overwhelming amount of support, prayer and love. Some of whom drove or flew hours to see me for a few minutes in the hospital. You cannot imagine how much this helps. Thank you all very much. I'll be sure to pay you back in spades during the victory tour.

So, long story short I'm kicking it in NYC with three hotties in a sweet apt on the Upper East Side for the next several weeks. Talk about coming full circle! My perspective and resolve are totally set and we are in full motion. The weird thing is just being around my wife and TWO daughters makes me think that life simply can't get any better. I'm definitely not in denial and very well aware of what lies ahead, but I just have too much stuff going for me to stop right now. As I've said before, don't feel any sympathy or pity for this situation because in the grand scheme of things it really ain't that bad and we are going to get through it one way or another. Period.

Please don't feel obligated to respond, I have limited access to email so just say a prayer and go have some fun.

Feel free to forward to anyone that may not have been included on the distribution list.

Until the next update, keep on rockin' in the free world!
RPM

—∞o🜚o∞—

ELIZABETH IS HAPPY TO HAVE HER
FUN DADDY BACK FOR A DAY

The next day, we took Elizabeth to the park. Ryan tried his best to follow her around and push her on the swings. Seeing the two of them together outdoors made me happier that I had been in months, and I know it lifted Ryan's spirits tremendously. He said it was going to be like that all of the time in just a few months. That day gave us hope.

Later that evening, Ryan felt awful. I took his temperature and he had a fever. He walked back to the hospital to get a check-up and he didn't come home. From June 19th–24th he was hospitalized due to fever and infection of the subcapsular hematoma. They felt he had developed pancreatitis as well. He needed more antibiotics. They again drained the hematoma.

My stepmother was staying with us to help with the babies and planned to take Elizabeth back to Michigan; she was getting to be too much for Ryan and I to handle. It physically hurt him to pick her up or hug her. It was wearing him out. He had trouble holding Sophie, but her stroller served as a useful walking aide for him around the city. I had never been without Elizabeth since she was born, and I dreaded the additional loss of control. But, it would be for the best. We could not fit comfortably into the one bedroom apartment, especially not with these circumstances where Ryan needed his peace and quiet. We of course, did not anticipate Ryan's re-admission to the hospital when we set these plans.

DATE: June 20, 2009
SUBJECT: Update.

Hello and thanks to everyone for your support! Here's the latest and greatest from NYC.

After several delays last week, they released me from the hospital and I was able to spend some serious quality time with Heather and the kids in our apartment, which was great. It's truly amazing that Elizabeth picked up right where we left off prior to the deployment and immediately remembered exactly who and what I was; a great big book reading jungle gym. While the energy levels aren't anywhere near pre-C levels, I am making progress (although way too slow for me) to the point where one of the doctors threw out 'next week' as a possible due date for the main event. Oh the joy!

Our great apartment is now rapidly getting smaller, not because of cabin fever but the insane amount of gifts being sent by all of you for which we are all very thankful but must ask that in lieu of any more baby clothes or toys, simply keep us in your prayers. I'm already guessing that we'll have to get the Army to fly the loot and us back to Clarksville in some type of huge military transport.

I will certainly admit that in the past few days there have been moments reminiscent of days immediately following 9/11 where I find myself walking around NYC and pondering the heavy side of life. Not bad, but just the usual near death 'what's my purpose' and 'am I satisfied with what I've done so far' kind of stuff; A very good exercise to periodically run through to ensure no regrets. The funny thing about this is

I'm weighing-in at or around 150 lbs. (down from about 185) obviously looking very gaunt and still yellow with yellow eyes which isn't too bad because it scares the hell out of possible muggers. When I walk, I'm totally focused on my immediate goal which is usually about 100m away and I've got the proverbial '1000 yd. stare', giving me a very zombie-like appearance.

Needless to say, this 150lb sack o' bones gets plenty of room on the sidewalk.

The biggest downer at the moment is the weather (rainy and grey), which of course, is delaying the U.S. Open, forcing me to watch some truly awful TV (reading is a bit of a challenge due to the drugs). I've been exposed to some programs on MTV of all stations, called 'Pregnant and 16' which scares the bejeezus out of me and again fortifies my desire to live if only to protect the sanctity of my two daughters by any means necessary. This wonderful show is followed by the 'World's Strictest Parents' which thankfully brings me back from the edge of considering our civilization beyond any sort of redemption. No more MTV for this kid.

Unfortunately, I had a small temperature last night and had to be readmitted to Sloan-Kettering. Of course when the doctors told me I earned a 48-hour stay, I immediately began planning my escape back to the family a block away. When the liver doctor explained the situation, I agreed to the stay. Long story short, is that I'm at a high risk of infection and any temperature increases need to be closely monitored. They're also looking at installing another drain to further decrease the levels of bilirubin so that the Main Event can be done under optimal conditions. Still no date for the Main Event.

So I'm here wearing some very obnoxious maroon pajamas that say 'Plump and Juicy' with giant hot dogs all over them, a bit of a departure than the usual hospital attire. The PJs along with my maniacal walking around the ward (15 laps = a mile) brings a smile to some of my fellow patients who have nicknamed me both Plump N' Juicy and the Marathon Man. A good sign, I assume, is that I tend to get a bit competitive to the point of almost being aggressive and try to lap anyone who happens to get in front of me including other patients (they're the easiest because most are 70+ years old and very slow) doctors, nurses, and the toughest of the competition is a guy in food service named Darryl who doesn't cut me any slack.

That being said, the continued outpouring of support from all my family, friends, and strangers makes this thing seem more beatable than ever. Having Heather and the kids by my side is amazing and of course, simply being back in New York is a source of energy. All combined, it makes the cancer seem more of a nuisance than anything. This doesn't mean that I'm underestimating anything, just that my confidence is pretty damn high.

As always, feel free to forward to anyone, as my email list is incomplete. Also, please don't respond unless absolutely necessary. Answering 50+ emails a day can be a bit time consuming. Thank God I'm not some sort of silly celebrity.

Until then, keep on rockin' in the free world!
RPM

There was an odd sense of security having Ryan back in Sloan-Kettering. The responsibility was out of my hands. And Ryan was in good hands. After a visit with us in the lobby one day, he was surprised with a baby shower thrown by all of his nurses. He said that they made him hold each item of clothing up as if he was the expectant mother. They had a great time with him, and Sophie had the best wardrobe any newborn girl could hope for, compliments of Ryan's nurses. They were so good with him, especially the younger ones, with whom he loved to flirt. Even on his deathbed, he just had a way with the ladies.

On Father's Day, I was busy trying to entertain my family in NYC, one of their least favorite places. Ryan insisted that we visit Central Park and take some pictures and videos for him. He was quite mad that we didn't make it but as usual it began to rain. I promised him that it would be our first stop when he got out of the hospital again. We instead visited the Museum of Natural History. I sent him photos of Elizabeth and Sophie with the dinosaur bones. I remembered that I had a gift for him in Tennessee. I had taken his large print from Hatch Show Prints in Nashville and had it custom-mounted and framed for him. He would have loved it. It was sitting at the frame shop, forgotten in the chaos. I had nothing at all to give him that day. I got him a balloon from the hospital gift shop and told him we would have to celebrate once he got home. Another reminder of how our real life was on hold.

Ryan asked me to come back alone that evening and have a date in his room. I brought him some take-out and sat in the recliner next to his bed, and we watched TV for several hours. He was impossible to feed. I would go to a gourmet grocer and get him at least five different options, and he would nibble at maybe one. For our date, I grabbed broiled lemon chicken with broccoli, roasted potatoes, salmon with dill sauce and lobster bisque; he maybe ate two bites. He just had no appetite. We found that ice cream was likely the best way to fatten him up. He was able to stomach Gatorade and Haagen–Dazs mint chocolate chip ice cream. However, he got into this annoying habit of eating the ice cream and spitting out the chocolate chips. He said that they made him sick. It was like force-feeding a toddler. I felt like I was miserably failing at my job of fattening him up before the surgery. It was also costing a lot of money in wasted food, and we were running low on cash. Friends and family realized that buying us credit at a local grocer was better than sending gifts, and soon we did not have to worry about grocery costs anymore. This came as a great relief because we had quickly drained our checking account once we landed in NYC. I wondered how we would ever recover financially, but the health recovery was what we needed to remain focused on for the time being. Money was tertiary in priority; Ryan and the baby girls were most important.

Once I returned home at night, we would call or text each other and both put on the same TV shows and talk as if we were in the same room, until one of us fell asleep. Oddly, it seemed like we were newly in love and long distance dating again. The "I love yous" were constant. We were just waiting for the next time both of our schedules, or at least his medical procedures, permitted a face-to-face visit.

The next day, I took Elizabeth to the hospital to say goodbye to Ryan. He stared and stared at her longingly. He couldn't keep up with her. He was having more shortness of breath and difficulty moving around. He watched my dad chase her around the lobby for a few moments, gave her the best hug he could give, and then we went on our way. I knew it was breaking his heart. This could be the last time they would ever see each other. He said he would only allow positive thoughts in his head though, and that got him through the day. He texted me a bit later and asked if she was gone. I replied, "'Yes, and I didn't cry in front of her, but I lost it when I got back to the apartment and saw her uneaten lunch and her toys sitting out. I feel like she was kidnapped.'"

Without Elizabeth, I became more aware of what was happening. It amazed me. I sat in that quiet apartment with Sophie, thinking that just a month ago, I was in our cozy home with Elizabeth praying for Ryan to return from Iraq and take care of our giant lawn before the new baby arrived. Now, I was staring out into the New York City rain, watching cars and cabs whiz by, holding this new child I did not yet know. Where did she come from? Where was Elizabeth? How did we get here? These thoughts raced through my head as my brain struggled to make sense of it all. It was unfathomable that life goes on as usual all around us, even though our world was upside down. How is it that everyone around doesn't sense that something is horribly wrong? How many times was I unaware that others were suffering as I went on enjoying my life? What a mad, mad world we live in.

Then Ryan called me. "We are going to make it. Everything is going to be just fine," he said. He was always right when he said those words. I had no choice but to believe him.

That evening he had yet another procedure done to remove blood from the hematoma and said it helped his breathing. Sophie and I took a walk across the Upper East Side, and I visited Ryan's old roommates. They have a daughter who is Elizabeth's age, and seeing her comforted me as she reminded me a lot of Elizabeth. It was just what I needed. I told Ryan about our visit and that my one source of humor right now was that every time I hit a curb or significant crack in the sidewalk with the stroller, Sophie would flail her arms and legs and her eyes would pop wide open for a second—the startle reflex—and for some reason this cracked me up and kept me going.

That night, as I sat in the hotel and Ryan lay in the hospital, we turned on *Jon & Kate Plus 8* and began the usual back and forth commentary and banter. He told me he had seen the episode twice already this week, but would watch it again with me. I think we were drawn to this program after Elizabeth was born. We thought it was amazing to watch two parents juggle eight kids, when we were sometimes overwhelmed with just one. I had the nerve to complain to Ryan that Sophie was restful all day and from 11 p.m. on, she was just a nightmare. She really had her days and nights mixed up. He suggested I sell her on Craigslist or deal with it. I was beginning to see what being a single parent was like, and I pitied poor Kate who was on her way there with her plus eight children.

Ryan's bilirubin levels continued to improve the next day and he reported that the drain they inserted had removed almost a liter of blood. I started the process of catching up on our bills. I spent the majority of my free time on the phone with my friends in Clarksville trying to get loose ends tied up. Our bills were piling up, I had a fence installed that I forgot to pay for, a lawn service that I forgot to cancel or pay for, and I was doing a terrible job of returning calls to the bill collectors, as it was the least of my worries. My fellow Army wife friends were there for me though. They took care of the house, dog, mail, yard, anything that needed to be done. And I never had to worry that it wouldn't be done. Their husbands were there for us as well. It is nothing short of awesome the way other Army families rally behind you when you need them the most. I don't know anyone stronger, more independent and brave, or as reliable as the Army wives and husbands that I call friends.

The next morning, June 24th, the doctors told Ryan he might need to stay in the hospital until the surgery. We just wanted to be back together, one night alone in the past six months would have been nice. A few hours later he called and said he was on his way back. I don't know how he got them to change their minds, but they decided to release him until the big date, which was determined to be July 1st. We began to think of that day as if it would be the first day of the rest of our lives together, like a second wedding day.

That night we took another walking tour of New York. We had beautiful walks in the summer evenings during that last week before surgery. We visited the 9/11 memorial, where we sat down and Ryan recounted the events of that day. He remembered vividly the search for his dear friend Adam. He talked about going to Adam's apartment and sorting through his belongings after his death. He said he hoped I would never have to go through the emotions that he did when Adam died, but if I did, I should know that by moving on and living my life and raising our kids in a way he would be proud, he will continue to live.

One evening Ryan's friends Ned, Tucky, and Russell came over to our makeshift apartment. We were able to serve some wine and snacks and chat without nurses and noisy machines speaking over us. A few of his other friends popped in and out over the next few days. It gave us some sense of normalcy. We were looking forward to the surgery and already planning our three-month stay to recover in NYC with the kids.

Over the weekend, Ryan decided he wanted to check out the Pride Parade. He said he never missed it when he lived in New York. We ventured to the other side of the city. It was absolutely the most fun, friendly and colorful display of lesbian, gay, bi-sexual, transgender, cross-dressing folks that I have ever witnessed. I'm more than glad that we went. At one point, I left him on the sidewalk with two week-old Sophie and ran into a few shops to buy a few non-maternity outfits and sunglasses. It was heaven. Ryan was quite pleased with himself that he managed to put a perma-grin on my face for the day.

We went to the Chelsea Market and talked about how great it would be to get out of Clarksville and move back to an energetic, cultured city.

We visited one of Ryan's favorite shops, Jeffrey New York. He grabbed a few suits, Armani and Hugo Boss and proceeded to try them on. Why on earth would he bother to try on suits when he was at least 40 pounds under his usual weight? Why would he spend $1,200 on a suit when he is in the Army? I wondered. He told me which one he liked, and that I should make a note of it in case I wanted to buy him a nice gift. It never occurred to me that he might be planning for his funeral. It just wasn't a topic we let ourselves discuss.

TINY SOPHIE ON HER FIRST DAY IN CENTRAL PARK

Central Park was one of Ryan's favorite places in his favorite city. He loved the history of it, the bridges, the people watching. Sophie and I were fortunate to experience the Ryan Means quick tour of his favorite corners of the park and bridges. He told us many stories of his days relaxing on the green grass of the Sheep Meadow, about the Jazz on the Great Hill and Opera in the Park concerts, which he faithfully attended. We watched some impromptu live musicians and the incredibly talented amateur roller skating dancers. We breezed through the Central Park

Zoo. We rested on the benches lining Poet's Walk holding hands, enjoying Sophie. I wished that Sophie would have some memory of this day. Luckily, Ryan always took his camera everywhere. I've never enjoyed being in front of the lens, especially not while I was still in my maternity clothes, two weeks post-baby. I was swollen and fat. Ryan looked like a sick anorexic Oompah-Loompah, and Sophie was so tiny that we received bad looks for having her in public. Some would even ask, "Do you think a new baby should be out like this?" But usually after making eye contact with Ryan's yellow sclera that bulged in his eye sockets, they would back off. We had just three days before he was to be operated on. We felt something most people will never comprehend. We were well aware that these could be the last three days of his life. We asked several people to take pictures of us together. I certainly wish I hadn't been so difficult about it now, as they will surely be the most precious photos that Sophie will ever own. I hated that Elizabeth couldn't be with us as

she was still in Michigan, but we planned to bring her to New York the following summer, and every summer thereafter as a way of remembering what our little family went through that summer and appreciating how far we have come each year.

RYAN WITH SOPHIE IN CENTRAL PARK, NYC

Chapter Five
The Super Bowel

DATE: June 27, 2009
SUBJECT: The adventure continues.

I'm happy to report the past few days have been filled with progress and good news. Perhaps the most important is the doctors have provided a date for the main event, which will be Wednesday July 1st. During the 10-hour operation, doctors will be removing my gall bladder, bile duct, some nodes and approximately 75% of my liver along with re-working my small intestine to create a new bile duct between what will remain of my liver and the small intestine. I cannot explain the excitement of going into this operation other than it's similar to all of the great sporting events: the Super Bowl, the Final Four, the Masters, the World Series etc, rolled into one (perhaps we call it the Super Bowel instead?). It stands to be the most exciting 10-hour ordeal with the outcome far more important than any sporting event I've ever witnessed. If only we could put it on pay per view!

That being said, the past few days have been terrific and I actually feel and apparently look better than I have since arriving in NYC. Prior to my release from the hospital, the doctors decided to install another drain in my gut. I believe this was a secret attempt to slow me down, as my walking dominance of the 15th floor recovery ward was just a bit too much for everyone to handle. Once the drain was installed, all of the blood that was complicating my recovery by presenting a serious risk of infection (not to mention was extremely uncomfortable) filled the bag several times over during the week, which was great. However, it proved disastrous for my lap-time almost tripling it to the certain delight of the other patients. Undaunted, I continued to walk or rather inch along the railing at a snail's pace. The most embarrassing moment came after being lapped by an elderly Japanese woman probably 95 years old who had both her colon and stomach recently removed. The only upside was the satisfaction she seemingly received after finally passing me as evidenced through her giggling and muttering of something in Japanese as she blew by me. I hope she enjoyed her moment of glory because Mr. Plump 'n Juicy will be back and will be out for blood next go around.

I left M15 the following day after a good 48-hour run as the fastest on the floor with my head held high. It was somewhat of a bittersweet experience leaving the floor and some of my patient friends. One of whom, was my roommate Alex, a Soviet helicopter pilot who spent five years fighting the mujahedeen in Afghanistan during the 1980s. I learned about his experiences after my teammate Phil was discussing his own in Afghanistan, which Alex happened to overhear. Needless to say, we had a very interesting and meaningful discussion on geopolitics and war. Only in New York City could that happen.

Just prior to being discharged, the primary surgeon, aka The Miracle Worker, Dr. Yuman Fong, stopped by to give me an update on the situation. He informed me that my blood work was improving, my bilirubin levels were coming down and the new drain was working well, all of which lessened the complications of the surgery.

I'm no statistician but I don't think these changes necessarily improved my odds of survival, which still stand at
40%, but they will make the surgery easier. Considering that
we started at 0% chance of survival, I of course hear 40% as
being 99%. Even had he thrown a lesser number out, my ears
and training have conditioned me to believe that I would be in
that number regardless if it was one or 70 and would still beat
this thing. In the grand scheme of things, I figure my job is the
easiest in the equation in that the only things I'm required
to do are maintain a positive mental attitude (check), lie on
a gurney and fall asleep (no problem there), and after my
guts are reworked, keep breathing and recover (no issues
here). The heavy lifting, as far as I'm concerned, lies with the
doctor, the operating staff and family and friends.

If you have not heard by now, we were fortunate enough
to be taken on by the best of the best and likely the only man
in the world capable of performing this procedure. Dr. Fong is
a very kind, skilled, competent and just all around good guy.
What else can I say? The man is quite literally holding my
life in his hands. Which is why Heather and I were more than
caught a little off guard when Dr. Fong informed us that he'll
be traveling to China for the next week and will return just
prior to the operation. As soon as he shut the door Heather
and I exchanged a nervous look for about five seconds before
both saying that we should kidnap the good doctor and keep
him under house arrest with the Operation Game so he could
hone his skills lest he travel across the globe and be detained
by the commies, catch the bird flu or God forbid damage his
delicate hands and fingers during this trip. Despite our quick

thinking, our plans were foiled by the overall complexity of kidnapping a world famous doctor in my condition (especially with the additional burden of having to care for a newborn) and lack of access to any weapons. With great consternation, we allowed the doctor to safely depart on his trip to China. Right now I'm in a solid holding pattern with my recovery, so until further notice please focus all prayers on the safe return of Dr. Fong.

Once released, I made my way back to my wife and new baby, which seemed to accelerate the recovery process until night time when the baby started crying and I immediately started considering voluntary self admission to the urgent care facility. Heather saw right through my charade and reassured me that the crying only lasts a few hours and restarts maybe a handful of times through the night until the early morning. The good news was that the baby sleeps almost the whole day. I again counted my many blessings and asked her for the first time since the ordeal began what I could do to help her. A truly great feeling even though deep down I sadly realized that I would not be able to fulfill her single request to grow a pair of milking breasts. Regardless, I am thankfully able to provide some support to her incredible skills at mothering.

The next day we were able to get out and spend the day walking around and enjoying ourselves like a semi normal family. We had lunch at a great little sushi restaurant and spent most of the time laughing and enjoying the unparalleled people watching that only New York can offer. As we walked home, Heather started telling me a very interesting story of which I am currently unable to recall any of the details, but about half way through, I noticed an older gentleman walking toward us wearing a University of Georgia shirt. I was wearing a UGA hat and as we passed, the man casually pulls his pipe out of his mouth, makes eye contact and almost on cue, we simultaneously shout "Go Dawgs!" This of course catches Heather completely off guard and she looks at me like I'm some sort of alien as I calmly turn and say, "Go on, I'm listening." She asked what in the hell that was all about not noticing the UGA gear to which I reply, "We are both Georgia fans."

For the next 15 minutes we walked in silence as she contemplated what just happened, thinking that we were both fans of the STATE of Georgia instead of the BULLDOG NATION, wondering how we knew that the other was from Georgia and what dogs had to do with any of it. Obviously, I've been deficient in educating my wife on the importance of Georgia football but will be sure to take time over the next week to fill her in.

This is likely the last update until the main event. Know that we are headed into this thing with a full head of steam and are supremely confident that we'll emerge victorious on the other side. I cannot thank everyone enough for all of the wonderful support that we've received over the past several weeks. Never in my wildest dreams did I imagine that so many people would take such an interest in our plight. The so called strength, courage and determination on display that so many of you have mentioned is not something I see as an inherent, special quality that only I possess, but rather, a direct result of the love and support from family and friends as well as the training that the Army has put me through over the past five years, both of which have simply not allowed me to consider anything else but winning and continuing on with my blessed life. The only thing I've found more important than maintaining a positive mental attitude is keeping a sense of humor throughout the ordeal. In my short life, I've found that even in the most dire of circumstances, being able to laugh in the face of adversity is critical to succeeding. Without that crucial trait, your chances at success are significantly lessened. Fortunately, my mother has reinforced the gallows humor concept from an early age and it still carries me through the difficult times. If the laughing ever stops, that's when you should become worried.

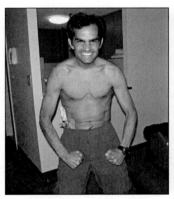

RYAN LOST OVER 25 POUNDS
IN ONE MONTH

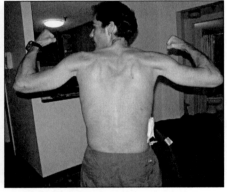

THE CANCER HAD DESTROYED THE BODY
HE RELIGIOUSLY TRAINED

PRE-CANCER BODY
FOR COMPARISON

Long story short; everybody can relax because right now we are too busy having fun to be overly concerned with this cancer thing.

Many thanks again to everyone for their thoughts, prayers, food, candles, baby clothes and many other gifts we've received over the past

several weeks. Your generosity is simply too much to comprehend. I am very much looking forward to the Super Bowel and
even more forward to celebrating and thanking everyone in
person once we kick this thing and start the Cholangiocarcinoma victory tour. Trust me when I say that it's going to rock.
As always, feel free to forward this on to other interested parties and be sure to send up a prayer or two on the 1st as both
me and Dr. Fong will need as many as we can get.

Until then, keep on rockin' in the free world.

Mary Jo, Al, Michael, Alfie, and Tommy returned to the city the day
before the surgery. They would be there for the big day. Ryan and I walked
over to a Mexican restaurant to meet them for lunch. When we walked
through the door, all eyes were focused on Ryan. I think Mary Jo did a
good job of feigning a smile and told him that he looked great, which
was nothing short of a well-intentioned lie. He needed to hear it though.
Everyone else looked like they were staring at a ghost. He looked bad,
really bad. As hard as I tried to feed him and get him stronger, he was
wasting away to nothing. He ate nothing at lunch that day. He seemed
to think that he was feeling better. I think it was just having his family
around that made him feel better, because he certainly wasn't improving
clinically speaking.

June 30th, 2009, the night before The Main Event, my stepmom
returned with Elizabeth and the Means family gathered in our apartment
for dinner after Ryan left to be admitted for prep work for the surgery.
I didn't sleep a wink the night before the surgery. I was at the hospital by
7 a.m. I had to race there early to elude Bryan, our Special Forces liaison
who replaced Phil at some point. I wanted these last couple of hours alone
with my husband. They could be our last. Bryan did not know Ryan per-

sonally, even though they were both in 5th Group. It was obvious by every word that came from his mouth that he was here on a mission. Detached. The Army had managed to insert many a perfect stranger into our lives to follow us and report on the events of their property, Ryan Means. Bryan, more so than other seasoned soldiers, took this daunting task seriously. Although I appreciate his babysitting skills, which kept dear Sophie alive on my frequent trips to the hospital, I was a little sick of having him in my family business. I tried to be appreciative, but it was difficult having so many strange men constantly around when all I really needed was a good amount of sleep, a few lactating nannies, and maybe a cure for cancer. Mary Jo jokingly began referring to me as Brittany Spears with all of her handlers and hangers-on pulling her in different directions and driving her to insanity. I started to wonder if that might be the case.

I stayed by Ryan's gurney as he signed all of the consent forms. We decided that if anything were to go drastically wrong, I would not prolong his life in order to keep him alive for my "viewing pleasure" as he called it. He reminded me to think with my head and not with my heart. "I know you can handle this, Heatwave," he said.

I sat on his bedside as Bryan entered the room. We were found. I gave Ryan my usual eye roll. He smiled knowingly. The three of us sat uncomfortably until he was wheeled away to his next holding room. I then gave Bryan a quick rundown of the game plan and went on my way. There was no need to tell him my plan for the day, as I knew he would track me down regardless. I wondered if for just a second, he imagined what his wife would be feeling if she were in my situation, as they also had a new baby. I don't believe it crossed his mind.

I returned home and sent Ryan one last text message before the surgery. It included a picture of Elizabeth, who now looked so grown, lying next to Sophie on our bed. I asked him to keep this image in his head as he drifted to sleep on the table. He replied, "My Perfect Angels," before his cell phone was confiscated.

The surgery was to take about six hours. We were asked to go home and keep our cell phones close, as we would be updated periodically via a nurse in the OR with Doctor Fong. The hours passed ever so slowly, and it was around noon when we received the first call. She told us that it was taking a little longer than expected as they ran into a situation that caused a change in their original plan, and that Dr. Fong was "doing the best that he can." Ryan was hanging in there and stable, although he tried to wake up a few times. They would call again in a few hours. Mary Jo and I decided to shop to pass the time. Ryan really would have wanted us to take in NYC while we could, and we did.

We were called to return to the hospital at 6 p.m. for a rundown of the surgery and treatment plan. Dr. Fong reported that the surgery was "challenging" but that there were "clean margins," meaning that he was quite certain that he removed all of the cancer cells.

Later that same day:

DATE: July 1, 2009
SUBJECT: Ryan's Surgery Update

Dear Friends and Family,

Thank you for your prayers for Ryan during his surgery. Your support has been overwhelming.

After nine hours, Ryan has just come out of his surgery. Dr. Fong successfully removed Ryan's tumor. Although the procedure was deemed a technical success, the tumor was more complicated to remove than expected. The bile duct tumor had also attached itself to the stomach, part of his small intestine, to an artery that feeds the liver and a major vein to the liver.

While we are feeling very positive that the cancer has been removed, the next 72 hours are very grave for Ryan as the liver must re-start to function. This is a perilous time for him, even though he is fighter, please continue your prayers.

Again, we cannot thank you enough for all of your prayers, love and support.

The Means Family

—ooo⊱◈⊰ooo—

That evening, after our meeting with the surgeon, we took our consistently optimistic selves home to rest and process the events of the day. I felt some relief. I was able to finally exhale. But, the Pavlovian response to the ring tone on my phone continued to be reinforced. We got the call at midnight to come to his bedside. I wrote this to my friend Carrie in Pennsylvania:

Sent: July 02, 2009
To: Thomas, C

I've spent the last hours reading old emails from Ryan. I was called in the middle of the night by the surgeon himself. He said the worst case is happening. Liver isn't starting up like it should. I'm praying my ass off. They are not telling Ryan in the hopes to not upset him. There's nothing they can do further but give blood products and wait. I was sent home.

I dread going back to hear the news. No news is better news right now. He's still intubated, not sedated, so he's writing like mad on this marker board. I can't make it out much. Something about the meat packing district? I sure hope he isn't referring to Jeffrey's—it's where he picked out and tried on a suit that he pointed out to me I could buy him in the future. I thought he should not bother trying it on, as he's 40+ pounds under his normal weight. Really bothering me. I hope he wasn't indicating it for his funeral.

He misses E so much and loves her and it makes me have a nervous breakdown in my head every time he says he can't wait to see her and toss her around and chase her again. He flat out asked me—well, wrote on the board—"Am I going to die?" And it was the first time I ever lied to him. I said "NO!" and started tearing up. I can't tell him his situation. Plus the doctor pulled me aside and told me that I'm the one who has to make the decision to wean him from the vent. He's coherent, why can't he? I guess maybe that's if he slips out of consciousness? Anyhow, I'm not telling anyone else at this point. I just need to be prepared. Maybe a miracle will happen?

I can't do this alone. E and Sophie—telling them about their dad all their lives? I almost wish he was an awful person. It would make this so much easier. But he's the best dad ever, which is why I chose him to have kids with in the first place. I haven't been saying this, but I will now: THIS IS NOT FAIR. Not to two baby girls. I don't get it.

Ryan was admitted to the ICU. Upon his arrival, we heard the nurse remark that "Dr. Fong's patients are never in ICU." The next few days consisted of a constant back and forth between the hospital and Helmsley, several times a day and night. The sick feeling no longer came and went with phone calls, but rather, it just stayed with me. I had trouble eating, sleeping, and taking care of Sophie. I didn't want to take care of myself or anyone else. Nothing was right in the world. I began to worry that Ryan's body was already dying.

The last time he was able to speak, he argued with his mother about a college landscaping job that she made him take, as well as her refusal to let him enjoy Sayulita with his brothers the past New Year's. He was irritable and starting to act confused, as was I. I felt like I couldn't take anymore. I needed someone to tell me if he was going to live or die. And no one would say either way. I would sit by his bedside wondering what I was supposed to do. Do I keep talking? If he were awake he would surely tell me to shut the hell up. He hated idle chit-chat.

The family was still gathered in NYC on July 3rd when Gabrey, Tommy's wife, arrived. I could breathe a tiny sigh of relief. Gabs is always an energetic and organized mommy. I was thrilled to have her take on the role of managing Sophie and Elizabeth while all of this was going on. She took both children along with Tommy to Central Park for an entire day. The girls got to experience New York as they would have with their own dad. They went to a few city parks, the boathouse, and to lunch with Josh, Michael, and Alfie.

Mary Jo, Al and I were at the hospital throughout the day. We were thrilled that Ryan was able to sit on the side of the bed and then with the help of his nurse, transfer to a chair. I sat on the bed next to his chair and he turned and looked at me and said, "Can I sit down in the chair?" in an angry tone. I replied "You are sitting down, you are in a chair, Ryan." He said that he wanted to sit where I was and the nurses placed him back in bed as they feared they would need to tie him down to make him sit where he did not want to stay. It scared me that he seemed so confused.

Mary Jo and I left for some fresh air and a walk. We passed one of our ICU nurses on the street and with great enthusiasm, told her that Dr. Fong reported to us that part of the liver was still working, and that dialysis would help out, and being that we had only heard bad news all day, we took this good news and ran with it, just like Ryan when he said he had 40% chance of surgical success and he took it as 99%. We had to remain positive as much as we knew these were not positive circumstances. Otherwise, we would not be able to go on living each day throughout this crisis. In retrospect, the nurse must have thought we were crazy, stupid, or maybe just felt plain pity for us, as she knew that the situation had little hope.

The night of July fourth, I could not celebrate. I believe some of our family went to the top of the Helmsley to catch a view of distant fireworks, and the brothers went into town to toast to one of Ryan's favorite holidays and watch fireworks together. I still had the consistent sick feeling and didn't feel like joining. Throughout the day with Ryan, I just felt like he was leaving his body, possibly he had left. There wasn't much of the Ryan I knew, but I didn't want to admit it at the time. I stayed in my room rocking Sophie and thinking about the fun Fourth of July holidays we spent at Gabrey's parent's lake house. As I sobbed in my chair, I felt the strangest feeling come over me. It was as if someone was standing behind me and put their hands on the back of my arms and was squeezing. It was terrifying and instantly calming at once. I don't believe in ghosts, and medically speaking, Ryan was still alive, but the feeling sent chills up my spine. I swore he was in the room. I wondered if I was losing my mind. I couldn't tell a soul about it. But immediately after those few seconds passed, I didn't feel like crying anymore. I pulled myself together and went to bed, ready to tackle the next day.

Email I sent to my girlfriends in Clarksville:

DATE: July 5, 2009
SUBJECT: Medically Speaking

Hi Gals,

Do I have any more mail that requires attention? I'm sure I
have hospital bills galore as we found out Sophie's birth wasn't
covered because I did not get authorization to switch hospitals from Nashville to New York. The whole issue of treating
a herniated disc during a stay for childbirth was the icing on
the cake of confusion. Denied, denied, denied. I sure hope Ryan
remembered to ask permission to get cancer or we will surely
be bankrupt, if we aren't from the hospital stay alone. There
is so much paperwork, red tape and codes to get reimbursed
by the Army for our room as well. They will not pay for meals,
cabs, etc. nor will they pay for Ryan to stay here unless it is in
the hospital. I have a few liaisons stalking me and trying to help
me with my stacks of military paperwork in my "free time" so
hopefully we will get it taken care of, but in the meantime, they
will only send correspondence to our home address. Fantastic. It's really the last thing I want to think of, but if we return
home penniless, Ryan may kill me for neglecting it. Thanks for
your help in getting everything forwarded here!

Today wasn't good, but not horrible relatively speaking
(in other words, he's alive). They drained two liters of fluid

from the right lung yesterday when they put the HD (dialysis) catheter/port in. It improved his breathing as far as chest expansion but he ended up more encephalopathic from being unable to process meds through his liver and kidneys.

He really isn't awake/alert at all (but NOT actually comatose), just out of it and in a ton of pain. He has his arms flexed/drawn in, really cold skin, grimacing and groaning all the time. He doesn't respond to a hand squeeze or follow any commands. The only word he's said wasn't very nice and it was when the nurses turned him! At least he responds to pain, right? I swear I try not to evaluate him as a patient, but if I did, I'd think he had some serious brain injury by these responses, and that this was not as correctable as they allow us to believe. The laughter has completely stopped at this point.

It's very upsetting, but the doctors tell us the situation is still reversible, so that's what I try to focus on. His O2 sats are low so they may have to restart the vent (intubate again), not sure. Abdomen is also distended so getting a CT tonight to see what's happening there. Hopefully, no more bad news with the results! Good news is... liver is not worse. Dialysis initiated last night. Could be a temporary thing, could be forever. It will take at least a month to assess kidney damage and reversibility (not a focus now).

I guess I'm growing impatient or maybe I became too optimistic when nothing went wrong the past two nights. He's very complex, they say, and his numbers (objective) never have and still aren't correlating with his clinical (subjective) presentation. So, it gives them a challenge. He has awesome Doctors though—and I'm the first to say if they were not. Dr.

Fong, his surgeon and Dr. Sanjay Chawla, the ICU doctor, are both amazing men with impeccable bedside manner, compassion and knowledge. I love them. What a change from the cold socialized healthcare we have in the Army.

E went to North Carolina for a little vacation today. Sophie is the gassiest baby and still doesn't know night from day!! I'm starting to not know or care about night from day myself! It doesn't really matter in New York, right?

Well, take care! Hope you guys are having some extra summer fun for me! I miss everyone and Jack and our house and I could go on...

Heather

Chapter 6
We Don't Say Goodbye

Michael, Alfie, and Josh returned to Atlanta on July 5th. Al, Mary Jo, and I took Sophie for a walk around the city and stumbled upon a French bistro that Ryan wanted to eat at while we were on one of our excursions, but it had been closed for lunch that day. I informed Al, and he decided he would treat us to dinner. We had a nice meal outside of the hospital that we could describe to Ryan when we next visited.

On July 6th, after our meeting with Dr. Fong, Mary Jo encouraged me to go get my hair done. She said that it was time to pull myself together and look good for Ryan. I went to a maniacal male hairdresser on the Upper East Side. I found him through a Google search going by price, location, and not much else. My main goal however, was to have it done as quickly as possible. He was running late quite from lunch. He asked a million questions as to what I was doing in the city and once it came out about Ryan's condition I asked him to please hurry. He assured me that all would turn out just fine, not only with my hair but also with Ryan. I'm so glad he could tell the future. Just as he was blow-drying my hair, I got a call from the hospital. We were to meet the doctors for an urgent update. I ran there in a panic.

When Al, Mary Jo, and I arrived, a new doctor greeted us. Our regular attending ICU doctor was off duty and the new doctor would be taking over for the next few days. No family likes to switch doctors, but no doctor can live in a hospital, so we would adjust. He certainly had a different bedside manner than we were used to, but he seemed confident that he would carry out the prior orders and address any new obstacles as they arose. He was clear in his explanations and very honest. This, I appreciated—a realistic approach to a real dilemma. He said that we were on high alert. The dialysis didn't seem to be doing what they had hoped, and we needed to be prepared for the worst. Dr. Fong, our hero, was looking at the liver numbers and had given us hope only in saying that the liver was not worse. The problem was, everything else was much worse. Kidneys not working, lungs not working, brain not working. I feared this was the end, but for some reason my heart and soul were taking over my brain and saying, "He's still alive, so there is hope." The call in the middle of the night still came as a shock.

I remember the phone ringing. It made me instantly numb, as if the blood emptied from my head and my guts and trickled out through my fingers and toes. I was instantly nauseated. They said to come to the hospital. He had taken a turn for the worse. This was it. This is how it ends.

Mary Jo and Al came to my room. We had to wait what seemed like hours but were really minutes for Bryan to come and stay with Sophie. There was no way I was going to miss being at the hospital, so I left the soldier some bottles and we started the walk.

I was shaking. My head was spinning. My heart was racing. I was in a full body cold, clammy sweat that summer night. The three of us were choking back our tears as we walked hand in hand on York Avenue to the hospital. Mary Jo said that we should be strong and support Ryan as he died. He didn't want us crying over him. I took in her words but still wondered what in the hell was going on. How could Ryan Means be dying?

We arrived at the hospital. They explained to us that his heart was no longer working. We lost the liver and kidneys, now heart and brain. Ryan had suffered a massive bleed. He was not responding to transfusions. He was only alive because of machines. With permission, they began to remove one machine at a time. The intubation remained. The priest came to perform the Last Rites (again). This was the third time in our journey that a priest was called for a sacrament to the sick and dying Ryan Means.

We stayed at his bedside telling stories. We told him how proud we all were of him and the way he lived his life. Mary Jo recalled his birth on the hospital gurney before she even made it into the delivery room. Al recalled his fishing trips. Mary Jo recalled all of the times she had bailed him out of trouble. She said that he was a gift from God that she was blessed to have and would give him back as God wished to take him now. He would be with his grandparents and with Adam. She said that when Ryan was 14 years old, he was at a party with some other kids and he ingested a large amount of alcohol, which put him into a coma. His respirations were six by the time his mother and brother got him to the emergency room, and even though the doctors felt he would not make it, Mary Jo prayed to God and Ryan was spared. At this moment, as her son died, she thanked God for giving her 21 more years with her beloved son.

I couldn't seem to think in that way. I thought only of the future. I told Ryan that he was and always will be the best husband and father that anyone could ask for, and I promised I would do my best to make sure Elizabeth and Sophie knew their dad. I told him that I knew he did not want to die and that I can always tell his daughters that he did everything in his power to stay alive for them; that he suffered through surgeries and excruciating pain in the hopes it would buy him a few more months of time with them. I would remember what he valued and make sure that they had the same values. He would live on through them. Mary Jo explained to him that the machines were being removed and that he would take his last breath as the sun was beginning to rise. She said that she will think of him as she begins each day with the light he leaves in her heart and mind. She was so reverent and composed, a true Catholic mother.

Mary Jo and Al left the room and the nurse drew the curtains and closed the sliding glass doors that made up Ryan's ICU. After all of those months in Iraq, after all of the weeks in this battle, at last we were alone. I put my head down on his chest. I wanted to hear his heart beat. It was the way I usually fell asleep when he was home with me. When he was healthy, Ryan's resting heart rate was around 45 bpm, but loud and strong. It was the most soothing sound to me since the first night we spent together. His skin was always smooth and tan, and he had no hair on his chest. It was once the perfect place to rest my head.

Now, the ventilator made his breaths rigid and painful—a loud and rapid explosion to expand the lungs, then a slow silent release. I couldn't hear his heart beat over the machines. So, I sat up. His skin was still warm. There were bandages all over his abdomen. I yanked his hospital gown from under his body and pulled back the bandage that was over his liver. I had to see. The ASW tattoo was unscathed and I told him this. I sat for a while holding his hand and telling him that I hoped he planned to watch over us. I admitted that I wished I was the one dying, because I didn't think I could do this alone, somewhat hoping that he would get angry at my words and wake up to tell me I should never talk that way and that everything was going to be just fine. He did not wake up; he did not squeeze my hand anymore. No more verbal reassurance that every-thing would be OK. His eyes and mouth were beginning to bleed from the internal injuries.

I took the last moments alone with him to look him over in the way a mother looks over her newborn baby. I touched his black hair, his thick eyelashes, the scar on his lip, the scar on his arm, his fingers, his feet and toes. I wanted to remember each part of him so that I could tell Elizabeth or Sophie what parts of them were just like their daddy's. Also, I just wanted to remember it all for myself. This was the last time I would ever see my husband alive. Then, for the very last time, I covered his body with the over-starched white hospital sheets and allowed the nurse to enter. She came in with her expressionless face, turning off the last of the life support and we all wept as quietly as any family ever had wept until the doctor entered to call the time of death at his last breath.

Ryan had managed to hold on until around 5:30 a.m., the same time he woke up every morning since I had known him; the same time he woke up Elizabeth to spend time alone with her before his long work days before laying her back in bed with me; the same time Sophie Ryan was born three weeks earlier.

The darkness and cold hospital lighting were gone. The orange sun was rising over the East River and appeared as a warm glow in his tiny room. We went to the waiting room as the nurse proceeded to extubate him and finally remove all of the lines, tubes and machines from his body. She wiped the bloody tears from his eyes and mouth.

As we waited, we started making phone calls. I never really thought about whom I would call first in this situation, but it just seemed like it happened automatically. The first person I called was Josh Cobb, Ryan's best friend. As he picked up the phone the words just came out "Ryan died." I told him what happened. Like all others we would speak to, there was confusion, followed by complete disbelief, followed by tears. I called each of my parents, I asked them to call the other family members and then my friends. I know it killed my family to not be able to be there for me, but at that point there was just no comforting me from anywhere. I was already aching to be alone to grieve.

We again entered the room, now completely lit by the sun. It was finally quiet. No equipment alarms ringing, no heartbeat monitors racing, just the sound of our stifled breathing as we choked back our tears to say goodbye. Mary Jo and Al said their last words.

Then Mary Jo said, "Heather, lie down with him one last time." I couldn't resist and for once in my life, I didn't care what people thought. I climbed up on the bed and lay next to the lifeless body, my head on his motionless chest and looked up at his face. It was unshaven for the last few days and although it was clouded by my tears, I could see his usual pattern of grays he said that he developed only since Elizabeth was born. Mary Jo reached over me and placed Ryan's arms around me and held me tight.

We wept on Ryan for a just a moment and then pulled ourselves together for him. He wouldn't have wanted that at all. He had clearly said so. I looked at my husband's face one final time. I whispered, "See you soon" as I walked away leaving my tears upon his chest, now covered in a clean white hospital gown. Neither Mary Jo nor I, shed another tear in public after that day.

PART VI

Life After Death

Chapter One
Farewell Sloan-Kettering and NYC

We got on the elevator. I remember trying to distract myself by saying, this is the last time you have to get in this elevator; this is the last time you have to step foot in this hospital; this is the last time you have to make this walk. No more terrifying midnight phone calls. It's over. Breathe. I wanted to run my fingers over the buttons and lay my hands on the cold steel elevators doors and take it all in. It was so bittersweet to have to leave this place that was keeping him alive. I pictured myself grabbing onto the handles and clinging for dear life as I fell to my knees in a giant puddle of tears. But I stood tall, next to Mary Jo and Al.

The three of us exited the hospital doors one last time. I forced myself to not look back. I didn't want to ever have to go through those doors again, but I didn't want to ever leave without him.

We staggered with a purpose through the daylight back to the Helmsley Medical Towers. We were in shock, traumatized by the night, and then stunned by the light of the day. I think that somewhere in my mind I thought that the sun would cease to shine and all life would die if Ryan should pass away. I had never had a loved one die since I was old enough to remember. I had no idea that we are expected to keep walking, one foot in front of the other and carry on with our lives. But traffic was about us and pedestrians brushed past on their way to work with no concern for our dazed little family staggering in shock along the early morning sidewalk of York Avenue. I felt like the three of us appeared as old black and white film, inserted into this city of digital color. We just didn't fit anymore. I still feel like that at times.

When we arrived back at the Helmsley Medical Towers, our family was there. The doorman and the desk attendants all seemed to understand. There was pity on their faces. They offered kind words that I cannot remember, and then they handed me a package that had been delivered. I assumed it was a baby gift from a friend and took it upstairs and set it aside. I tended to Sophie after reporting to Bryan one last time. Then I opened the box as I prepared to start packing for our trip home. What I saw inside the box made me almost faint. It was a designer diaper bag that I had more than hinted to Ryan that I wanted. I was hoping he would get it for me for Mother's Day, but it never came. According to the packing slip it had been on backorder and eventually sent to my house. My friends sent it to NYC for me, and my gift from Ryan was delivered on the day of his death. This led to the first time after his death that I would try to converse with him. I thanked him. I asked him why he monogrammed Elizabeth's initials instead of mine, since we would have two babies using it. No reply. I was uncomfortable with the silliness of talking to a dead man.

It was time to inform the rest of our friends of Ryan's death. Al sent out the following email. The responses were of shock and disbelief followed by sympathy.

DATE: July 7, 2009
SUBJECT: Ryan Patman Means, July 7th, 2009

On the morning of July 7th, at 5:30 a.m. the sun rose on New York City as Ryan passed on to heaven. His wife Heather and his parents Mary Jo and Al held him closely.

Ryan was not in pain as his once strong body relinquished its long and courageous struggle to stay with us. For six days Ryan fought with the strength and honor of a Special Forces soldier, but the complications from surgery to remove a cancerous tumor in his bile duct were far too great. We will remember Ryan as a sweet son, a doting father, a wild-man brother, an unwavering friend, and a fearless soldier. But most of all, we will remember Ryan as our hero.

At St. Catherine's of Siena church directly across the street from Memorial Sloan-Kettering Cancer Center, next to the statue of St. Theresa, is a prayer that gave his father, Al, comfort during daily Mass:

Let nothing disturb you
Let nothing frighten you
All things pass away;
God never changes.
Patience obtains all things.
He who has God
Finds he lacks nothing.
God alone suffices.

Ryan's family thanks everyone for their prayers, thoughts, and comfort in this time of great heartache. Details and arrangements will soon follow.

Love,
The Means Family

Ryan left instructions for Michael to give me a password for a document he had left on the computer. My heart was racing as I opened the document. It was nothing but passwords and information that I may need if he died. I hoped it was a final letter and was beyond disappointed that it was just a bunch of impersonal crap. I kept searching, as Ryan loved creating a good mystery. He never handed me a present. He always handed me a note with a clue as to where I could find it or he would try to make me guess what it was before he would give it to me. Even if it took days, he would make me wait. This time I finally managed to find a letter he wrote to each of his parents along with a few other writings. It baffled me that he didn't write me a personal letter since that is what I had come to expect from him.

When he was hospitalized, he told me that he refused to write a "goodbye" letter, as that would make it seem as though he was ready to say goodbye...and he never would use those words. All he ever said when I asked him if he wrote to me or the girls "just in case" was that, if I didn't understand how much he loved me and our children by now, I never would. I sent the following email to our friends:

DATE: July 8, 2009
SUBJECT: A Letter from Ryan and Heather

Dear family and friends,

In the last 38 days, I watched the love of my life slowly die. During this surreal time, Ryan managed to write the sincere updates you received from him.

At first, I was selfishly bitter. He took our time to write to all of his friends and family (I was calling it his fan club), but he didn't sit down and write a specific Heather letter, Elizabeth letter, or a letter to Sophie who barely made it here in time to meet her father. I searched our computers per a clue that the letter was on a computer because he couldn't write while on all of the medications and machines.

Ryan is known to me for hiding presents and making me
open clues and solve puzzles to find them. Christmas 2007
was an hour-long scavenger hunt through snow and dirty
diapers to find a diamond ring ultimately hiding in his green
beret on the coat rack! This was no different.

Maybe there are more letters, I don't know. But this is
what I found; it was unfinished, so I am completing it for him.
I have often been his editor and think I can do this justice. It is
not for me or my children alone. It is for everyone who knew
Ryan. I'm no longer bitter about that fact. I have received
plenty of love and letters from Ryan...it is time to share, as
you will see—"men who mean just what they say, the brave
men of the Green Beret."

"While I'm still supremely confident about the outcome,
I wanted to share something about myself which isn't very
easy especially considering how extremely tough I am, that
I'm an unstoppable member of the nation's elite fighting force,
a barrel-chested freedom fighter and generally someone who
was born without feelings or a conscience. The secret to my
attitude is what I consider a gift from God; Something that I
don't think I've ever mentioned to anyone but now somehow
feel obligated to share with the world, which I really don't like.

The one thing that has always managed to get me through
the darkest of times—and there have been more than I can
really remember—is this strange and uncontrollable ability
to see beauty where I really don't think other people can. It's
odd because I'll be in the midst of a hellish situation or simply
walking down the street and just for an instant, something
will catch my eye, whether it be the flight of a bird, wind rus-

tling through some trees, a person in the midst of a genuine emotion, the way my daughter looks at me; really it can be anything or everything but in the blink of an eye my heart fills with such passion, joy and happiness that I almost clutch my chest because I think that my heart is literally going to explode and at that moment I know that no matter what may happen, everything is, in the long run, going to be ok.

The way I see this strange phenomenon is that God is telling me that He is all around us and everything is simply going to be ok."

Please live each day as Ryan always has lived. Appreciate everything. Fight hard, love even harder. And to conclude, here is a prayer that was sent after his death that seems like it was written just for him:

Do not stand at my grave and weep.
I am not there; I do not sleep.
I am a thousand winds that blow.
I am the diamond glints on snow.
I am the sunlight on ripened grain.
I am the gentle autumn's rain.
When you awaken in the morning's hush
I am the swift uplifting rush
Of quiet birds in circled flight.
I am the soft stars that shine at night.
Do not stand at my grave and cry.
I am not there. I did not die.

                        –By Mary Elizabeth Frye, 1932

Ryan lives on through his daughters, and also all of us. He touched more lives than we could have ever, ever imagined. Let's "keep on rockin' in the free world" for him—no tears, as he is all around us. I know I feel it when I dance with Elizabeth or rock Sophie to sleep. His strong arms are wrapped around us—his girls. And, he is with you, too.

Love,
Heather and Ryan Means

Al, Mary Jo, and I were immediately ready to return home. However, we were technically under orders of the Army and not allowed to leave NYC without their permission. Bryan informed us that he had never been in this situation and was unclear of the protocol. His duty ended after he reported the death to the command. Another liaison would take over at this point. They sent a woman from a local base to walk me through paperwork. She too had never seen this situation before, as New York City was not the final destination for many wounded warriors. She needed a death certificate from the hospital, and we did not have one. The City of New York was not quick in this department, and she could not issue the Army death certificate without this information. And without the military death certificate, we could not get orders to book a flight home. We were at the end of our tolerance for Army regulations.

The officer was also unclear as to how we would get Ryan's body to Atlanta. We planned to have a funeral there and then a burial in Arlington. So the body would have to be moved twice. She explained that the Army would pay to move it once, to the site of burial. But since we wanted it in

Atlanta for the funeral first, we were making matters more complicated. We would have to pay for his body to be flown to Atlanta.

Ryan had filled out the required forms before deployment as to whether he wanted to be cremated or buried, but not much else. He was very unclear, and like many of the young men in the Army, he just didn't take it as seriously as he should have, since he felt it was unlikely that I would ever read it under these circumstances.

I needed to choose a wood or metal casket. Ryan wrote that he wanted to be buried in civilian attire rather than his Army uniform, which brought me back to the suit at Jeffrey New York. How could I get there? Which suit was it again? Would he want me to spend that much money on a suit he would only wear to be buried in the ground? Do they even bury them in their clothes or do they give the clothes back to you as a keepsake? Will the casket be open or closed? He had said closed if he was disfigured, otherwise it was up to the loved ones to decide. I chose a closed metal casket. His beloved American flag was proudly draped across it at all times.

The woman told us that another liaison would be sent directly from Fort Campbell where Ryan was stationed. She referred to him as my "Casualty Assistance Officer" or CAO. Normally, he would be the one to knock on my door and inform me of my husband's death in Iraq. In this case, I guess we called him. Ryan's group was still deployed, and thus my CAO was from another battalion. He had never met Ryan, however he was from 5th group and would get us home and attempt to lead us through the rest of the process. It took him a day longer than planned to get to New York. By the time he arrived, we had grown angry and anxious to get home. None of us could sleep, so the days and nights seemed endless and the sense of normalcy we had been lacking for so long had still not been granted back to us. We were short with him, and for the first time in this whole process, we began to express our disgust out loud. Del was about the same height as Ryan with dark skin, and dark features also like Ryan. And of course, he entered wearing the same uniform we were used to seeing Ryan wear. It had been awhile since we saw a man in this uniform, and Mary Jo and I thought this resemblance was both ironic and eerie.

Del's CAO training and experience in combat must have prepared him for our family. He remained calm throughout the entire confusing process. He was older and obviously more seasoned in dealing with people than Bryan. Poor Bryan was likely hoping to fight terrorists and spend time with his own newborn when he was assigned to NYC to our family. Del had compassion and true sympathy, which in my book trumps the ability to feign empathy. It was somewhat comforting to me. I believe that he conducted himself in a manner similar to that which Ryan would have, had he been in his same shoes. He looked out for the two children and me for the next few months, never making us feel like he would rather be somewhere else.

Del eventually made arrangements for us to fly back to Atlanta, and he would arrange for the body to be flown there as well. I completed a daunting stack of paperwork, with Al overseeing my decisions. It was once again Al's turn to take over and direct the family. Mary Jo and I were the decision makers in the hospital; Al was best in the business world. He would not let me sign my name on a slip of paper without reading it himself first and having it explained in full detail. I probably would have signed what was left of my life away at that point, since I felt I had no reason to live. I just wanted to sign anything necessary to get on with what was left of our lives. I wanted to get back to Elizabeth and out of that dreary room at the Helmsley.

In order to make use of my time and resources in NYC, I decided to shop for my dress for the funeral. It had to be done. I thought that I would need a simple black skirt suit. Jackie Kennedy instantly flashed into my mind. What did she wear? A pillbox hat. No, I certainly wasn't going to wear a hat, even in the South. The first time I ventured out, I returned in tears, telling Mary Jo that I couldn't even find anything that I might want to try on, and that I was looking for a suit. She told me that Ryan wouldn't want me to find something that I thought I should wear, but isn't really me. She said "Find a sexy dress, that's what Ryan would want."

"What's a sexy funeral dress?!" I replied.

"Something classy that shows your legs. Ryan loved your legs," she said. So I went out for a second time. I felt like a zombie going up and down the escalators in Bloomingdales. There were so many gorgeous clothes that I could never afford. And I wondered if I would ever even shop again. I had no reason to want to get dressed and leave my house once I returned home. I thought of where I could wear each cute dress or blouse that I saw when Ryan and I went out next. It was just how my mind was used to thinking. That started to get quite depressing, but I held up my chin and carried on through the process.

I was in the dressing room with at least five dresses that looked to me to fit the "sexy funeral" category. And then the conversation that I knew was inevitable: "What is the dress for?" the sales woman asked.

"Funeral," I replied.

"Ah, someone in your family?" she continued.

"Yes." I said, trying to remain calm.

"Were you close to them?" she asked.

"Yes, it was my husband," I said, hoping it would end the conversation. But it did not work. She wanted to know how he died. Seriously? Does she really want me to go into this? I redirected her back to the dress issue.

She attempted to zip me into a second dress that would not accommodate my breasts, same as the first. I was breast-feeding Sophie, and it was about time for me to get back to our apartment for the next feeding.

I had those God-awful pads on that absorb the milk, and they were nearing the end of their lifespan.

I hated breast-feeding. I never understood how people thought it was such a beautiful bonding experience. My good friend Ali is the poster-perfect mother for breast-feeding. She would be happy to feed and nurture any baby that needed it. I, on the other hand, would be lying if I didn't say that it just made me miserable and bored. They really push you to do it these days though and I didn't want the guilt hanging over my head if something should go wrong due to my unwillingness to breast-feed. Years from now, Sophie could be on trial and blame her acts on the fact that her father died when she was born and her mother didn't breast feed. Who knows? So I continued to do it until the stress and schedule of the funerals dried my supply prematurely.

The woman commented on my voluptuous (gigantic and unconventional is more accurate) boobs, and I told her the issue. This made her grow even more interested in my story. So I let her hear it. She started crying, then I started crying and she left to grab some tissues. I sat down on the floor of the dressing room looking at myself in the full-length mirror. My breasts were leaking, my stomach was deflated and flabby from the recent birth, I was bleeding to death as you do after birthing a baby, and I had to find a sexy funeral dress for my own husband's funeral. This was far worse than the aggravation of prom dress shopping or finding a bikini in the winter, and I thought that was as bad as it would ever get. Not so. This was a real problem that I could have never imagined back when I was trying on those awful prom dresses years ago. It was hell.

Whose life is this, anyway? I wondered. I had always wanted to live in New York City and shop at the finest stores. I wanted to know what it was like to buy something without caring if it was on sale. I promised myself I would do that on this day. But I was more miserable than ever.

Those things mean nothing. As a matter of fact, they mean less than nothing, which I knew before, but I didn't truly understand until now. This was humbling. I suddenly realized that it doesn't matter if I lived in Clarksville, Tenn., where there isn't a decent mall within an hour of my home or if I lived in the center of Manhattan. Without Ryan, I was fucking miserable. He always said that would be the case. Was he laughing and saying, "I told you so"? I wondered. I bet he was saying it, not laughing, but rather wishing he could come and pick me up off of that fitting room floor and carry me home.

The woman returned with Kleenex and a Cynthia Steffe dress in two sizes. It had some stretch and some ruching on the sides. A long silver zipper ran up the entire length of the backside in a sexy manner. The length was right at the knee. This was it—or at least as good as it would get in these conditions. I had my dress. I grabbed a pair of Spanx and returned home to prevent any further wallowing in self-pity.

Our NYC network of friends arrived at the Helmsley with condolences and boxes. They retrieved the extra strollers, baby toys, and large items that we would already have at home and took them to local shelters. Tucky and Ned, along with Charlie, whose generous wife, Jamie, had given us an entire nursery for our room, helped box up our belongings. A few boxes were for Sophie containing formula, diapers, and baby necessities and would be sent to Atlanta where we would go first for the funeral. The others were my clothes, Ryan's clothes, and all of our belongings, which would go to Clarksville. Tucky made sure to put all of Ryan's clothes and belongings in a single box with a notation on it, so that I would not open it until I was sure I was ready to examine the contents. Charlie, being one of the few people in the city with a car, took on the daunting task of mailing the many heavy boxes containing my life to their correct homes.

We have some fantastic friends.

Chapter Two
Atlanta: Active Duty Death Beneficiary

Al, Mary Jo, and I, along with Sophie, returned to Atlanta with only two days to spare before the funeral. When we arrived at the airport, the USO and family members were greeting their loved ones with hugs and tears. I was numb. I didn't look up at them for fear that I would lose my composure. That should have been us. It was about the time that Ryan would have been coming home from Iraq.

To this day, I cannot enter the baggage claim area where the USO and families wait for their home-coming soldiers without choking up and sometimes actually crying. No matter how I try to stop it, my mind always flashes back to this awful day when I came home from NYC with my fatherless child and was greeted by a casualty officer.

When I finally picked-up my head, there were two dark-haired men with Green Berets as well as another taller man with traditional Army formal dress. It was Del and another SF team member Pat, who would be assisting us through the funeral process. The third soldier, Paul was from a local base. He was technically assigned to Al and Mary Jo but would walk me through the signing of all future documents at Fort McPherson. Apparently, besides accepting and dealing with my husband's death, I had to "check out" of the Army system myself. The soldiers would remain in contact with Ryan's fellow Special Ops family and inform them of all funeral details.

I was taken to Fort McPherson to hand in my military ID. They didn't make me wait the usual eight hours but took me straight to the back. Others looked angry with this, as I would have, too, knowing how long it can take to get an ID in those places. When we got married, I waited five hours for my ID, and they closed before they ever got to my number and told us to return the next day. I had to lose two days of work to get the ID since I needed it to apply for healthcare benefits. But this time was different. The woman assisting me understood. I told her I didn't know I had to have my picture taken this day and she gave me a minute to straighten myself. She explained to me that I would still have Ryan's ID number on my card, but rather than "Active Duty Spouse", I was now titled "Active Duty Death Beneficiary." We had at least three other stops on post where I filled out paper work that would ensure that Sophie and Elizabeth got what they were entitled to as far as educational and healthcare benefits, and I was introduced to a number of women representing various grief organizations. Many were geared towards the sudden killing of a soldier in another country and coping without ever saying goodbye. I didn't feel I was that bad off compared to them and didn't want to join the groups. I didn't feel like I fit into that category, so it seemed selfish to use their time and resources. I also didn't fit in to the traditional widow groups where almost everyone is over 60 years old. And I wasn't ready for anything church affiliated, as I was no longer on speaking terms with God.

An email was sent out to my parents and family up North, and they made arrangements to drive or fly to Atlanta. It was pure hell trying to coordinate everything. For some reason, I had it in my mind that once we left NYC we would all be at peace. We would sit down and remember Ryan quietly and reflect on all that we just went through. I would possibly even get some sleep despite the schedules of a newborn and a toddler. I just wanted so badly to be alone and sort out my mind. Between family, Army liaisons, and children, I hadn't been alone in weeks. And it wasn't going to happen now—quite the opposite—it was about to get worse.

I suppose I have never been the most patient person. And throughout all of this traveling, cancer-battling surgery, baby birthing, toddler raising, husband dying, and arguing with the Army, I lost what very little patience I once possessed. I wanted these funerals over with, and I wanted to finally be alone with my kids. But, everyone else seemed to want to be around me. My parents, of course, wanted to be there. I'm sure if my daughter's husband died, I would want to be there for her and do anything possible to take away the pain. The Army liaisons had a duty to check on me constantly and keep me moving though the many services and checkout processes that needed to be done. The massive number of people that Ryan knew in Atlanta wanted to individually offer their condolences. But there was nothing anyone could do, and I'm the type of person who wants to be alone when I'm not feeling my personal best. So, the constant influx of calls and emails became more than overwhelming. Simple questions seemed to throw me over the edge. I wasn't at my personal best as far as congeniality goes.

I began to shut out all of my married friends, which really cut down the number of wonderful people I had to rely on over the next months. There was no husband to lean on when I needed his strength the most. There was no partner to parent with anymore. I was on my own with two children. I could choose to resort back to the days when I had to ask my parents to help me and it hurt to know that I was regressing. I wanted to move on from my old life as a child and conquer the world with my husband. Now, seeing my family gather around me, comforting me like a sad little child made me realize even more what I had lost with Ryan's death.

A year later, I'm thankful that my children have three sets of amazing grandparents, but I still can't shake the feeling that I have been shortchanged, as I am no longer part of a set. I can call any of the three couples and brag on the children, but it doesn't give me the same satisfaction as sharing with their own doting father. Any milestone in the girls' lives is happiness followed by instant sadness that I can't turn to him and say, "Did you just see that?"

—∞∘❮❮◉❯❯∘∞—

Next on the agenda was meeting Ryan's body at the airport. We went to Hartsfield-Jackson International Airport and were led to a receiving area where his body would arrive. It never occurred to me that there were often coffins flying with the luggage below during our domestic flights. It seemed cruel to me that my husband was placed below deck with the luggage; However, I don't think a casket would be well-received in first-class passenger seating, where he truly belonged. There was, however, a soldier assigned to receive his body in New York and accompany it to Atlanta. We waited in a small area with vending machines until he arrived, and then we were directed into a much larger room.

The honor guard was present to ceremoniously lead the casket, which was draped honorably in the American flag, to the hearse. The hearse took the body to Patterson's Funeral Home where Ryan would be dressed. Al, his brother Bo and I met at the funeral home to complete the necessary arrangements. I was still conflicted about choosing a tie for Ryan, as the one I asked my friends to send had not yet made it to town. Bo suggested that Ryan may like his UGA Bulldogs tie and Al and I agreed. This is what he wore, with his own black suit and shoes.

I never asked to see his body for two reasons. First, I was afraid the image would terrify me and be forever imprinted in my memory. I had already watched as he died and I didn't think I could bear to see him after he had been artificially preserved. The thought repulsed me. The second reason was made on a more sub-conscious level. I think that somewhere inside my grieving mind, I thought that if I did not see it, it was not happening. I could still pretend that maybe there was a mistake, that maybe he would come back to me in time. I'm glad I didn't see him, as I still pretend sometimes. It's a way of coping that few would understand.

Chapter Three
The Girls Keep Me Going

The evening before the funeral, a wake was held at the Rybert's beautiful home in Brookhaven, a short walk from where Ryan grew up. They are close friend's of the Meanses, and they graciously offered their home to a party of 100 that easily tripled in size by the end of the night. A band played "Keep on Rockin' in the Free World." Since his death, we have forever marked Neil Young's hit as "Ryan's song" amongst our family and friends. They played the "Ballad of the Green Berets" as well and there was not a dry eye, except for Mary Jo and myself, who were still adhering to the "no tears" policy.

For at least the first hour, I was standing next to a table of photos of Ryan, receiving sympathetic guests, most of whom I had never met. I was trapped in that corner for well over an hour. My legs were tired and my knees felt as though they would surely buckle from standing with them locked for so long. I felt like I was running out of energy and the will to talk. It was always the same question: "How are you doing, dear?"

What the hell was I supposed to say? "I don't know" was the true answer, but usually I said "I'm doing well, all things considered...The girls keep me going." It seemed to be the answer that most wanted to hear.

I finally found a comfortable chair in the library with the Chi Psi crowd. Again, there was an instant connection. I felt like I had known them all for as long as Ryan. I had met some of them before, but never did we think we would meet again like this. They were a group of friends you could bare your soul to, and I huddled up with them as we exchanged Ryan stories.

After the wake, I joined the Chi Psi family, our friends, and Ryan's Special Forces team members at a local bar. We had our own Ryan-style celebration with those in our age group—a less formal wake that he would have loved to attend. Just as we arrived, it felt like he was in fact there. It was a quiet night, with a sprinkling of rain, but as we exited our cars, torrential downpours ensued. We were all completely drenched. I overheard at least a dozen people say things like, "This was Ryan conducting the evening from his new home."

THE BOULDER CREW – THROUGH THE YEARS

AT RYAN'S WAKE IN BROOKHAVEN

Chapter Four
The Funeral: Atlanta

The next morning, Monday July 13th, the funeral was held at Ryan's church, Christ the King. He was a student there as a young boy and his family had been lifelong members. Mary Jo and Al expected around 500 people, which seemed just a little overwhelming to me. There were two traffic lights out on Peachtree Road, so we were advised to hire traffic directors in case the actual mass of 500 people attended.

The immediate family met at the Means' condo, and Al rented a limousine to take us all to the church together. We gathered in the church rectory as the other guests arrived and took their seats. Word travelled to us that there was standing room only in the church. My heart began to race faster. As we headed to the church from the neighboring building, we walked past the hearse with Ryan's body inside. His team was ready with solemn faces to escort him into the service. We turned the corner around the side of the church, where there were crowds of people.

The expected group of 500 turned into 1,500! People were gathered outside, in the parish hall, along the walls, and outside aisles of the pews. It was a hot July Monday in Atlanta, and everyone was standing in the heat, with a raised American flag to honor Ryan as the casket made its journey from hearse to altar. It was overwhelming to see hundreds and hundreds of flags painting a sea of red, white and blue in the name of Ryan Means.

Mary Jo and Al would lead the way, along with me cradling Sophie, now one-month-old, in her long white cotton gown. Alfie accompanied Daisy, the Means' housekeeper who had quite a role in raising the four boys. Elizabeth was attached at the hip to her Aunt Gabrey and Uncle Tommy, Teddy and Lilli, followed by Michael and his soon-to-be fiancé, Angela. People, overflowing the church, belted out verses of "America the

Beautiful," accompanied by organ pipes resonating the melody in a way that gave chills to all in attendance.

As I walked slowly down the aisle, two things were running simultaneously through my racing mind. First, I told myself not to look to either side. I didn't want to see the tears, the sadness, the grief on anyone's face. I promised Ryan that I would not cry and if it meant detaching myself, I would do it. I held my chin up and drew my shoulder blades together, as Ryan often would stand behind me and pull my arms together behind my back in order to correct my terrible posture. "How is it that you are a physical therapist with posture like this?" he would ask.

Second, I thought to Ryan, 'How dare you do this to me?' We decided together that we would not have a wedding; neither of us could bear to be the center of such pomp and circumstance—his words—and now, here I was alone. I was walking down the very aisle that we might have walked down at our wedding. Only I was without Ryan, expressionless in my black funeral attire, newborn baby nestled in my arms, publicly advancing up this endless aisle, his flag-draped coffin following closely behind. This was far worse than any wedding scenario that we avoided.

After the funeral, we were led into the Parish Hall where the crowd had gathered around tables adorned with exquisite flower arrangements, and a rather extensive menu of brunch items along with Mimosas and Bloody Mary drinks. I was under the impression that after the wake the previous night and the service today, we would finally take a rest until the burial at Arlington, for which we were not yet given a date. Once again, chin up, shoulders back, no time for rest. I thought I was tired after Elizabeth's uneventful birth; boy, was I wrong. This was a fight to stay upright. I was completely and utterly exhausted. I worked frantically with my mother, and my "mommy" friends to keep Sophie away from germ infested hands and sneezes and to get her fed and home safely in all of this chaos. She still managed to catch the eye of many visitors and was passed around more than I was comfortable with, but I seemed to always be blocked from her by another friend or relative speaking their sympathies.

Being on the receiving end of sympathies when a loved one dies is not what I imagined, not that I really sat around imagining any such thing. "I'm sorry for your loss" is probably the simplest expression of sympathy you can receive. I like it. It's to the point and it doesn't pretend to be any more knowledgeable about the situation. It isn't religious or flowery; it is just simply stated.

On the other hand, some choose to be religious in their sentiment: "It was God's plan." Really? It was? Did you talk to him? Did he tell you this was his exact plan? Or, "It was his time; he was ready to go." Actually, I can vouch for the fact that he wasn't ready. Ryan was 35 and happy. Trust me, it was NOT his time.

And my personal favorite, "You are so beautiful and young. You will meet someone else." And I heard it more than once...not from anyone my age, of course. My friends and Ryan's, with or without children, seemed to understand that it was more a matter of raising two babies alone without the man I wanted to grow old with at my side. At no point have ever I felt blessed to be young and wrinkle-free when Ryan died, so that I may snatch up another husband. In my opinion, people might as well have followed the ridiculous comment with, "It's too bad you have those two little babies, though. That's going to make your game a lot more difficult."

I realize that no one intends to say hurtful things at a funeral. It stands to reason that few will understand where a widow's heart and mind has gone if they have not been a widow themselves. Others will not remember how it was to be in young love and have all of your hopes

and dreams ahead of you. To them it would seem that losing a spouse
before "growing attached" over the years would be easier than losing
them later in life. Who am I to say if it is or if it isn't? I've not grown
old with anyone.

—∞∘❋∘∞—

RYAN PATMAN MEANS
NOVEMBER 5, 1973 – JULY 7, 2009

July 9th, 2009

Ryan's obituary, *The Atlanta
Journal Constitution*
Ryan Patman Means

Staff Sergeant Ryan
Patman Means, a U.S. Special
Forces soldier died on Tuesday,
July 7th in New York City at
the age of 35. The cause was
complications after surgery
to remove a cancerous tumor,
Cholangiocarcinoma, from his bile duct. Ryan was serving in
Iraq at the time of his diagnosis on May 28, 2009.

Born in Atlanta to Al and Mary Jo Means, Ryan attended
Christ the King grade school and graduated from Marist
School in 1992. Ryan attended college at the University of
Colorado at Boulder and later graduated from the University
of Georgia.

Ryan's professional career began in Atlanta working in
telecommunications for BellSouth and later for Williams
Communications in New York City. It was on the morning of

September 11, 2001, when two airliners crashed into the Twin Towers that set in motion Ryan's incredible journey from his childhood neighborhood of Brookhaven to the neighborhoods of Iraq.

This journey began with Ryan's close friendship with Adam White. Ryan and Adam were best friends since the first grade. They were fraternity brothers, roommates, drinking buddies, and climbing partners while students at Boulder. Their shared thirst for adventure was forged while bivouacking in a snowstorm near the summit of Mt. Ranier.

Adam and Ryan continued to climb together even after they both moved to New York City. On the day of the September 11th attacks, Ryan became greatly concerned when he could not contact Adam, as Adam worked in the North Tower. Ryan rode his bike around the city for weeks posting flyers with Adam's picture and searching the city's hospitals. Ryan never found Adam and he was profoundly affected by his best friend's death. He simply had to do something.

Ryan's friends and family were shocked but not surprised when at the age of 31 he enlisted in the Army. Many remember Ryan as child wearing fatigues everyday. For his 7th birthday his mother planned an Army birthday party at a military themed restaurant. When Ryan was eight, two Marine Corps recruitment officer knocked on his parent's front door because Ryan filled out and mailed in a recruitment postcard that he tore from a *Boys Life* magazine. Ryan hit the jackpot when an Army-Navy Surplus store opened in the neighborhood. To his parents great concern, he brought home various Army helmets, pocket-knives, gas masks, nunchucks, smoke grenades, and cammo face paint. Brookhaven was kept very safe by their beloved nine-year-old neighborhood commando.

Ryan did not take this decision to enlist lightly. Deep in Ryan's heart was a love for his country and a great historical perspective of the sacrifices that young men and women have made to defend America's peace and security.

One night at the Buckhead Lions Club, Ryan listened intently to a speech about the global war on terror given by Major General Julian Burns. After the speech, Ryan introduced himself and informed General Burns of his decision to join the fight. General Burns was so fired up about Ryan's commitment that he and Ryan both got down on the floor and pumped out fifty push-ups together.

After basic training and Airborne school at Fort Benning, Ryan was selected to tryout for Special Forces at Fort Bragg. At 32, Ryan was one of the oldest candidates in his class. The training was physically and mentally grueling. He emerged from the program successfully and graduated to become a member of one of the most elite fighting forces in the world.

During his time at Fort Bragg, Ryan and his buddies would often road-trip to Wrightsville Beach North Carolina. One morning while overlooking his motel room balcony, Ryan spotted a beautiful young woman pull into the parking lot driving a convertible. Her name was Heather and she was radiant, demure, intelligent and gorgeous. Ryan had to utilize every bit of his elite Special Forces skills to allure her into his life. Mission accomplished.

Their love affair was easy. The two simply decided to get

married while holding hands and walking around Chastain
Park. After an intimate, flip-flop-wearing courthouse wedding, they settled in Clarksville, Tenn. just outside of his base
at Fort Campbell. Their first child Elizabeth was one year old
and Heather was three months pregnant with their second
child when Ryan was deployed to Iraq in January 2009.

Ryan's letters from Iraq did not elaborate on his daily missions and he very much downplayed the fact that he was in
harm's way. Although he was a courageous and tough warrior,
Ryan felt great empathy for the Iraqi people and he particu-
larly felt compassion for the Iraqi children. He always made
an effort to share things like lip balm, toilet paper, soccer
balls and school supplies with the kids. His was living out his
dream but his letters always ended with his desire to be back
home with Heather and having bath-time with Elizabeth.

After six months in Iraq, Ryan noticed that he was jaun-
diced and was airlifted to Baghdad for further testing. Ryan
was diagnosed with Cholangiocarcinoma at the end of May
and immediately medevac'd to Walter Reed Army Hospital in
Washington, D.C. for initial treatment, and later to Memorial
Sloan-Kettering Cancer Center in New York City for surgery.
He was met in New York by his immediate family and his wife
Heather who was nine months pregnant.

Directly across the street from Sloan-Kettering Hospital is
New York Presbyterian Hospital. This was very convenient for
the Means Family because Heather went into labor and was
wheeled across the street by an Army Special Forces liaison
officer. He then ran back across the street to Sloan-Kettering
where he pulled out Ryan's IV's and wheeled him into Heath-

er's delivery room just in time for the birth of their second daughter, Sophie Ryan Means.

Ryan, Heather, 18-month-old Elizabeth and newborn Sophie spent the following days convalescing. Ryan would show his wife and daughters his old New York City haunts and tell stories about his old friend Adam. And everyday after their long easy strolls through Central Park, Ryan would bring his children home for bath-time.

On the morning of July 7th, the sun rose in New York City as Ryan passed onto heaven. His wife Heather and his parents Mary Jo and Al held him closely. Ryan was not in pain as his once strong body relinquished its long and courageous struggle to stay with us.

For six days Ryan fought with the strength and honor of a Special Forces soldier, but the complications from surgery to remove the cancerous tumor in his bile duct were far too great.

We will remember Ryan as a sweet son, a loving husband, a doting father, a wild-man brother, an unwavering friend, and a fearless soldier. But most of all, we will remember Ryan as our hero.

Ryan ended all of his letters with a simple thought: "Keep on rockin' in the free world."

Chapter Five
Back to the Hospital

As it turns out, even in the summer months, it isn't a good idea to pass an infant around a crowded church. Sophie developed a fever high enough to warrant an emergency room visit just a day after the funeral. We rushed her to Scottish Rite Children's Hospital.

They ran some tests and decided to admit her to the hospital. Since I was still attempting to breastfeed, I was admitted as well. I finally had time to myself. Just me and my new baby in a private hospital room, alone at last. I explained to the nurses that I did not want a single visitor. No one was permitted to visit during our entire stay for the sake of Sophie's health and my sanity. It was a three-day stay that might have saved my life. The nurses were kind enough to take care of Sophie through the nights and not wake me often. It was like rehab, a recovery center for me. That stay gave me the moments alone that I had been dreaming of for weeks. Thank heaven for the staff on our floor. Children's Hospital of Atlanta was hands-down the best of all of the hospitals I visited that summer.

I asked the nurses for some paper and a pen, and Mary Jo left me a *People* magazine and some gossip rags. I began journaling my thoughts, which to me is the most therapeutic of processes. This was my escape. I wish we could have stayed longer. I knew that Elizabeth was well taken care of, and she certainly didn't seem to mind that we were once again separated.

To this day, neither of my kids shed a tear when we part. This tragic experience at a young age has made them very well adjusted to change compared to their competition. As long as I'm not going to heaven, they are fine with me leaving for a few days.

—◦◦◦❦◯❦◦◦◦—

Elizabeth spent several hours each day going to Capital City Club swimming pool in Brookhaven with the Means family. Ryan and the other Means boys grew up in a house that faced the golf course and spent their childhood terrorizing the members and employees of the club on a daily basis.

Capital City is a rather tight-knit group of individuals who are only really divided into cliques by age and parental status, and maybe tennis or golf preferences. At least 30 different women, most of them young mothers like me, had met Elizabeth at the pool during this stay in Atlanta. I only knew a handful of people from our few visits to the club when we were in town, but the first time I walked through the gates that summer, I realized many knew me. Word travels lightening fast in these social circles, and I felt many eyes upon me as I came to pick up Elizabeth.

One after another, young mothers introduced themselves, offered their sympathies and made it known that they would love to babysit or help out in anyway. What made their sentiments most sincere is that they weren't silly phrases like, "Thank God he met Sophie before he died," or "At least he wasn't shot overseas." I hated the ridiculous notion of reaching to find some tiny ray of light in Ryan's death. No, these were true sentiments such as, "I cannot even imagine what you are going through. Your story has made me appreciate each day that I have with my husband and children, no matter how crazy they make me."

People still tell me to this day that when everything seems wrong or impossible to manage, they remember back to the summer of 2009 and know that it could be so much worse. They followed our story through Ryan's emails from NYC as they played by the pool with their families, thankful that it wasn't them and sad that it was someone they cared about. This makes me proud, not because I want to be an example of such a tragedy, but because if something like this must happen, let it have a profound and positive effect on others, not be completely in vain. I love to hear that people still think of Ryan in this way, as I too have to remind myself often that the day is not as bad as those of July 2009.

Finally, the time came for the road trip back to Tennessee. I thought once I pulled into my driveway, I would be reduced to tears, but I wasn't. I was relieved to be back in the house that I shared with Ryan. As I lay in bed writing that night, I realized the reason I was so at peace with being home: I was waiting for him to get there. It had only been two months since I had been lying in that same bed, pregnant with Sophie, waiting to hear a date as to when he would arrive in Nashville from Iraq.

Once inside the walls of that same house, my mind wandered back to that time period when we were optimistic about reuniting after the deployment. It was oddly comforting. It happened subconsciously, and I knew consciously that I had to control it. I could have likely lived an entire year pretending that he was deployed, reading old letters and messages over and over and keeping myself busy preparing our home for his return. But I knew that when the day came that I was forced to face the fact that he would not return, it wouldn't be a healthy course for me or my children.

The next morning I started by taking Ryan's clothing and personal effects and sorting them into two stacks: Keep and Goodwill. I suppose I went overboard, as I eventually wished that I had many of the articles back, but it was part of the healing process. I kept many of his favorite shirts, hats, sunglasses, watches and trinkets that I found in boxes, even though I didn't know the story behind many of them. I threw away his Army fatigues and his boots, as well as most of his 100 different T-shirts, which I sometimes regret. Ryan's weapons went to his brothers and Josh. His books went into Rubbermaid containers with the remainder of his belongings. Del, as part of his casualty assistance, helped remove boxes upon boxes of items from our attic. Mary Jo and I sorted through them with a realistic, matter-of-fact approach. If it seemed like something neither I nor the girls would use, like ice-climbing boots for example, it was offered to the brothers and then trashed if they were not interested. I didn't want to be one of those widows living in a hoarded mess of a shrine to my dead husband. On the contrary, I wanted to simplify. I knew that no good would result from me sitting around crying over Ryan's photos and wearing his unwashed T-shirts. That's not to say that there wasn't a lot saved. I was just particular about what I chose to save and those belongings are within reach in my new home. I sometimes find myself sleeping in his soft British Army fatigue pants.

A few days after we arrived in Clarksville, Ryan's personal effects from Iraq were delivered to my door. I was told to expect that someone would bring his belongings in the coming days, but the manner in which they arrived was still a bit unexpected. Del knocked on the door in his full dress uniform and Green Beret. He had a huge black footlocker as well as a middle-sized tote. In the footlocker was everything that was taken from Ryan's room in Iraq. Each item was packaged in the appropriate sized Baggie from loose coins in tiny bags to a giant green foam cowboy hat. We had to run through the list per Army protocol. This meant Del would read aloud the contents of each of the 75 Baggies, and I would check off that it was in fact Ryan's and that I received it. When we finally got to "one large green foam cowboy hat," Del gave me a look. I explained to him that Ryan was playing on the fact that the Iraqis made reference to American men as cowboys, likely from TV that they had seen, and Ryan was always one to make people laugh. I believe he was also reprimanded for this hat. We decided to keep it.

Some of the belongings were expected: the Oakleys, the Northface sneakers, REI shirts, cargo shorts and pants, uniforms and boots. Others were not as expected: First, he never even opened one set of the sheets that I sent him after all of the pleading for soft sheets. I imagine he must have been made fun of for having fancy sheets or something. More interesting, each DVD or CD was returned in a new freshly labeled envelope. This seemed odd because they were my DVDs I had given him along with my blue-sequined girly disc holder to take to Iraq for entertainment. Upon questioning, I was informed that the Army watched each disc to make sure there was nothing top secret on there and that they were in fact labeled appropriately. They also have an IT person go through the contents of the deceased's computer to make sure of the same, as well as for the purpose of removing any pornography that might offend the surviving spouse. As it was, Ryan was able to bring his own laptop back to the states and Apple had the pleasure of finding and removing all of that "information" when I bought a new computer. I learned nothing more than I already knew: Ryan loved Bob Marley and women with large breasts. Nothing top secret there.

Next on the agenda was the Special Forces funeral on post at Fort Campbell. My sister tended to the girls at our house while my mother and I attended the service escorted by Del, along with Josh and the immediate Means family. Again, the intended group was to be his team of 12 and any other 5th group Special Ops men that were on post that day, and it ended up being over 100 people. There was a large poster of Ryan and a slide-show presentation put together by his team. Stories were told. I learned that many times, when Ryan had told me he had no Internet and that "nothing was going on over there" he was in fact the target of men who aimed to see him dead. He never wanted me to know he was in danger, and he did this at the risk of my constantly complaining that he should come home if he's sitting around on his ass doing nothing in Iraq. He always told me that I wouldn't know what he was up to and, boy, did he mean it. My jaw dropped at the service when I heard the stories. But my chin was once again held high during the "Ballad of the Green Berets."

From the time we lived in Wilmington, that song was on my iPod, and Ryan had coached me, to the point of tears, for this very day. He never planned on dying from cancer, but in the line of duty. So, I was likely more prepared than other wives with less-abrasive husbands. I didn't shed a tear. Prior to the service, Del had warned me that the song would be played, and I informed him that I was well aware of the lyrics and that I would be just fine. He did not, however, warn me that they needed Ryan's rifle and boots. The rifle was left in Iraq, but the black dress boots were already at Goodwill. How awful I felt. I'm sure that no soldier would judge my grieving process, but I'm sure they wondered why it didn't occur to me to save his precious boots. Thankfully, a teammate lent his for the service, and the full effect was still there.

Now, as we waited for the date of the burial at Arlington, I had another decision to make. Where should we live? For the last few years, the Army had made this decision. Ryan and I both longed for the day that we could move to a larger city. New York was, of course, out of the question due to cost, but we were hoping that Alexandria, Va., or Washington, D.C., would be the next stop. We were tired of small-town life. There was no reason to stay in Clarksville, as my friends there were, like myself, only staying until the Army moved their husbands on to the next base. Financially, it would have been best for me to stay; there is a much lower cost of living. But what kind of quality of life would I have there, as the Army widow alone with her two children?

I ruled out Pa., where my mother, grandmothers and most of my family still remain, as well as Mich., where my dad and his family live. I am a grown woman, and as much as I love my family, I like to have my own life, freedom and space to live. I'm independent, believe in my own abilities, and choose to be in charge of my life and future—another reason Ryan's death was unimaginable to me; it just wasn't in my plan. Moving back to Pittsburgh was another option I toyed with, but I really didn't know anyone there; it had been years since I lived in the city, and as much as I liked Pittsburgh all summer, the long, harsh northern winters are unbearable.

Since I first vacationed in South Carolina after high school graduation, I had said I would live in the South. I accomplished that goal, and I really didn't want to turn back. With an invitation from Ryan's family and our friends, I chose Atlanta. I still hope with all of my heart to own a beach property in Wrightsville Beach so that my children can spend their summers where their father and I met and fell in love. I just don't think living there full time would have afforded Sophie and Elizabeth the opportunities that their father's legacy left for them in Atlanta.

Alfie invited the three of us to stay at his home in Atlanta while I searched for a new home. Initially, I planned to rent in case I changed my mind once the initial shock of Ryan's death passed. I was told you should not make any major decisions within the first year after your spouse or close family member dies, as your judgment is clouded. This is true. But at the time, I wasn't listening to anything I heard about death and grief. I felt like I was the only one who had ever gone through it and that nobody could possibly understand me, so I would make my own rules.

Michael's friend Anna K, is a kind young real-estate agent in Atlanta. She lost her mother to cancer and took a special interest in me, and she offered to help me find a place to live. We drove for hours a day to different homes with one major roadblock for me—I never knew where the hell we were. It was hard to choose a home when I had no clue who or what was around me. By the second week, we decided there was nothing worth renting, so we looked with the intention to buy. Anna, thankfully, loves her job and was patient.

Next, I contacted Felicia, the agent we used to buy our home in Clarksville. I remember when we were buying, saying to Ryan, "If we ever sell, I want Felicia," and he agreed. She is a spitfire to put it mildly. I knew she would sell my home. And she did, in about a week, which is almost unheard of in this market.

In the meantime, the burial at Arlington was set for August 3, 2009. It never occurred to me how Ryan's body arrived in Arlington, so I asked family for answers and received the following email from his Aunt Sherry, an essay she wrote to Ryan to help her through the healing process:

First of all, let me just say, when someone you love so much dies, you are truly out of your mind with grief. I mean to the point of not knowing what you are saying, hearing or doing. When Ryan left our large and very close knit family, we were honestly zombies...I would venture to say for weeks, maybe months.

Ryan's father, Al, called us early that morning of July 7th to tell us about Ryan's passing. I could not tell you one word he said, except that Ryan died. I think we were on the phone for at least 15 minutes between talking to Al and Mary Jo, but I can't recount a single sentence that we said...only that awful word "died." I truly don't remember much of anything between the time of death and the funeral, hence explaining how this uncanny twist of fate occurred.

Al had many, many phone calls to make, not only concerning the funeral plans, but also to relatives, friends, Army personnel, etc. When it was decided that Ryan would be laid to rest

at Arlington Memorial, Al began the long and arduous task of
helping family and friends with the logistics of travel to D.C., as
well as lodging, services (religious as well as military) and dinners and celebrations, which Ryan would have insisted upon. I
would imagine that Bo and I were among the first few calls he
made. I immediately made our plane reservations just as Al
had told us. In the next few days, we were mostly together with
Ryan's family and friends. It was comforting to all be together,
but at the same time, it made me so sad. Nobody would have
loved having us all together more than Ryan...especially since
we were all recounting funny "Ryan stories" and it was heart-
breaking that he couldn't be there. He always loved being the
center of attention! In all of our togetherness, we began com-
paring travel plans—if we would be on the same flight or at the
same hotel. Bo and I quickly figured out that everyone, with the
exception of us, was flying into National, as Al had instructed.
In our collective stupor, either Al told us (and only us) to fly
into Dulles, or we thought he said to fly into Dulles. We tossed
around the idea of changing our flight to fly into National, but
for some reason, we didn't. As the date neared, we told Al we
were flying into Dulles, and he said that he thought Ryan was
being flown into Dulles. The time and date of Ryan's flight was
totally at the discretion of the military and Delta airlines...the
family had no say so in the matter. Now keep in mind, Ryan
could have been flown from Atlanta to Washington, D.C. any of
the 21 days between his death and his burial. And also, keep
in mind that Delta probably has at least 12-15 flights a day
between Atlanta and D.C.. The day before our departure date
to Washington, Al found out that Ryan would indeed be flying

to Washington Dulles the same day as us, and that Ryan would indeed be on our flight.

Neither Delta nor the U.S. Army knew that Bo and I would be on that flight, but Ryan did. I truly believe that it was his last little gift to me to be his escort to his final resting place. I loved taking care of him as a child. He spent many days and nights with me. I adored him, and he always knew it, and I believe it was mutual.

I must say that Bo and I were overwhelmed when it was confirmed that Ryan would be on our flight. I felt so honored to be the only family members with him, but at the same time, I felt a responsibility that I wasn't sure I could handle. It was up to me to take care of Ryan, who as a member of the most elite group in the U.S. Army had taken such good care of the entire free world. I cried for 24 straight hours, and prayed that I could be strong for him. I failed miserably at the strong part.

Bo and I went to Atlanta Hartsfield-Jackson early the morning of our trip. We were being met at the Delta gate by one of Ryan's fellow Special Forces team. We weren't sure which one it would be, but as we neared the gate, we spotted Joe. We had met Joe at Ryan's memorial service in Atlanta, and so admired him. Instead of feeling a blanket of comfort, as I expected, I only felt an unbearable sadness. I knew that Joe was hurting as much as we were, but he had to be strong for Ryan, the US and us. When I say I cried buckets, that's not enough. It was more like barrels. Joe and Bo and I were escorted down to the tarmac. I wanted to make sure they got Ryan on safely and treated him with the respect that he deserved. The Delta agents did both. Joe saluted him and the baggage handlers treated him as if he were a Faberge egg. We then boarded the plane. I cannot begin to explain the feeling of responsibility I felt knowing that Ryan was under us. It was MY duty to get him there safely. No one on the plane knew the nature of our trip. We were not seated with Joe. As we began descending into Dulles, I began to feel a slight sense of relief. I almost had him there. The captain came on the intercom and asked that everyone please remain seated upon arrival because we were carrying the remains of a great American soldier. As a courtesy to his family traveling with him, the captain requested that we de-plane first. Mind you...90% of the plane was very ambitious business travelers, who normally would have knocked each other down to get off first and get to their business meeting. We touched down and taxied to the gate. I begged God to help me get off of that plane without making a terrible crying scene. He didn't grant me that prayer.

We were seated five rows from the back, and Joe was somewhere behind us. We had at least 40 rows until we got to the door, and I promise you, I drenched each and every one of the passengers that was seated in an aisle. As Joe, Bo and I left, not one traveller moved. No one got up to retrieve brief cases or carry-ons until we were gone. There was total silence and reverence. One person started to clap in appreciation of Ryan's service, but then no one really knew if that were a tribute or irreverent, so they stopped. They only wanted to do what was respectful and right, but they, like us, just didn't know what to do. We felt the admiration for Ryan and we felt the appreciation in every one of their hearts.

Joe, Bo and I were met at the gate by Army personnel and a

Delta agent. We were, once again, escorted to the tarmac. Ryan came out first. The military, as well as the baggage handlers, saluted him. They ever so gently lowered him and placed him in the hearse. My job was done. He had protected all of us and now I had protected him. He was on his way to his final resting place and I was able to play a small role in getting him there. Joe saluted him until you could no longer see the hearse that carried our great American. Through my non-stop bevy of tears, I thought I saw a single tear roll down Joe's face, which he discreetly wiped away with the completion of his salute.

You could try for a million years, but you could never convince me that Ryan didn't put us on that flight with him. It just would have been way too much to put his loving wife, Heather and his beautiful daughters, Elizabeth and Sophie Ryan, or his mom or dad, or any of his brothers in that position. I guess I was the next best thing. I think, also, that he got a little bit of a kick seeing me crying like an idiot...Ryan always got the last laugh.

I love and appreciate you always, Ryan, YFA.

Chapter Six
Another Funeral: Arlington

We drove through Washington, D.C., to arrive at Arlington National Cemetery. Being back in the city brought me back to the time we were at Walter Reed, and the nauseated stomach recommenced.

It seemed that morning I was no longer able to smile and celebrate Ryan. I didn't want to take photos or talk anymore. I didn't want to bury him either. The reality of seeing his body lowered into the grave would be too much for me to see. I just wanted to go home and pretend that he was deployed. Del did his best to keep me in the background away from any conversations and cameras. I had confided in him that I was done. I couldn't put on this face any longer. He reminded me that I had every right to just sit alone and talk to Ryan rather than worry about entertaining everyone. And so, I did.

The officials at the cemetery took me, Mary Jo, and Al into a cubicle prior to the burial. They told us where we would walk, the order of seating, and what to expect at the gravesite. Although they performed this operation all day, everyday, we were treated with the utmost respect and compassion. They caught me off guard though. I had to fill out instructions for Ryan's headstone. I hadn't given this a single thought. We were only allowed a few words, and I can be a dramatic woman of many words when it comes to writing about my husband. I wanted to come up with something clever to

CHILDHOOD ATLANTA FRIENDS IN ARLINGTON

honor him: "Ryan Patman Means, Liberator of the Oppressed, the most passionate of Scorpios, a brave and noble barrel-chested freedom fighter, worldly scholar and philosopher...hands down the most extraordinary husband and father that ever lived. The world will mourn the untimely loss of this man with hearts that bleed until the end of time."

This proved to be too much for the traditional Arlington headstone, so Mary Jo and Al agreed upon:

RYAN PATMAN MEANS
SSG (Staff Sergeant)
U.S. ARMY
IRAQ
Nov. 5, 1973
July 7, 2009
BELOVED HUSBAND, FATHER AND SON

We asked to have "BROTHER" included as well, but the wording was too long. It pained me to put such a typical headstone on such an amazing man's grave, but such is the story off all who rest in peace at Arlington cemetery.

The immediate family was transported by a car, which followed the hearse to the gravesite. I believe the other guests were asked to walk behind to avoid congesting the cemetery with automobile traffic. Six members of the casket team respectfully lifted Ryan's body from the hearse, with a seventh at the head. Dressed in their crisp dress blues, they placed the steel grey coffin precisely over the gravesite. His fellow soldiers saluted Ryan. The chaplain took his position in front of us and performed his duty. It was to the word, exactly as I had seen on TV and in the movies.

Afterwards, family and friends each took a turn walking to the casket to say good–bye in their own special way and lay flowers upon him. When my turn came, I knelt down in front of the casket and took a moment to place both hands upon it and rest my cheek upon the warm metal. I would have knelt there until the end of time if it meant never having to say goodbye. I only wished I could lay my head on Ryan's chest one last time and feel his arms around me. I finally started to understand that day would never come. Why, why was our time cut so short? I rose to my feet and returned to my seat feeling more alone than I have ever felt in my life.

Silence fell over the crowd as the rifle team was instructed to begin their salute. The shots were fired. Seven men, simultaneously firing three consecutive shots only interrupted by the quiet space between each pull of the trigger. The haunting melody of "Taps" echoed in the summer breeze in perfect harmony with the billowing trees around us.

Finally, the flag was systematically raised over the coffin and folded into a triangle. It was passed to the soldier at the head of the casket and placed between his two palms, one held over the other. He walked toward me slowly. When he was directly in front of me he knelt upon one knee and looked me directly in the eye. He was so young, and I could tell he was either nervous or choked up himself. I assumed the first, as I imagined he had done this many times.

He said, "This flag is presented on behalf of a grateful nation and the United States Army as a token of appreciation for your loved one's honorable and faithful service. God bless you, and God bless the United States of America."

The same words were said to Mary Jo and Al as they were presented their flags. I remember hearing Mary Jo thank the young man, as she sat next to me. I did not thank him. In my mind, at that moment in time, it seemed to me that the Army, their inability to get Ryan home from Iraq in a timely manner, and their medical treatment may have somehow led to his demise, and I wasn't thanking anyone for anything until I was sure I truly meant it.

As the service concluded, a Lady of Arlington, one of the Gold Star Wives of America, introduced herself and welcomed me to a club where nobody actively seeks membership, as you must have a spouse or son/daughter die during active duty or as a result sickness or disability acquired on active duty in order to become a member. I was given a lapel pin and a book of information. These strong women fight hard to ensure that our lawmakers do not forget the wives and mothers who are left behind when a service member dies.

RECEIVING THE FLAG THAT ONCE DRAPED THE COFFIN

Immediately following the burial, a brunch was held at Bobby Van's Steakhouse. Al received a call the night before from the commanding officer of 5th Group who reported that Joe Hickey, the owner of Bobby Van's restaurant, planned to be at the interment at Arlington. He graciously extended an invitation to family and friends for lunch at his restaurant after the service. Al reported the number of guests, which again tripled but without complaint from our host. The restaurant was closed to the public, and everyone was served a perfectly prepared salmon or filet mignon. It was the first time I had really sat down to eat in weeks, and we were all very grateful for the generous gesture. Ryan's teammates each took a turn telling a "Ryan story" from the most recent deployment. Once again, I learned that Ryan was never as safe as I thought him to be overseas.

Del and I had to leave the brunch shortly after eating to catch our flight back to Tennessee. I was still wearing my funeral attire: the black "Jackie O" skirt-suit and silk blouse; and Del, his full Army dress uniform. I carried the flag through security wondering if they would force me to unfold it. It occurred to me that they had seen this many times before, and Del assured me that they would do no such thing. I sat in the airport with the folded flag on my lap. A few people looked at the flag, looked at me, then instantly turned away, avoiding the risk of making any uncomfortable eye contact.

On the other hand, a woman about my mother's age as well as an elderly couple in town to visit their son's grave, spoke to me and expressed their sympathies.

RIP RPM

Chapter 7
Finding life (or Living)

The flight home was sobering. I sat quietly alone, holding my flag upon my lap as my mind wandered on fast play through the events of the last three months. It seemed to me that summer never really happened—just a series of impossible events...and here I was left to deal with the aftermath. No husband, just an American flag and my memories.

I was happy to return home to Sophie and Elizabeth. And although hesitant, I was anxious to complete the move to Atlanta. Once we began to settle into our new home, it was time for the holiday routine to begin.

Halloween, being Ryan's favorite holiday, was tough, but we made it through as a family. Thanksgiving and Christmas felt like rituals that must be completed for the sake of the children, but the pain was difficult to mask for all of us. It killed me to watch Elizabeth and Sophie opening presents on Christmas morning because I knew that Ryan could not be there to see it for himself, and more so, he never would.

ELIZABETH AND SOPHIE AFTER DADDY'S FUNERAL

—∞⊸❉⊷∞—

New Year's Eve, 2010, I climbed into bed and began thinking about our New Year's celebration the prior year in Mexico. The trip to Sayulita, the embrace we slept in that last night in paradise before returning to the states for that the deployment. I thought about the year 2009 and all that it brought to our family, and I continued keeping a journal, as Ryan did when Adam died:

As it turns out, this Cholangiocarcinoma thing is a pretty big deal and pretty rare. I'd say that suits you. I just know from your words and letters that you were not ready to die at its hands though. It means the world to me that you never gave up and always wanted me next to you. It was no fun watching you die, but I enjoyed being with you those last months, nonetheless.

Before your coma state, you joked that I could find a good Catholic migrant worker to do what you do at home, and maybe even teach E a second language. There are so many things that I love about you but never told you about because I knew you would either say I was lazy for not being that way myself or get an even more inflated ego. Neither of which I cared to deal with. Now, I can tell you, as I need to find ways to perpetuate them now that you are gone. E and Sophie can't be without just because you aren't physically here anymore. So, here goes...

I started listing his finer qualities: his loyalty to me, our girls, and his family; the way he felt responsible for taking care of us, even if it was from another country; his persistence, athleticism, and the way he formed unbreakable bonds with people; and how he was the eternal optimist in the face of adversity—it even made him stronger.

Ryan was as patriotic as an American could be although often surrounded by people who took their freedom for granted. A free-flying American flag would make him stop and gaze with pride until a tear would almost form in his eye. He loved his country and its citizens, especially his family and friends. It was hard for me to comprehend how he could give up his freedom and become the property of the Army to keep all of us safe. "Green Berets are brave men who stand watch at night, they risk their lives so that you may sleep safely," he would tell me.

Ryan always made me feel safe; he challenged my brain and my soul to be better. He was fearless, adventurous, and more confident than any man I ever met. He was a get-it-done guy. He never procrastinated. He was an excellent public speaker and communicator. He talked me into more things than I ever knew I was capable of doing or even wanted to do. He NEVER gave up and NEVER gave in to anyone or anything. He was a true lover and a true fighter.

This was about as far as I got in my first journal entry when I heard a beeping noise. It sounded like Ryan's watch alarm. I searched the room in the glow of the streetlight and finally discovered the noise was coming from the wood chest that the Army gave me to hold his keepsakes. I call it the little coffin. I opened the box and was forced to search through Ryan's clothes and personal items to find this watch. It was the first time I had opened the chest since I filled it with his belongings. The watch beeped incessantly until I found it and despite my efforts, I couldn't get any button to make it stop.

I started bawling my eyes out sitting amidst all of his clothes, his passport, wallet, sunglasses, and hats. I put on the British Army pants and his T-shirt. I climbed in bed with the watch and cried myself to sleep as I listened to the fireworks at midnight, just as I had the previous year in Mexico when he coined me the "best wife ever." The blasting sounds and lights reminded me of our breezy oceanfront bedroom in Mexico, the waves crashing on the shore, the sand sprinkled about the cool clay floor, the shower that always ran cold, Ryan throwing Elizabeth 10 feet into the air over the ocean while Michael and I tried to capture the perfect photo. It brought me back to the swimming pool that I stood in for hours reading, *A Prayer for Owen Meany* as requested by Ryan. It brought me back to the time he hit the gas instead of the brake when we were parking the rental car. I could almost hear his voice speaking to me that night: "Never give up, never ever give up."

I finally realized he was dead. He wasn't going to come to this new home and find me. But he was still alive in me.

It took me a few days to start writing again. The watch still beeps periodically but never at midnight to my knowledge. I don't believe in ghosts or signs, but it bothered me nonetheless. I decided to use the journal as a means of communicating with Ryan, since I wasn't sure about the afterlife or if it was a great idea to get in the habit of talking to dead people.

Ryan,

I've had some serious God issues lately. I've looked into it and apparently being mad at the Man isn't as bad as denying his existence altogether, so I'm not as bad off as I was when you died...at least in that department. I consider myself spiritually challenged at this time. I'm no longer on speaking terms with God. From May 26th until July 7th, I literally prayed upon my knees with clenched hands and tears in my eyes several times a day. I bargained with God. I offered him anything...myself, my undying faith, my promise to raise my kids as God's children, anything I could think of, as though that would work even just to keep you here with us for Elizabeth and Sophie's youngest years, so that they could know you the way I do, so that they could just have their own memories of you.

E has pictures and videos with you to remind her and I will always show them to her. Sweet Sophie has just two pictures with you and you don't even look like yourself at all. It just isn't fair to either of them. I'm terrified of how this will affect their lives and ruin the innocence that little children should be allowed. We had so many dreams and plans for our future, their future, and now I feel like they are gone. I can't do it myself. You were so much better than me in so many ways. It's funny that you used to say the same thing to me. And I wished I asked you in what ways I was better, because I can't seem to find them now.

Part of my delusional grieving mind wonders if I should go around pretending that I have this imaginary friend, a guardian angel watching over me and our daughters, in order to maintain my sanity. Is that even a sane idea? The only certain thing I know about life these days is that it is uncertain. Maybe that is some-thing that other people will never truly grasp so I'm thankful for the knowledge only, not the grief. Right now it seems ridiculous for me to even plan on next week, or tomorrow for that matter as something is likely to destroy the plans and I can't take much of that destruction these days.

I've been reading books and websites about grieving. Many say that it is good to write about it. I agree, thus this journal. But one specifically asks the reader to write, "how your loved one's death made you feel."

I was surprised at what I wrote:

"A creature came from behind. I never saw him coming. He swiftly hit me on the back of the head with a Louisville Slugger. My skull shattered into tiny pieces and my brain matter spilled on the cold tile floor as I fell to the ground in slow motion. As I lay there dumbfounded but not dead, the creature, which almost appeared human, reached into my chest with his claw and ripped out my heart. I felt the thicker veins and arteries snapping as the beating organ exited my body. He proceeded to jump on my ribcage with his heavy black boots expelling every last molecule of air that was left in me. He began twisting the boots harder into my motionless body. I tried to kick, to punch and to push his foot off of me but I couldn't move a limb. I couldn't make a noise come from my mouth. I was helpless. I wondered if this creature was the Grim Reaper, but I was not dead to the world, just completely paralyzed and frozen with disbelief. I wondered if this creature was God."

As you can see, it is going to take a lot of time and work for me to get over this confusion I have about God. I've never believed in Satan, and have been rather agnostic. But, I always wanted to believe that there was a God. Different religions see him in different ways but all things said, he is a higher power by any name. If this is the case, how can our Christian friends believe that God said it was your time to go? That he would take my devoted husband, a loving father from his babies? The God I was raised with would not take my heart from me nor crush my soul by letting that happen. Would I have felt the same about God if a terrorist killed you? I honestly have no idea. Do you see why I am so confused, Ryan?

I guess all religion aside and all blame aside, cancer is what ultimately took my heart and soul but left me to live. Cholangiocarcinoma ended your life, and changed Elizabeth and Sophie's lives and my life... and RPM, you have changed my life forever.

I'm starting to learn how to talk to people and answer their questions about my dealing with your death. It has taken almost a year, but I've found that when they ask "How are you doing?" they don't really want to know all of the details. It's depressing to know the truth and I can see it on their faces when I start to tell them how it really feels to live without you. They look uncertain what to say in reply (nothing is expected, I mean what CAN you say??), and the situation is uncomfortable. So now my favorite response is, "Staying strong!" followed by "We're hanging in there!"—both of which are followed by my giant fake smile and hopefully a look in my eyes that is not too telling of the truth.

The fact of the matter is, every second of every day is a conscious wholehearted effort to continuously remind myself why I must live after you have died. I can be having a conversation with a friend, listening intently, responding appropriately sometimes I even manage to be witty, but there is a constant static, like a song you cannot get out of your head, and it is saying "DEAR GOD WHY? WHY? WHY? WHY RYAN? WHY Elizabeth and Sophie? WHY did he die? Why on Earth couldn't I have gone too?"

No one knows what to say to me, so they just seem talk and talk about nothing. No matter what the topic is, I'm forced to hold back from replying that "I'm 31, I have a new baby and a 2-year-old and my incredible young husband just came home from Iraq so that I could watch him die. Not to mention, I now live in a strange new city and I can't even find my way to the grocery store to buy diapers without using my navigation system let alone begin to think about how I will provide for these two babies on my own for the next 18+ years!" I'm aware that it can't be easy for anyone to address the matter with me, so I try to be patient.

That said, I've really got to find a way to be kind and compassionate again. I can never go back to work as a physical therapist with this attitude. I can never stay in this area of Atlanta for that matter, unless I figure out how to reintegrate myself into a society that doesn't get me anymore. I'm not the same person I was a year ago. My values have changed, my soul has changed. The appreciation you found for life and human kind after Adam died is inspirational to me. You've had a profound affect on my inner soul and as you wrote in your journal, "This is the greatest tribute..." "To be inspired in such a way that you alter the greatest possession that a person could own...their life."

Over the next months, the children and I watched a lot of "Daddy movies" in our home. Elizabeth still knows Ryan's voice or face when she sees it. Although the videos make me homesick for my old house, my old life as an Army wife in a simple town, my life with Ryan, I still find it necessary to watch them because I need to see him and hear his voice. I think about all of the doors that I slammed when Ryan made me angry. I think about complaining that we never had enough money; that I had to work so hard while I was pregnant and tired; that I wanted a bigger house; that I wanted to live in a real city; that Ryan wasn't home enough; and that, when he was, it seemed we were always surrounded by friends or traveling, not alone enjoying each other. I was so unappreciative of the health that we had, the life that we shared. That old house now looks perfect to me in those videos, as does Ryan. It baffles me to think I will watch these movies in years to come and he will remain the same age as I grow older.

Maybe I feel that life isn't fair, but it isn't fair to my children to hear me say that we don't deserve this life. Many people would love to have our life. We are fortunate. Just as Ryan was fortunate when he was left jobless and penniless after losing his best friend in the WTC attacks. He was rich with the knowledge that he was something great, and that life and living it to the fullest is something great, and that's all we really need. He may have died without a penny, but he died a hero. Sophie and Elizabeth will always have this knowledge, as I have promised Ryan that I will instill it within them.

When I visit Ryan's grave, I plan to tell him that I have a strange unwavering feeling that I will see him again one day. And that this adventure has taught me what is important in life. It isn't about possessions; it is about having each other. We had unconditional love for each other and that could never be taken from us. I know from living with Ryan that life should never be about what you want to be, but who you want to be.

I will let go of the guilt I feel for ever making him feel like he wasn't enough for me, and the guilt I felt that I was never good enough for him. I loved our life together more than I ever would have realized if he was still alive. My judgment was often clouded by day-to-day issues that in the grand scheme of things really didn't matter. It now occurs to me daily, that we complain about such petty things. Traffic, irritable clients, creaky old houses, and screaming babies....they never should have had an effect on the way we love and treat people. I no longer worry about a little fender bender or the baby's diaper leaking on my new dress before I leave the house. I never thought of life like this before Ryan died.

I think of what he went through those last few months without a single complaint. How could he not complain about being told he would die in thirty days when he loved his life so dearly? I think about how he said complaining and stressing out is not productive. He would always tell me, "Nobody is being shot at and nobody died today." I need to remember that nothing I deal with on a daily basis is as horrible as the day I lost him. I know that everything is really going to be okay.

I want to tell Ryan that if he could just come back, we would be more phenomenal than ever. If we started over, knowing what we know now about this life on Earth, the relatively short period of time we have on this planet, we would be the wisest young couple that ever lived. It cannot be, so I hope to make our children understand what I have learned from this, as it can be the only good that can come of our tragedy.

You are alive, thus you have it all. Those who are left to live are those with a gift from their deceased; a life full of knowledge, if you choose to accept it.

As much as I long for the eternal sunshine of a spotless mind, a mind free of the memories, good and bad, I cannot learn from what I have not experienced. The proposal on the swing of the home we never bought, the doting father that followed the nurses around the delivery room watching over his new babies, the hugs that caused a good hurt in my back, the warm breath I felt on my neck at night as I slept, the call from Iraq, the cry on his chest as he took his last breath.

I don't want to remember any of it because it is the worst pain imaginable. But if all of these memories were erased, if the pain disappeared, I would be a shell of the woman, the mother, the friend that I am now. I would be ordinary. Ryan granted me a new life and left me a handbook by which to live it, and I wouldn't trade that for an easy life without the hurt. I have my days where I dream of doing so, but never in a million years would I trade lives with anyone.

Epilogue

The sadness never completely leaves. It comes and goes like the ocean waves. The waves are constant and variable all through my days and nights. Sometimes a wave will give me a little push and I will barely notice. I will stand strong on my feet and continue to walk in the shallow ocean water of grief without even realizing where I am. Other times, a powerful wave will come out of nowhere and pull me under to the point I fear I will surely drown. I miss my life when I knew no such pain, when life was purely about 'what may be', not 'what once was'. I miss Ryan so damn much.

There is an emptiness, an immeasurable void that not even our beautiful children can fill. This void makes me who I am and makes me better and stronger and ready to live my life to the fullest.

"Tis better to have loved and lost than never to have loved at all."
—*Alfred Lord Tennyson*

One year later, I can say that I now truly understand the love that I lost. And, only because of what I have learned, can I say that it truly is better to have loved and lost, than to have never loved at all. Most importantly, it is best to have been loved....loved in the way we were loved by Ryan. He loved us with the powerful intensity of which fusion occurs in stars. It was the only way he knew to love. Some will live and die never knowing the love that we felt. We will be

OK, knowing we had it briefly and that it is the truest love that can exist on earth or in heaven.

"In the end, if everything is not OK.... it is not the end."

See you soon, RPM.

"The mystery of love is greater than the mystery of death."

–Anonymous

RYAN IS BURIED IN SECTION 59, SITE 3662
ARLINGTON NATIONAL CEMETERY (PHOTOGRAPHY BY MATTHEW KOVACIK, ATLANTA, GA)

DATE: Dec 2, 2006
FROM: MG Julian Burns
TO: Ryan Means

You have done well. you have performed nobly. And, you inspire me to an upwelling of pride in all that you have achieved.

You by now, too, have no doubt come to realize the wonderful benefits that come from a life of service. Your time in the Army may be brief or lifelong. No matter, for a thing done well is done well forever....whether in a blink of an eye, or to the very end of days.

There is a statue not far from here in Washington: The confederate soldier on the main street in Alexandria, looking south, not looking north as do so many of the statues that you will find further south in GA, SC, or NC, from the civil war. It is a simple thing. And like the most profound things in life, it has a simple inscription, that says "In recognition of duty nobly performed." Such words echo those in Micah, chapter six "to do justly, love mercy, and walk humbly with thy God."

You now enter that sublime company of warriors, at the pinnacle of fighting acumen—Special Forces. But, it is what inspired you to serve thusly that distinguishes you, not your beret, or your skills and your physical ability. The distinguishing character that places you above the common race of men is your submission to the well being of all mankind, by the imposition of your life blood between them and those that would do them harm.

As did our Lord and Savior 2000 years ago.

Do well, care for one another on the team, remember your heritage, and when it is over, come by and tell me your story.

—MG Julian Burns

"Life without liberty is like a body without spirit."
                                                —Kahlil Gibran

With great pride along with the most humble and heartfelt thank-you, this book is dedicated to those Americans who serve and their families. In order to truly appreciate our freedom, we Americans must remember the sacrifices you, and those before you, have made in order that we may live in the land of the free, home of the brave.

Thank you.

Acknowledgments

Thank you to my family for allowing and encouraging me to share Ryan's story. Thank you also to my friends for never asking me to drop the idea or move on to something else. Writing this book was better therapy than any psychologist could have provided. It healed me.

Countless thanks to the following:

— **MG Julian Burns** for mentoring and inspiring countless patriotic spirits and for your kind words of encouragement & support

— **Susan Soper** (*obitkit.com*), who copy-edited stacks of papers and made them into something my children will cherish for life. You made me believe that it was possible to share Ryan's story with the free world. **Wendy McSweeny** (*photolively.com*), for making this into a real book. You two sisters took this on as a labor of love and made my dream come true.

— **Cassie Brkich** (*brkichdesign.com*), for turning my crayon sketches into a beautiful cover and polishing up the entire book for sales.

— **Valentine Brkich** (*valentinebrkich.com*), for tirelessly correcting my mediocre grammar.

— **Beau Parry** (*www.brivas.org*), for your laser-like focus and determination to get this book out into the free world and the cyber-world for Ryan.

— Thank you to Ryan's **Chi Psi Brothers and their families,** not just for the charity and getting my little family through the first year, but for continuing to be ever present in our lives

— Thank you to the **Green Berets** and **Army friends** that continue to check-up on us and watch over Ryan's girls.

And of course, thank you to all of you—both friends and family—who supported us, both with your words and your generosity. You make me realize that I have a team of friends that will never let this story die.

Ryan will live on through us. Thank you all. Please visit us at **www.ryanpmeans.com** for more about Ryan and his legacy.

313

Mission Statement

The Special Operations Warrior Foundation provides full scholarship grants and educational and family counseling to the surviving children of special operations personnel who die in operational or training missions and immediate financial assistance to severely wounded special operations personnel and their families.